# Voyage of the Forest Dream

To Bob Mills,

Captain Niels Thomsen

# VOYAGE
# OF THE
# FOREST DREAM

## AND OTHER SEA ADVENTURES

**A MEMOIR**

*by Captain Niels Peter Thomsen*

Vancouver, Washington

ISBN: 0-9631232-6-2
Thomsen, Niels Peter
VOYAGE OF THE FOREST DREAM
Includes index


Cover design by Mary Rose
Cover photo Puget Sound Maritime Historical Society

# TABLE OF CONTENTS

# ACKNOWLEDGEMENTS

To the renowned maritime historian and noted collector of sailing ship memorabilia, Captain Harold D. Huycke of Edmonds, Washington, I express my great appreciation and gratitude. It is due to his spirited generosity that the seventy year old diary of my beloved shipmate, Malcolm Chisholm was made available to me. By virtue of this action, this tale of the sea has become a reality for the enjoyment and edification of those of us who have dreamt of being a part of the adventurous era of tall ships, billowing sails and following seas.

To my secretary Diana James, I owe a standing ovation for her enthusiasm over our project, her tactful, unbelievable patience, and the multitude of skills that she brought to this endeavor.

I thank my youthful, tempestuous wife, Airdrie, for her forbearance with my ten-year obsession with the voyage of the *Forest Dream.*

I extend my heartfelt gratitude to Suzanne Price, my former neighbor, who presented me with a copy of an East Coast marine historical magazine, wherein a minuscule "letter to the editor" eventually led me to Malcolm's seventy year old diary.

# PROLOGUE

The voyage of the *Forest Dream* is contained in book one of three volumes of the JOURNEY OF AN IMPATIENT HEART, a chronicle of my life which I commenced for my children and their children as family history. It was highly personal and written with total honesty without thought of publication.

In the beginning the voyage of the *Forest Dream* in 1925 was but a chapter in my memory until five years into my story when, by an incredible series of events the seventy year old diary of my closest friend and shipmate, Malcolm Chisholm, came into my possession. This was the diary that Malcolm read to me almost daily during the fourteen month long voyage of the *Forest Dream*.

The remarkable set of circumstances which resulted in my recovery of Malcolm's diary convinced me that as the only survivor it was my duty to my shipmates to present our story as Malcolm had intended, to those who love the wonder, beauty and mystery of the sea as did Mac and I, and my watchmate Frank who paid with his life when he fell from aloft one dark night during a gale while we were furling the upper topgallant sail. To those beloved shipmates of so many long years ago this book is dedicated.

# NAUTICAL GLOSSARY

ABACK  The sails in an unmanageable condition because of a sudden shift of wind striking the sails opposite from that to which they are trimmed.

ASTERN  Going backwards.

A-LEE  Putting the helm (wheel) down to bring the ship up into the wind, as in tacking ship.

BACKSTAY  A rope or shroud slanting sharply aft from the top of the mast of a ship to help support the mast.

BARK  A sailing vessel with two forward masts square-rigged and its rear mast rigged fore and aft.

BARKENTINE  A sailing ship square-rigged on the foremast with two or more fore and aft (schooner) masts behind.

BELAYING PIN  A removable wooden or metal pin in the rail, around which the lines (ropes ) can be fastened.

BOAT FALLS  A hoisting apparatus.

BOW  The forward end of the ship.

BOWSPRIT  A large tapered pole or plank extending forward from the bow of a sailing vessel with the foremast stays fastened to it.

BULWARKS  A part of the ship's side above the decks.

BUNTLINE  One of the ropes attached to the footrope of a square sail to prevent the sail from bellying when drawn up to be furled.

CAPSTAN  An apparatus used mainly on ships for hauling in cables and hawsers, consisting of a large spool-shaped cylinder with a cable or hawser wound round it, revolving on an inner shaft.

CHOCK  The woodwork on a ship's deck where the lifeboat rests.

CLOSE-HAULED  Having the sails adjusted for heading as nearly as possible in the direction from which the wind is blowing.

DEAD RECKONING  (deduced reckoning) The finding of a ship's position by using compass readings and data recorded in the log (speed, course and distance travelled), rather than astronomical observations used in storms, fog and other weather conditions.

DOGWATCH  Either of two duty periods from 1600 to 1800 and from 1800 to 2000 half the length of a normal four hour watch period.

DOLDRUMS Equatorial ocean regions noted for dead calms and light fluctuations of winds.

DONKEY BOILER A small boiler used for generating power to assist in hoisting a ship's anchor.

DONKEYMAN A crew member who tends to all machinery, lighting and tending the lamps, as well as carpenter work.

FID A small, round, pointed wood tool used for splicing rope.

FIFE RAIL A rail with holes, around a ship's mast to hold belaying pins for the rigging lines to be attached to.

FORECASTLE  (foc'sle) The upper deck in front of the foremast where the crew is berthed.

FOREMAST The mast nearest to the bow of the ship.

FORESAIL  (fors'l) The lower main square sail on the foremast of a square-rigged ship.

GANTLINE  A working rope for raising or lowering sails, blocks, or anything from aloft to the deck or vice versa.

GALLEY Ship's kitchen.

GUDGEON A socket for a pin or shaft into which a pin (pintle) on a ship's rudder is attached; similar to a hinge.

HALF DECK A separate house on deck in front of the poop.

HALYARD  A rope or tackle for raising or lowering a sail.

HATCH  A rectangular opening in a ship's deck through which cargo can be loaded into the ship's hold.

HAWSE That part of the bow of a ship containing the hawse holes through which cables are run for mooring.

HAWSE PIPE  The anchor hawse hole.

HAWSER  A large rope or small cable, often made of steel, by which a ship is towed or moored.

HEADSAIL  Any sail forward of the mast or foremast.

HELM  The wheel or tiller by which the ship is steered.

HORSE LATITUDES Either of two belts of calms, light winds and high barometric pressure situated about 30° north and south of the equator.

LEEWARD  The direction toward which the wind blows (opposed to windward).

MAINMAST The principal mast of the vessel; in a schooner, brig, bark and similar vessels, the second from the bow.

MARLINSPIKE A  pointed wooden or iron instrument for separating the strands of a rope when splicing.

MIZZENMAST  The mast closest to the stern of a

ship with two or more masts.

PAY OFF  To cause or allow a vessel to veer to leeward.

POOP The area containing separate quarters for the captain, mates and stewards, a large storage space for sails; a separate galley for the captain.

POOP DECK On sailing ships, a raised deck at the stern, also the roof of the after cabin.

PORT  The left-hand side of a ship as one faces forward, towards the bow. Larboard is opposite to starboard.

ROYAL MAST The smallest (highest) mast above the topgallant mast.

SCUPPER An opening in the ship's side to allow water to run overboard off the main deck.

SHEET A rope or chain attached to a lower corner of a sail; it can be shortened or slackened to control the set of the sail.

SHROUD One of a set of ropes or cables stretched from the ship's side to the masthead to offset lateral strain on the mast.

STANCHION An upright bar, beam or post used as a support.

STARBOARD  The right hand side of the ship as one faces forward, towards the bow; opposed to port (larboard ).

STAY A heavy rope or cable, usually of wire used as a brace or support for the mast of a ship.

STEM 1) The most forward part of the ship; 2) the upright piece to which the side timbers or plates are attached to form the prow of the ship.

SWELL A large wave that moves steadily without breaking.

TACK To change the course of a ship's heading by turning her head into the wind.

TOPGALLANT  Adjective used to describe any mast, sail or spar that is above the topmast and below the royal mast on a square-rigged sailing ship.

TOPMAST The second mast above the deck of a sailing ship, supported by the lower mast and often supporting a topgallant mast in turn.

TOPSAIL In a square-rigged ship, the square sail next above the lowest sail on the mast.

TRADE WIND Easterly winds that blow toward the equator from the northeast side of the equator, and from the southeast on the south side.

TRUCK A small wooden block or disk with holes for halyards, especially on top of the mast.

WEARING To turn or bring a ship about on the other tack by swinging the bow away from the wind; as opposed to tacking, usually done in heavy seas as a precautionary measure.

WINDWARD  In the direction from which the wind blows.

YARD (yardarm) A pole or spar fastened at right angles across the mast for the support of the square sails.

YAW  To deviate temporarily from the ship's course when steering.

# Life

We cannot quell
The raging seas
Or decree
What winds will blow
Nor will the set
Of our sails
And the trim
Of our jib
Determine the way we go.

For some of us
It's an easy reach
With a wind
That is flowing free
And for whom
There is always
A flooding tide
And the rush
Of a following sea.

But for most of us
It's a tack
Or a wear
Against the wind
And the tide
And some of us
Never reach our goals
As we run aground
On hidden shoals.

Though our arms
Grow weary
And the night is long
And we have kept our hands
On the tiller strong
We may never make
The port of our dreams
Or attain
Our heart's desire.

Thomsen

CHAPTER ONE

# NIELS
# 1910

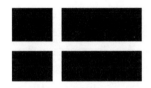 I was three years old, confined in the Ribe General Hospital with scarlet fever. It was a cold snowy day, and I was standing up in my crib looking out the window where a nurse had rubbed a hole in the frosted glass so I could wave goodbye to my mother, Adelheid, who was leaving the hospital.

I can recall the large walled-in, cobblestoned courtyard, completely surrounded by the apartments of the five Thomsen brothers, whose back doors all opened into the court. Christian Thomsen, my father, was one of a family of twelve children. He had no formal schooling beyond his eighth birthday, when he was sent away from home to work on a farm as a Bondboy. At the time of his marriage to Adelheid he worked as a hod carrier in the building trade, carrying heavy loads of cement on his shoulder in a "V" shaped wooden container called a hod. It was incredibly hard and painful work, and I can remember Adelheid having to anoint and bandage the sores on his shoulders each evening when he came home from work.

Like most of his fellow workers, he invariably stopped at a local tavern on Saturday evenings on his way home from work, arriving intoxicated and having to be undressed and put to bed by Adelheid.

This was the custom of the laboring class in that era, and women accepted it without complaint as a fact of life. It was strictly a man's world, divorce being unthinkable.

Ribe was a city of great historic significance, having been the seat of the first kings of Denmark, and the location of the eight hundred year old Ribe Domkirke Cathedral. It was a lovely old town, filled every weekend with farmers coming from miles around to sell their produce and livestock. There were no automobiles, and all the streets were paved with cobblestones. I doubt if there was a house in Ribe under 200 years old, and most of the houses had been occupied by the same families for several hundred years or longer.

The narrow, slowly moving river running through the center of the town was a fascinating and never ending delight. I can recall the many times when I was punished for running away, and found to be sitting on the retaining wall bordering the river watching the fishing boats passing through to the North Sea.

Ribe was famous throughout Denmark for the many long-legged storks that arrived every spring from Spain and the south of France. Their nests could be seen on scores of chimneys across the town, the same storks returning year after year to their particular chimney. A family with a stork's nest on their chimney was deemed to be especially blessed.

I have a recollection of crossing the Atlantic on the steamship *Hellig Olav* of the Scandinavian American Steamship Line, and arriving at Ellis Island along with hundreds of other immigrants. Our first destination was to be Keystone, Iowa, where Adelheid had a brother named Jorgen who owned and farmed a quarter section of land that he had homesteaded.

The trip on the train was an exciting adventure for a inquisitive five-year old boy. It was crowded to capacity with open-hearted, kind unpretentious foreigners, all filled with pure anticipation and wonder at this strange new world where they would surely own their own land and prosper. Most families carried their own food, such as roast chickens, pork and beef roasts, which in a warm and friendly fashion they shared and traded back and forth. At every train stop, vendors boarded the train, selling box lunches and refreshments. The people were from a dozen different countries, yet there seemed to be no barriers, only expressions of bright hopes with a common concern for one another's welfare. These memories still linger as an especially happy time. I remember asking Adelheid why we were only three in our family, while other families had five or six children.

I cannot recall any particular memorable event during our two month stay on Jorgen Jorgensen's homestead. They had two sons, Harold, who was my age, and Jorgen, two years older. From Iowa, we traveled by train to Fresno, California, in the fertile San Joaquin Valley. Fresno had a large population of Europeans, predominately Armenians and Scandinavians.

Fresno was the home of Adelheid's aunt, Mrs. Jensen, whose husband had recently passed away. It was she who had loaned Chris and Adelheid the money for the voyage from Denmark to Fresno. Mrs. Jensen was quite wealthy, her husband having been one of the earliest settlers in the San Joaquin Valley, and he had the distinction of being the person who introduced the first gasoline engine into the valley for irrigation purposes. She had extensive property holdings in downtown Fresno, her residence occupying an entire block on Divisadero Street in the center of town.

Mrs. Jensen's two sons, Chris and Andrew were prominent in city and county affairs, both being graduates of Stanford University. Chris was the County Surveyor and Andrew the City Engineer. Andrew was the inventor of a highway paving substance called Jensenite, still in use on California highways. He was an admirable person, who always had time to talk to and counsel a small boy.

I had the impression that Mrs. Jensen felt that Adelheid had married beneath her, as I do not recall that Chris was ever invited to their home. Adelheid became a daytime housekeeper for Mrs. Jensen who lived in a rather grand style. She was one of the first persons in Fresno to have an electric-driven automobile.

Fresno's economy in 1912 was almost entirely agricultural, dominated by vineyards, along with vast fig, peach and apricot orchards. The city had a population of about 30,000 and the dome of the courthouse in the downtown city park with its bandstand for Sunday concerts, although no taller than a two-storied building, could be seen from a distance of ten miles. I recall that the fountain in the park featured a small boy peeing into the fountain basin.

Chris bought an acre of land for $150 with a $20 down payment. It was on Maple Avenue in the Recreation Park area about four miles from the courthouse in downtown Fresno. Close by were the county fairgrounds, the combined county hospital and poor farm. The general area was planted in wheat fields and vineyards bordered by rows of fig trees.

Chris worked as a hod carrier and general

laborer. As soon as he acquired his acre of land, he spent his evenings and weekends digging the cellar with a hand shovel. Through one of the Danish Brotherhood Societies, the Dania, Chris and Adelheid became close friends with two couples, Marius and Hulda Madsen, who had three sons, Einar, Holger and Rudolf. The other family was the Jorgensens, Hans and Lena who also had three sons, Hans, Ernest and Louie. Hans Jorgensen was a butcher, and Marius Madsen and Chris worked together as construction laborers. These three families would remain friends all of their lives.

There were no girls in the three families, and the seven boys became a close-knit group of growing youths. By virtue of being the eldest, I became the leader of the group, which may to some extent account for my driving quest for authority throughout my life.

The Madsens bought an acre of land adjoining ours. Chris and Marius worked together to build their homes, buying materials every week. When our cellar was dug and the floors of the house laid we moved into the cellar to live while the rest of the house was being built. The construction of the house was a lengthy project. Chris and Marius worked ten hours a day in town, carrying cement up ladders on their shoulders, and there were many times when they were too exhausted to work on their homes. Every day except Sunday, Adelheid worked at the home of her aunt and as a consequence, I spent a great deal of my time with the Madsen family next door.

Hulda Madsen was a warm, intelligent woman, and treated me as one of her own children. One of the greatest joys of my boyhood were the evenings when she would read Grimm's fairy tales to us. The illustrations in the book were so fascinating. I was now seven years old, carefree, and in a practical sense, mature far beyond my years.

I have vivid memories of spring, when thousands of wild geese flew across the sky in "V's" at great heights, honking their way north. If I pause for a moment I can still hear the symphony of singing bluebirds, meadowlarks, cooing doves, and feel the warm sand caressing my bare feet, and trickling between my toes as I ran across the fields between the rows of grapevines.

The neighbors I remember with much affection were the Vargas family from Mexico. They had three children, Ray, Joe and Hortense. Affectionate, demonstrative people, they lived next door with an open kitchen to all of us neighboring boys. On their back porch, always available to us, stood a large barrel of black olives in brine. We ate at whatever house we happened to be in at supper time. Because of them I have always had a warm regard for Mexican people. One of the boys, Ray, became a prize fighter. After several years he came to a tragic end when only 24 years old. The daughter, Hortense, was three years older than me, and we all wanted to pair off with her when we played "hide and seek" amongst the grapevines. She would sometimes lift her dress and delight us by showing how girls were built differently from boys.

Another neighbor was the Fred Dow family, an older, childless couple in their early fifties. They were the principal pioneer landowners in the area. They lived in a large house, had servants who waited on them at dinner, and were held in awe by their neighbors. They liked to have me at their house, usually for dinner, and to walk about the ranch with Mr. Dow. Whenever Mr. Dow had to travel to San Francisco on business, I would be invited over to their house to be company for Mrs. Dow during his absence. Mrs. Dow mothered me, and being a college educated woman, helped me with my school work. Mr. Dow had an electric automobile, and on his trips to town, he always took me along. We would stop at a drug store and have a strawberry ice cream soda.

Our pleasures as children were simple. We never had any store-bought toys, except at

Christmas. We made our own games, such as a popular game called peewee, which consisted of a two-inch length of broomstick, sharpened to a point at each end, and a bat made from a two-foot length of broomstick. The small piece would be placed in a narrow three-inch deep slot in the ground, and propelled some distance with the longer stick. The object of the game was to strike the tip of the small piece, flipping it into the air, and batting it towards the slot in the ground, a game likened to golf.

There were the seasonal marble games, when every boy of any consequence carried a sackful of marbles to school. During recesses we would play "for keeps," thereby increasing or decreasing our supply of marbles; such as dobies (clay) marbles, agates and puries, each according to his skill. There was "Annie Over," where persons on opposite sides of the house would toss a ball back and forth over the roof, while shouting "Annie Over."

When I became six I enrolled in Jackson School, three miles from home. Grades from the first to the eighth grade were taught in eight tiny rooms. For years I had the same teacher, Miss McIntyre, in a room with twenty desks, and a large pot bellied wood stove in front of the teacher's desk. In 1913 there were few male or married teachers, and the principals were always men.

I caught on rapidly and skipped several grades while in grammar school. At times I must have been bored. One cold day with a fire raging in the stove, Miss McIntyre came from behind and caught me engrossed in a *Nick Carter* dreadful featuring a bloodcurdling train robbery, hidden in my history book. Held by one ear, I was marched up to the stove, and while Miss McIntyre lifted the stove top, I had to commit *Nick Carter* to the flames. I received 10 whacks with a ruler on the palms of both hands.

On my first day in school I showed up dressed in Danish attire, consisting of a woolen knitted cap, and trousers that stopped halfway between my knees and ankles. That, coupled with my always sober mein, earned me the name of "Grandpa". That title stuck with me through all my school years, even following me to high school. Although I could be outgoing and companionable with the Madsen and Jorgensen boys, I was quiet to a degree that other youths found disturbing. I knew a few words of English, but had difficulty in putting together a sentence. Chris and Adelheid spoke only Danish at home, as did the Madsen and Jorgensen families.

I always had the lowest obtainable grade in deportment and unfortunately, this was the only grade that was of any importance to Chris and Adelheid. I could have all "A's" in English, geography and history, but a "D" in deportment called for an appointment with Chris and the razor strap, a heavy leather one. Sometimes I thought of running away from home, rather than face Chris with a poor grade in deportment.

There were three special attractions that we never failed to religiously attend on our way home from school. The most important and exciting being the detention home for wayward girls. It was a large two-storied, red brick building about a quarter of a mile before we reached the County Hospital and Poor Farm. It was surrounded by a high, wire mesh fence. On our way home we would gather outside the fence, observing and listening to the girls at the open windows shouting sexual salutations. To our great delight, they made interesting lewd gestures with their hands and bodies, a great subject for future analysis by me and the Madsen boys. We invented names for some of the girls, and of course we had our favorites. We never passed up this landmark without at least 20 minutes of sex education. We were sworn never to tell our parents about this entertaining stop.

The next stop was the leper, good for at least 15 minutes. On one corner of the hospital grounds was a five hundred foot square of pasture land. The leper's tent was in the middle of this pasture, and at a halfway point to the edge of the pasture was a smaller tent. The hospital attendant would bring the food to the smaller tent, and hurry away from the area when the leper came to fetch his food. The leper was in residence there for about five years.

Our third and final stop was at a row of benches just outside the County Hospital and Poor Farm, which was also the end of the Recreation Park street car line. There was always a group of 10 to 15 old men sitting on the benches, for the most part full-bearded and dressed in ragged clothes that were smelly and stained with tobacco juice. At this spot the Madsen boys left me. They were forbidden by their mother to linger or talk to this group of men. In my case there were no such restrictions, Adelheid being at work.

I knew most of the men by their given names and always stayed to visit. They were eager to talk to an interested young boy who listened to their stories of ships and far away places. This stop might take a half hour or longer, so they could finish their tales of adventure. Later, when I had a newspaper route and could afford it, I would bring each of them a sack of Bull Durham tobacco, cigarette papers and matches. I was always sad and wept when told that one of them had died or was ill in the hospital.

Next to the County Hospital was the site of the Fresno County Fair Grounds, which boasted the largest wooden racing tracks in the United States. It was the forerunner of the Indianapolis 500 automobile races of today. World famous drivers such as Barney Oldfield were racing in those days. World champion boxing and wrestling took place there. I can recall that one year "Farmer Burns" was a competitor for the world's wrestling championship.

Another event I looked forward to each week was Saturday evening when Chris returned home from the saloon, where he tended bar that night. We lived on a side road one half mile from the main dirt road that led to town. Towards dusk, Adelheid and

I would watch for his horse and buggy to appear. Should the horse fail to turn into our side road, hesitate, and slowly meander on, we would know that Chris had passed out in the bottom of the buggy. Then I would dash barefooted across the sandy fields, get into the buggy and proudly drive home with my feet on Chris lying on the floor of the buggy. When we reached the house, Adelheid and I would carry him off to bed.

After several years, Chris and Marius Madsen formed a small cement contracting company. Chris stopped drinking, and Adelheid worked long hours at the laundry, saving every spare dollar towards their dream of returning to Denmark and buying a small farm. Chris had no formal education, and Adelheid, while a good wife and mother whose world did not extend beyond the care of her family, did not consider my education of much importance. It had no priority.

There was no communication between Chris and me that could establish or sustain a father and son relationship. Sometimes I sensed a hostility, as though he resented Adelheid's loving regard for me. I do not find myself able to blame him for his feelings, for, reading the above words, I have been startled to discover that the sad, regrettable relationship I had with my own children is almost identical to my relationship with Chris. Probably that has something to do with my inability to condemn him now. History repeating itself. How could I have been so blind?

These years of my life until the age of twelve, were fairly good years. Living in a world of my own, I had no way of measuring the quality of my existence.

I brought home books from the library every week, eager to learn about the world. I collected labels from every product that gave away prizes, one in particular being Nabisco box ends. I carried on a regular correspondence with the United States Patent Office with inventive ideas, collected postage stamps, raised pigeons so I could sell squabs. I also made my own wireless receiver from drawings in *Popular Mechanics* magazine, so that with a piece of crystal ore I could receive dots and dashes. At age 11, I graduated from grammar school and looked forward to attending Longfellow High School at the close of summer. I would have earned enough money to attend by picking grapes, but that was not to be.

The cement contracting business had prospered and Chris felt that with the sale of the house, their savings, and the sale of his part of the business to Marius Madsen, we would have enough money to return to Denmark. There they would fulfill their dream of owning a small farm.

I remember the day World War I ended, and the flu epidemic when everyone had to wear white gauze masks on street cars on city streets and in all public places. I remember the day finally arrived when we packed all of our belongings and set out by train to New York to sail across the Atlantic on the *S/S Hellig Olav*, the same ship which had brought us to America seven years earlier. This ship would carry us to Copenhagen, and from there we would go by train to Ribe, the town of my birth.

On our arrival in Ribe, we moved into the Thomsen brothers compound. I was bewildered and confused about my dreams and ambitions. Except between major cities connected by trains, most transportation in Denmark was by horse-drawn vehicles or bicycles, and even to travel a hundred kilometers (60 miles) was considered a major journey. In contrast to communications today, news moved very slowly. In small towns and on farms, news of happenings outside their immediate vicinity was of little interest to the average inhabitant.

We made our headquarters at the home of Chris's family, while Chris and I traveled about the countryside in a horse and buggy searching for a small farm. I vividly recall every detail of the third farm we visited and eventually purchased.

It was near the village of Faurholdt, approximately ten miles from Ribe, and on a clear day, the spires of Ribe Domkirke Cathedral could be seen on the horizon. It was a dairy farm with 12 cows and the usual farm animals such as hogs, ducks and chickens. The farm produced all the feed for the livestock. Adjacent to the farmhouse was a large garden with berries, fruit trees and vegetables. The farm building was one long stone structure with a thatched straw roof.

The living area was separated from the stables by a pantry and washroom, where stood a hand pump made from a bored-out tree trunk. There was no inside plumbing. There was a small two room apartment at the opposite end of the building, which, as part of the sales agreement, was to be occupied by the old couple selling the property. Most farms in Denmark have such quarters attached, so when their offspring take over the farm, their parents retain a lifetime tenancy on the property, as well as subsistence provided by the one taking possession of the farm.

When a Danish farmer decides to retire, the eldest son has first right to the farm. If he does not desire the farm, then it is offered to the next child in order of precedence by age. A standing committee of perhaps a dozen local farmers then evaluate the farm property and arrive at a sum the person assuming ownership must pay in compensation to his brothers and sisters as their share of inheritance rights.

The owner of the farm and his housekeeper, both in their late eighties, had lived on the farm their entire lives. The first evening was a memorable one. We sat down to supper at a round wooden table in the kitchen, bare except for a horn spoon in front of each of the four chairs. A large wooden bowl of pea soup was placed in the middle of the table. After saying grace, the old couple dipped their spoons into the soup bowl and began their meal. With a warning look at me, Chris followed suit, as reluctantly did I. The old couple was slurping up their soup with loud noises. Soup dripping down the old man's long beard made it quite an ordeal to finish the course. The soup was followed by meat and potatoes. Half way through the meal a piece of meat became stuck in the old man's throat, whereupon the housekeeper jumped up, ran to the stove after a lamp-chimney cleaner, a piece of wire with a large dirty piece of cotton at one end. She stuffed this down his throat while slapping him on the back. He recovered and resumed eating.

At bedtime we retired to the one living room in the house. On opposite sides of the room were two sets of double doors opening into what I thought were closets or cupboards. When the doors were opened, lower and upper berths were revealed on each side of the room. Each cubicle was fitted with a ventilation outlet to the loft. Chris and the farmer took the berths on one side, while I was assigned to the upper berth above the housekeeper on the other side. The doors were then tightly closed, and in these tombs, we spent the night. Chris must have had as uncomfortable a night as did I for the next morning he was up very early. We left for Ribe to negotiate for the purchase of the farm. In about six weeks we took possession.

It had no modern improvements whatsoever, and the methods of farming had not been upgraded for at least two hundred years. The only motive power consisted of one tired old horse. In the garden adjacent to the house was a cleared circle about 30 feet in diameter, with an upright post with a large carriage wheel fastened horizontally to the top. From the wheel another pole extended horizontally about 10 feet. The horse's collar was attached to the end of this pole. By walking in a circle about the post, a series of rods and gears led to the straw cutting machine in the small threshing room. In the winter months sheaves of wheat and barley would be tossed down from the storage loft, where the kernels would be thrashed out with a hand flail. The straw would then be sliced to tiny bits by the horse-powered straw slicer as winter feed for the livestock.

The farm consisted of sixty acres, of which 15 was a grove of tall fir trees planted in rows. Twenty acres were pasture land, and the remainder was allocated to the planting of wheat, oats, barley and sugar beets. There were also three deep clay pits about fifty feet in diameter, stocked with pike and pickerel. In the winter the ice on these ponds was up to 10 inches thick, fine for skating. Under the ice one could see fish up to two feet in length, caught by stunning them with a blow on the ice with the back of an axe and retrieving them by chopping a hole in the ice.

There was an antique, pin-fired, double barreled 12-gauge shotgun on the farm, and in the winter months I often hunted white rabbits for food and pelts. The gun had a terrible recoil, and when fired would throw me backwards several feet, as well as bruising my shoulder.

The farm was isolated, and there were no children my own age in the vicinity. Chris and I got up at five every morning while it was still dark. I quickly learned to milk cows and feed the hogs. My first task in the morning would be to shovel up the cow dung from the trough behind the cows and trundle it in a wheelbarrow to the top of the manure pile outside. Much to the disgust of Chris, I was always running to the pump to wash the dung from under my fingernails. The urine from the cows and pigs stored itself in an underground holding tank, and in the spring we would pump it into a small horse-drawn tank cart and spray it over the fields as fertilizer, not a pleasant task. The cow barn and the pig sty had to be scrubbed out twice daily. The care of the chickens and ducks was allocated to Adelheid.

I do not recall that Chris or Adelheid ever

attended church during our years in the United States. I had never been exposed to any contact with religion, other than singing "God Bless America" every morning in school, or seeing "In God We Trust" on silver dollars. My introduction to religious training came that first winter in Faurholdt. It having been decreed that, for the good of my soul I should be confirmed. So when the snow started to fall and the temperatures dropped below zero, and there was no outside work to be done on the farm, I trudged through the snow banks five days a week to the nearest rectory three miles distant. There, with a dozen other children, I studied the Bible in preparation for my confirmation to take place the coming spring.

Confirmation was an important milestone for Danish youths, comparable to the Jewish "Bar Mitzvah" coming of age ritual. It was an occasion where boys for the first time would wear long trousers, always hand tailored of heavy blue serge, and accompanied by a silver watch and chain from the family.

As an American I was considered somewhat of a curiosity by the other children attending confirmation classes that winter. In the spring I was duly confirmed.

Spring and summer passed and it was harvest time. The work methods in the fields were primitive. Even at my tender age, and knowing nothing about farming, I could see dozens of ways of doing things more efficiently. Chris would walk ahead of us cutting the grain with a long sweep of his scythe. Adelheid and I followed behind with bent backs, gathering up the oats, barley and wheat, and binding them into sheaves as Rachel did in the Bible 2,000 years ago. After drying and curing them in the sun, we hauled the sheaves to the house for storage in the loft. We dug pits in the soil, where wrapped in straw against freezing, we would store potatoes for our winter use, as well as a winter supply of sugar beets for the farm animals. Chris

and Adelheid, with my limited help (I was small for my age) worked long hours in the fields plus we cared for the livestock. Chris had spent some years on a farm as a boy, but there was much knowledge necessary to being a successful farmer which he did not possess, and there were no close neighbors to counsel him.

After the first year, Chris began to wish that he was back in Fresno in the cement business. He and Adelheid decided to sell the farm and return to the United States. A buyer for the farm was found, and we moved back to the Thomsen compound in Ribe, where we would remain for approximately six months until the sale was finalized. I was not unhappy over the turn of events, and looked forward to the day when we would be back in Fresno. I could get on with my schooling and my dreams. In Ribe I spent most of my days fishing in the river, and one evening each week I attended dancing school conducted by a man named Stockholm Simmonsen.

Then one day Adelheid told me that Chris thought it best that I remain in Denmark to acquire a trade that would be of use to me when I later joined them in Fresno. An apprenticeship was a four year period. I was more than a little shocked. Adelheid had a sister, timid and not very bright, who was married to a German saddle maker in the town of Tonder, 200 kilometers from Ribe, near the border with Germany. Her husband was Wilhelm Nixdorf, a man well over six feet, with a long handlebar mustache and a dour nature. So off I was shipped to the tender mercies of Wilhelm Nixdorf.

I liked the smell of tanned leather, of which there was very little. The chief product turned out by this saddle shop was horsehair mattresses. Ninety percent of my working hours was spent cooking horsehair, which had first to be coiled in tight loops, tied and placed in a large steaming vat of boiling water. I would tend this by keeping the coils pushed under the surface of the water, using a four-foot long broom handle. When the coils were removed from the vat they were cooled, by which process they retained their springy texture. The bundles were then opened up, and the horsehair sewn into small cloth sacks. Although I was far from the happiest worker in this dawn to dusk mattress factory, I was at least learning something. Most of the time we worked three or four hours after supper, and rose at six the next morning. Wilhelm was an unfeeling taskmaster not above giving me an occasional clout on the side of the head with a coil of horsehair if I did not move fast enough to please him.

I stuck with it for three months before putting my belongings in a paper bag, and without notifying anyone, set out walking to Ribe. My arrival was greeted with disgust by Chris and joy by Adelheid. A week later Chris had me apprenticed to a watchmaker in Ribe. To become an apprentice to a Tradesman, one would pledge his services for four years in exchange for being taught the trade. He would reside with the Tradesman's family, receiving board and room, clothing and a stipulated small amount of spending money. In effect, he was to be treated as a member of the Tradesman's family who had the equivalent of parental control over him, or his status might also be likened to a sixteenth century bonded servant.

The watchmaker was an elderly, kindly man, and we liked each other from the start. I ran errands, cleaned the shop, and assisted wherever I could. I was quite content with the arrangement.

A short time later, Chris received the farm settlement, and the necessary papers from the United States permitting him to return to America. Adelheid insisted that I not be left behind in Denmark. The three of us set out on the journey back to Fresno, California.

On the steamer crossing the Atlantic, I struck up an acquaintance with several crew members. I spent time each day in the crew's quarters, storing up information that would be of use to me sooner than I knew.

The voyage to Fresno was uneventful. My father's farm venture had been disastrous. On arrival in Fresno he had very little money left. He had hoped to rejoin Marius Madsen as a partner in the cement construction business they had built together some years before, but the business had grown considerably in Chris's absence. Marius was not interested in resuming the partnership. Chris went to work for Marius as a hod carrier, back where he had started years before. Adelheid resumed her position at the laundry, and I began my first year at Longfellow High School. We no longer lived near the Madsens or the Jorgensens, so I saw them only on occasional Sundays when the three families had picnics together at Kings River Dam.

To buy a bicycle, clothes and have spending money, I took on two paper routes. I would leave home at 5:30 in the morning and deliver the *Fresno Republican,* and evenings after school deliver the *Evening Herald.* On Saturdays I mowed lawns. At school I was strictly a loner. My nickname "Grandpa" had followed me from Jackson School.

I found it depressing to have my former classmates now one or two grades ahead of me. I was a better than average student in spite of my two year absence. Slightly built, with delicate features and a dreamy, imaginative nature, I had no interest in any sports or group activity. I had an additional problem in that I invariably became the "Teacher's Pet," a dubious honor. This did not increase my popularity with my peers. More often than not, I was a regular participant in after school fights held in the eucalyptus grove behind the school.

In retrospect, I can see the chip on my shoulder. I was never a member of any group. Many a Friday evening I arrived home with my shirt torn to pieces from a "coming home from school" encounter. Whenever possible, I joined a group of neighborhood girls, who came to my aid if I was threatened.

My closest friends were three Armenian boys from "across the tracks." One of them was William Saroyan who later became a Hollywood playwright. He was the author of a number of books, one entitled, *The Time of Our Lives*. Bill and I, along with John Hagopian, and a boy named Haig, had a habit of playing hooky from school to swim in the irrigation ditches on hot summer days. A number of times the school principal, Mr. Munson, had us in his office bent over a chair for some lashes with a strap. Except for some damage to our pride it could not have bothered us too much or we would not have had so many repeat performances. Bill Saroyan and I corresponded off and on when he was struggling with his writing career in San Francisco.

In my first year at Longfellow, a beautiful person entered my life. It would be impossible to describe the feelings that were brought forth and nurtured in this relationship in which I felt so unselfishly loved and cared for. She was my English teacher, Jessie K. Paxton, about 25 years old, with flaming red hair and beautiful legs, and she loved me. She belonged to a well-to-do family and had graduated from an Eastern college. She was the only teacher with an automobile, and every school day she would come by our house and drive me to school. On Fridays she would take me to the library and select four or five books for me to read during the week. I devoured Joyce, Conrad, Tolstoy, Shakespeare, and the English poets. These books brought a golden glow into my life and set my reading habits during the many years I spent at sea. Years later I visited Miss Paxton in San Diego, California, when she was in her sixties, still single.

My thoughts and attitudes towards women were decidedly Victorian. I viewed girls as mysterious, untouchable creatures to be placed on pedestals and worshipped, an affliction that possessed me until my early thirties. I remember in detail while in high school, falling in love with two sisters, both at the same time. Their names were Gladys and Thelma Duckett. They had recently come to Fresno from France and lived in the Marlborough Apartments downtown, which in itself was glamorous and a distinction of no small dimension. They had been brought up in Paris, spoke with a charming accent, and did not associate with the "Group" at school. After school, having to go downtown to the *Evening Herald* for my newspapers, I carried their books home for them. All winter long my heart sang with happiness at being near them, and I was the envy of all the regulars whom they pointedly ignored.

While top grades came easily to me at Longfellow High School, socially I was a complete failure. Except for my relationship with the Madsen and Jorgensen boys prior to going back to Denmark, I do not recall ever having attended a party or played a sport of any kind. I always presented a serious demeanor. Except for emotional immaturity, I had had from the age of seven the temperament, outlook and disposition of an adult.

A photo of me at that tender age bears this out. It was as though I had skipped over childhood. I did not achieve any emotional security until after the age of 70. Deeply rooted in me was a degree of insecurity stemming from my early life which demanded that I never relinquish control of my actions or destiny to others. I needed complete self-sufficiency. This might explain in part why even at 90 I find it difficult, except in a few instances, to develop a closeness with any group or individual.

On weekends I would take with me a blanket, books, food and fishing gear, and walk five miles to Fancher Creek, a densely wooded stream that flowed through the deserted countryside. There I would read, catch and cook fish, and search after pearls in freshwater clams. Sometimes I would have a substitute take care of my paper routes and would stay away for several days. No one ever questioned my absence, except to ask where I was going and when I would be home. My world consisted of books, school studies, my two newspaper routes, and these weekends at Fancher Creek. Adelheid was a warm uncomplicated person, and protective of me. Through no fault of his own, Chris was unable to be demonstrative as a father, and our home was completely devoid of any intellectual atmosphere. Sometimes I felt as though I was a stranger at home as well as in school, seemingly not a part of anything.

Chris had a brother named Hans, who with his wife and family drove out from Kansas City to Fresno to visit us for two weeks. The eldest daughter, thirteen year old Carla, in the course of a childish argument, told me that Chris and Adelheid were not my real parents, that I had been given to them by my mother who had been unable to keep me. She had overheard her parents discussing this in their automobile while enroute to Fresno.

I brooded over this for several weeks before I had the courage to ask Adelheid if it were true that I was not her child and Chris not my father. Adelheid, a completely honest person unable to lie, told me that after caring for me the first four years of my life, when she received my birth mother's letter saying that my parents were to be married and would be coming to reclaim me, she could not bear to give me up. She had persuaded Chris to emigrate to America, taking me along. It was a very emotional scene, as she was all I had.

That night, after Chris and Adelheid had gone to bed, I got up and dressed. With a bundle containing several shirts and socks, and my savings of $13, I climbed out of my bedroom window and made my way to the railroad tracks on the other side of town. I passed through Chinatown, where I stopped at a restaurant for a cup of coffee and a doughnut, as well as to find out where to catch a freight train to San Francisco. The restaurant proprietor directed me to an area along the railroad tracks where he said men gathered to board freight trains passing through Fresno. In the darkness I

headed in that direction alone. My mind was full of unanswered questions about my birth and natural parents. I felt as though my entire world had fallen apart.

# CHAPTER TWO

# JENNY

Jenny was the strikingly beautiful, well-educated, headstrong and unconventional daughter born in 1887 to a Lutheran minister in Denmark. The tragic death of her mother followed shortly after her ninth birthday. Jenny was devastated when her father dutifully remarried to provide a new mother for her and her younger sister Anna. Distance grew between Jenny and her father as he became utterly absorbed in the work of saving souls and preoccupied with his new wife. Jenny's world became schoolwork, books and dreams of romantic love. The ensuing eight years produced eight more children in the Andersen family, including Jens whom Jenny bore unwed at the tender age of eighteen, causing stinging disgrace and embarrassment to her father. She steadfastly refused to marry the child's father and kept her son despite heated arguments.

Desperate to leave her father's house, Jenny took employment on the grand estate of Peter von Buchholdt, the grandson of a titled count. She was able to have Jens with her and settled nicely into her duties, becoming the favorite of the lady of the manor, who quickly reassigned Jenny to be her personal maid. Jenny loved the elegant, exquisite surroundings and enjoyed her position.

The von Buchholdt's son, Hans Christian, was a student at the military academy in Kiel, Germany. Returning to the manor on leave, Hans Christian was drawn to the spirited young girl and Jenny was swept off her feet by the dashing and handsome young cadet. Jenny was stunned when she found herself with child. The family opposed marriage, citing the fact that Hans Christian would be expelled from the academy should he marry before graduation. Frau von Buchholdt asked her to remain. But Jenny was convinced that social and class distinction were at the root of the von Buchholdt's decision to deny the lovers' request to marry. She left the manor and moved to Ribe, an ancient city several hundred kilometers distant. There she found employment at the local hospital.

Ribe was the largest market center in Southern Jylland and a town of great historical significance: the site of the First Kings of Denmark, and the location of an 800 year old Ribe Domkirke Cathedral. It was a beautiful, quiet city with a river flowing through the center of town.

At two o'clock on the morning on March 20, 1907, Jenny gave birth to a son in a small two room house facing the bank of the river. When he was two weeks old, Jenny had Niels baptized in Ribe Domkirke, giving him the name Niels Peter Andersen von Buchholdt, after her Great Grandfather Niels Rytter and Hans Christian's father, Peter von Buchholdt.

Needing to have her two boys cared for during the day, Jenny found a newly married couple, Chris and Adelheid Thomsen. Chris was a laborer and one of a family of twelve children. Adelheid, of a better educated class, was one of eight children of a Lutheran minister.

Jenny remained in Ribe for approximately one year. Extremely independent and high-spirited, she refused to have any contact with the family von Buchholdt. Adelheid Thomsen had full time day and night care of both children while Jenny worked. Jenny received a letter from her aunt in Copenhagen stating that she had purchased a small pension (hotel), and offered Jenny a position. Jenny accepted. She discussed the matter with Adelheid, who, unable to have children, had become very attached to Niels. She expressed a desire to continue taking care of him without any monetary compensation. Jenny decided to leave Niels with the Thomsens, and departed with Jens for Copenhagen.

The next four years were a relatively quiet, uneventful period in Jenny's life. She got along well with her aunt, and periodically she traveled to Ribe to spend a day or two with Adelheid and Niels. During these years there was limited correspondence with Hans Christian, who was still in love with her. He graduated from the academy, but received no affirmative response to his written declarations of affection and proposals of marriage.

There were indications that Jenny was not particularly interested in marrying Hans Christian, a very serious-minded career officer. Mr. Jorgensen, visiting from the United States, and a guest at the pension struck up a friendship with Jenny. They corresponded after he returned to the United States. A few months later he wrote to Jenny proposing marriage. Jenny, ever adventurous, agreed to marry him. Mr. Jorgensen farmed a section of land in Nebraska and made all arrangements for her to travel there, sending her railroad and steamship tickets that would take her to Nebraska.

For some unknown reason Jenny made no use of the steamship ticket, relegating it to a bureau drawer. An examination of this 85 year old ticket reveals that passengers listed are Jenny and her son, Jens. It is presumed that she had made no mention of Niels to Mr Jorgensen and could not bring herself to abandon him.

Hans Christian took leave from his duty station on the German border and came to Copenhagen. For the first time since they had parted at the von Buchholdt estate these star-crossed lovers met face to face. Hans Christian again asked her to marry him, and Jenny accepted. Jenny wrote to the Thomsens that they were to be married and after a month-long honeymoon in Switzerland, they would stop in Ribe to pick up Niels. From there the family would proceed to Hans Christian's duty station as second in command on the German border.

Jenny and Hans Christian were married in Copenhagen on October 12, 1912, spending a month on their honeymoon in Switzerland and Germany. They returned to Copenhagen travelling by train to pick up Niels. On arrival in Ribe they were stunned to learn that the Thomsens, together with Niels, had emigrated to America. This was a heartbreaking development. They would not have with them the son they had created. Bereft by the realization that Niels had been abducted, Jenny and Hans Christian went to the cathedral where Hans Christian signed the baptismal certificate register declaring Niels' birth legitimate.

CHAPTER THREE

# RUNAWAY

 After walking about a half mile along the railroad track from the Chinese restaurant I came upon eight or ten men, bearded and roughly-dressed, each man with a role of bedding on his back. They were sitting around a campfire waiting to board a box car on a freight train for San Francisco. No one questioned my presence and when a string of freight cars came by at low speed, I jumped in a box car along with them. Once the train had cleared the outskirts of Fresno, several of the men questioned me, wanting to know where I was going. I told them of my intention to take the train to San Francisco where I hoped to find a sailing ship.

They were helpful with advice, telling me that the next stop would be Livermore, and when the train slowed on entering the town limits we would all leap from the train. The plan then was to camp by a stream and rest until nightfall, when we would hop another freight train bound for South San Francisco.

I had thirteen dollars and felt well off, bolstered by the belief that in all likelihood I was richer than any of my companions. One of the men showed me how to leap from the moving train to keep from being hurt, for which I was grateful. Livermore was two thirds of the way to San Francisco and when the train slowed on entering Livermore railroad yards, we all leaped off before it came to a stop. The area along the track was wooded, and there was a small stream nearby.

Two of the men gathered branches to build a fire, one producing a tin pot, and some searched the area for tin cans to use as cups. One of the men asked if I would come with them to some rows of houses and help beg food. They told me what to say after knocking at the back door. We then headed for different streets, and in an hour we returned to camp.

Perhaps my youthful appearance evoked greater empathy in this pan-handling operation, for I proudly returned with my arms full of bread, butter, jam, cheese and a large slice of ham. The food was placed on newspapers and shared equally, together with coffee made in the large pot. The men joked about making me a permanent member of their group and continuing with them to their final destination in Arizona. Their comments gave me a sense of security and self-confidence.

After our meal we laid down to rest, except for two men who went into town to find out when the next northbound freight train was due to pass through Livermore. They soon returned, saying the train would be passing at midnight. At eleven o'clock we walked to the far side of town and lay in wait for the train. When it came by at slow speed, with one of my companions by my side, we hopped into an empty box car. We left the door open and as it slowed entering South San Francisco, we leaped from the train. One of the men directed me towards the San Francisco waterfront. Amid exchanged shouts of "Good luck," we went our separate ways.

After an hour long walk I reached the Embarcadero, a very busy street skirting a long line of piers where ships of all shapes and sizes were loading and discharging cargo. I stopped at an open street stand and bought a cup of coffee and a doughnut for fifteen cents. I started walking the full length of Embarcadero Street, eagerly looking for the tall masts of a sailing ship, such as I had visualized from reading Joseph Conrad's tales of the sea. Most of the piers were taken up by wooden ships called steam schooners. These shallow draft vessels were powered by steam, and all served in the lumber trade between San Francisco and outports on the Northern California, Oregon, and Washington coasts. They carried a general cargo north and lumber south. They had to be small and of shallow draft to cross the bars at Northwest river ports. The average vessel carried a ten man crew, and the vessels were loaded and unloaded by the deck crews of each ship. Later, the formation of longshore unions made it mandatory that all cargo be loaded and unloaded by longshoremen.

I walked the entire length of the Embarcadero without seeing any sailing ships. Finally I asked some men sitting on a crab fishing boat if they knew where I might find one. They seemed to think that I was joking. I then asked how to find a berth on one of the small steam schooners I had seen. They told me to go on board one of them and ask for the mate. They also suggested that I was too young and too small to be a sailor where I had to work cargo. I should tell the mate that I was eighteen and looking for berth as a cabin boy. All that first day I tramped

up and down the waterfront looking at ships and asking questions. I was having difficulty screwing up enough courage to go on board and ask for work. Several times I got as far as halfway up the gangway and went back on shore without speaking to anyone. That night I rented a room at the Bay Hotel on the waterfront for seventy-five cents a night. At a nearby restaurant I had a complete dinner for twenty-five cents.

The next morning I was up early, had coffee and hotcakes for twenty cents and resumed my search, determined to overcome my timidity. The first vessel I came to was the *Silverado*, a small wooden steam schooner with some men working at loading the ship. I watched for a while and soon was able to pinpoint the man in charge, whom I took to be the mate. For some reason I felt that he would not rebuff me, so I walked on board after asking permission as I had been instructed by my previous day informants. He asked what I wanted. I said I was an experienced cabin boy looking for work. When he asked my age, I added two years and said I was seventeen.

He remarked, "Our cabin boy has been absent for two days, stay around, and if he does not show up by noon, you can have the job." The cabin boy did not show up, and I was hired at twenty-five dollars a month. The vessel was loading cargo for Coos Bay, Oregon, and was to sail early the following day.

I bought some work clothes at a Navy surplus store and was left with six dollars, but I had a job on a ship. I came on board with my belongings and was shown a berth forward by the kindly Chinese cook. He attempted to familiarize me with my duties, speaking half Chinese and half English, and difficult to understand. Except for myself he was the only crew member on board who was sober. The crew had been passing whiskey bottles around all afternoon in celebration of the ship being loaded.

My duties would be taking care of the officers

in the after cabin, where the captain, mate, and the two engineers lived. I was to keep that end of the ship clean, the beds made, set the table, carry aft the food from the galley forward, and stand by to wait on the table. With the help of the cook I made it through the evening meal, after which all of the crew, except the cook and I, went ashore.

I stayed up, waiting for the officers to return from ashore. Just after midnight the crew began to board the ship, all very drunk, staggering about. The mate fell down the companionway where he stayed and went to sleep. There were no electric lights on board, and a lamp was knocked off the wall, almost setting fire to the ship. I was apprehensive because of the condition of the officers. Had it not been for the support of the cook who said everything was normal, I doubt if I could have stayed on board. My experience with Chris's drinking now stood me in good stead, and strangely enough I slept until the cook called me at five o'clock. The mate and the engineers appeared at breakfast, but the captain did not show up until several hours later, about ten minutes before we sailed. I carried his breakfast up to the bridge. None of the officers or crew seemed any the worse for wear despite their long night of drinking.

The lines were cast off and with a wheezing of the engine, clouds of black smoke poured from the stack. We steamed out of San Francisco Bay, out through the Golden Gate, bound up the Coast to Coos Bay. There was a strong northwest head wind and sea. After an hour I became deathly seasick, bringing up my breakfast and thinking I might be dying. I was totally incapacitated, and again the kindly Chinese cook carried me through the day. The wind and sea abated during the night and though not in the best of shape, I was able to perform my duties. The captain and the mate were sympathetic to my condition and appreciated my determination to continue with my work.

On arriving off the mouth of the river at Coos Bay, we had to stand offshore for one day because of unfavorable bar conditions. Coos Bay was a small town completely surrounded by dense woods. It took a number of days at the dock to discharge cargo and load lumber for San Francisco. The main topic of conversation at the dinner table was descriptions of the many fine whorehouses in the town.

I made six round trips on the *Silverado* in the next four months. My ambition was to advance from cabin boy to "ordinary seaman" in the deck department. To accomplish this, it was necessary to accumulate time on a larger ship.

To progress in the deck (sailors') department, one had first to pass an examination, both written and practical. It included lowering a lifeboat into the water and being able to row a lifeboat. After passing this test, and receiving a certificate of proficiency, one became eligible to apply for an ordinary seaman's berth. After sailing for two years as an ordinary seaman, with sea time certified by discharges, he then would be eligible to take an examination for an "able seaman's" certificate. That required an examination in seamanship conducted before an official of the Department of Marine Inspection, an agency which had jurisdiction over the American Merchant Marine. All these functions are now performed by the United States Coast Guard.

On small, coastwise vessels sailors performed the loading and unloading of cargo. I was neither old enough nor had the build and strength needed for this work, so advancement in the deck department on a *Silverado* class vessel was impossible. I made no particular friends and wrote to no one, not even to Adelheid. I was carrying a deep wound, and my emotions seemed frozen.

I joined the Sailors' Union of the Pacific, giving my age as sixteen. As a member of the union I would have a place to while away the time between ships, waiting for a job to come up on the hiring board. With the assistance of the Union, I was examined and received my lifeboat certificate, making me eligible for an ordinary seaman's berth. The hiring system operated on a seniority system based on when you checked in and registered as available for an assignment. My name and number were now on the ordinary seamans' register. Whenever a job came into the hall it was placed on the blackboard and anyone interested would hand in his card. The man with the oldest-dated card would then be assigned to the ship.

I took a room on the Embarcadero which cost three dollars and fifty cents a week, and I felt that I could survive several months waiting for an ordinary seaman's berth. After a five week wait I shipped out on the United States Shipping Board oil tanker *Dilworth* as an ordinary seaman at thirty dollars a month. The *Dilworth* was a 6,000 ton vessel, and was to carry a cargo of fuel oil to Manila in the Philippine Islands.

We sailed on August 25, 1924. I was seventeen years old and looked forward to the time when I would have accumulated two years of sea service as an ordinary seaman and could apply for an able seaman's certificate.

The captain of the ship was a man about sixty, a dour, quiet, chunky Scotsman by the name of Dawson. The chief mate was from Finland, a tall craggy faced man in his forties.

There were three watches in the deck department, each watch consisting of one able seaman and one ordinary seaman. The watches were four hours on and eight hours off. Each deckhand steered the vessel for two hours out of each four hour watch. For the other two hours he stood lookout watch on the bow of the forecastlehead. The duties of the lookout were to keep a sharp lookout for ship or shore lights and report them immediately by hailing the watch officer on the bridge. He had also to keep watch on the red and green running lights on each wing of the bridge.

Every half hour, in response to bells being struck on the bridge, he would strike the same number in reply while shouting to the bridge, "All lights are bright, Sir." Bells on the bridge were struck at half hour intervals twenty-four hours daily, with one bell struck on the first half hour of each four hours, with an additional stroke every half hour to the end of the four hour watch, a total of eight bells.

My watchmate was a red-headed able seaman from New Zealand named Gordon Campbell. The Pacific crossing took about twenty-five days to the entrance of the Straits of San Bernadino, where we would pick up San Bernadino light. No ships had been sighted on our long crossing, and the lookouts had become lax in their duties. It happened that on the night we were scheduled to sight San Bernadino light it was very cold. To warm myself I had crawled in between the drums of the anchor winch to sit on the steam chest which for some reason had been turned on. Unfortunately, I fell asleep, and when the light was seen by the bridge deck officer it was not reported by me, the lookout.

The mate on watch took over the helm and sent Campbell forward to look for me. Campbell did not think of looking between the winch drums and reported to the mate that I was not on the bow. The mate then sent Campbell to search the messroom, lavatories, and other sections of the ship and when I could not be found, he called the captain and the chief mate. The crew quarters, messroom and toilets were searched a second time. The captain and the mates then considered the possibility that I might have fallen overboard, but decided it would be futile to retrace the ship's course and search in the darkness for a man overboard, and so the ship continued on her course. The chief mate decided to make another search of the bow and as a consequence found me asleep. With a foot in my rear end, he assisted me to the bridge for a conference with an irate, Scottish captain named Dawson. The following day, a Captain's Mast (court) was held, and I, Niels Thomsen was fined two weeks' pay without shore leave in the next port.

On arrival in Manila, we anchored in the Bay and prepared to take barges alongside and commence the discharging of our cargo of fuel oil. That night the entire crew went ashore, with the exception of the chief engineer, the first mate and myself, I being restricted to the ship. Around midnight one of the sailors, a large bearded man in his forties, came back to the ship in a local rowboat. It was the only transportation except for a midnight harbor launch which made nightly rounds of vessels in the harbor.

He was wildly drunk and attempted to get into my bunk with the intention of raping me. I kept pounding at him with my fists, terrorized by his bleeding face, and the fear that I was not going to be able to knock him unconscious. Finally I broke away from him and made my way to the chief mate's room, and between us we managed to handcuff him to the iron pipes of his berth. The following day Captain Dawson lifted my shore leave restriction and I could go ashore. I loved the sights and sounds of the city, and exploring the great once-fortified, stone walls surrounding the inner city of Manila. After two days, the captain called me to his cabin, and told me the two weeks' fine imposed at the Captain's Mast was cancelled.

Every evening after sunset, thousands of small fishing boats set sail for the fishing grounds to work until daylight. Each boat had a lantern in the rigging, and the bay looked as though filled with thousands of fireflies, a beautiful sight.

I went ashore almost every evening and made friends with some young Swedish seamen of my own age, crew members of a ship anchored nearby. This association brought about some astounding, latent, behavioral changes in me. For the first time I drank alcoholic beverages, such as beer, and a local rum called anisette, made of licorice root. I also frequented a dance hall called Lerna Park where hundreds of petite Filipino girls in colorful native dance costumes were available as dancing partners and companions. Fortunately, mainly out of fear of venereal disease and female entanglement, I confined my activities to dancing, drinking and sight-seeing.

After three weeks in port the captain and the chief mate, who were becoming concerned over my welfare and conduct, restricted me (much to my indignation) to three nights ashore weekly. I had to be back on board by midnight which meant I had to return to the ship on the midnight harbor launch. On most of these nights ashore, despite the daily lectures doled out by the captain and the chief mate, I managed to return to the ship many nights in a semi-intoxicated state, a complete reversal of my former sober, austere lifestyle. One blurry evening, to promote the image of a seasoned able seaman, I had a butterfly tattooed on my left shoulder. In my own way, I was rapidly qualifying for my able seaman's certificate, or so I convinced myself. Orders were received for the *Dilworth* to proceed to the island of Cebu.

On departing from Manila we sailed several hundred miles to the island of Cebu, where we would remain for two or three months while more than two hundred loin-clad workmen cleaned and polished the interior of the ship's cargo tanks in preparation for loading the ship with a full cargo of bulk coconut oil for San Pedro, California. To clean fuel oil from every square inch of our six tanks was a gigantic undertaking. The tanks, with their heating coils turned on were washed with hot water provided by the engine room. Stages were erected in the holds and swarms of loin-clad native Filipinos armed with a pot of coconut oil and baskets of small hand-made reed brushes, commenced to scrub every square inch of the holds.

Cebu was more like a small insular community than a city. In the center of the town square stood a statue of Ferdinand Magellan, who in 1521, was slain in this same square by the ancestors of these men now scrubbing the holds of the *Dilworth*. Something to think about. The local people were poor, gentle and hospitable, showering us with kindness during our long stay. Having parted company with my Swedish friends who had led me astray in Manila, I had returned to my normal self, quiet and solitary, devoted to my ambition to advance to able seaman and hopefully in time, to a ship's officer. When the tanks were clean, the ship was pumped full of hot coconut oil from heated tanks on shore. On the return trip to San Pedro the ship's steam lines would have to keep the cargo at a high temperature to maintain the oil in a liquid state for pumping ashore at our destination.

After departing from Cebu, the captain and the chief mate had again taken me under their wing, spending much time instructing me in seamanship. The heat of the tropics, combined with the cargo of heated coconut oil, made the entire ship unbearably hot, especially in the crew quarters. Sleeping below decks was virtually impossible. I was still on the twelve to four watch with Gordon Campbell.

One afternoon while on wheel watch the captain came into the wheelhouse clad only in his shorts, carrying a bottle of Sloan's liniment. He said, "Niels, I will take the wheel while you rub some liniment on my back." I stood in great awe of the captain, ranking him next to God, so with trembling hands I proceeded to rub his back with Sloan's liniment. In my nervousness I tipped the bottle too far, and a stream of liniment ran down his spine and between his buttocks. The stinging pain caused him to let out a roar and rush off the bridge to sit in his bathtub, leaving me prepared to jump overboard. Captain Dawson never mentioned the incident. The second mate on watch thought it hilarious.

We arrived in San Pedro after a thirty day voyage. We began pumping out our cargo and paying off the crew. I now had sufficient sea time to

enable me to take an examination for an able seaman's certificate, and so I boarded a Greyhound bus for Seattle, where I intended to sit for the examination. I had a strong attachment to Seattle, perhaps because of the predominantly Scandinavian population on the waterfront in that era. There were many Japanese restaurants where a complete dinner with dessert could be had for only twenty-five cents. I was known at several hotels on First Avenue where a room cost less than five dollars a week, and if I was to run out of money, I could always get credit. My favorite was the Columbia Hotel on First at Seneca. It was operated by a blind man whose wife was stone deaf. I registered at the Sailors' Union Hall of the Pacific just around the corner on Seneca Street.

A week after arriving in Seattle I shipped out as an ordinary seaman on the *Admiral Evans* of the Pacific Coast Steamship Company, which operated a fleet of passenger vessels between Seattle and the Southeastern Alaska ports of Ketchikan, Wrangel, Petersburg and Juneau. I made a number of trips until I had enough money to stay ashore and take the examination for a certificate.

I will always remember this milestone in my life. For months I would awaken at night, take the certificate out from under my pillow and admire it. The next step would be a third mate's license, requiring two years of able seaman time, or better still, a second mate's license, requiring three years as an able seaman, and to be twenty-one years of age.

Two days later I shipped out as an able seaman on the *Dorothy Alexander*. It operated on the coastal run between Seattle and the California coastal ports of San Francisco and Los Angeles (San Pedro Harbor). On the second trip, one of the quartermasters had to leave the ship because of illness. The chief mate asked if I wanted to be a quartermaster. It seemed definitely a step up, and I accepted. The position of quartermaster required an able seaman's certificate and could be likened somewhat to the traditional British system of midshipmen and cadet officer training. His primary duties were steering ship when underway, keeping the pilot house and bridge in order, and when in port, to man the gangway. His work station was on the bridge. The quartermaster worked in the company of deck officers, which gave him the opportunity to observe them performing their navigational and ship-handling duties.

For the next four months I served as relief quartermaster on two coastal passenger vessels of the company, the *Emma Alexander* and the *Dorothy Alexander*. Next I served as quartermaster on the *Harvard*, a fast overnight, high speed passenger vessel operating between San Francisco and Los Angeles. When the *Harvard* went into the shipyard in Seattle for an annual overhaul on September 3, 1925, I left the ship.

Although I had been steadily employed for seven months, I was penniless and in debt. I had spent a great deal of time learning to play poker, dice and blackjack in the steward's quarters on the *Harvard*. I had become a gambling addict in the worst sense of the word. The ambitious career I had set for myself was completely derailed. I had enough sense left to know that I needed to make a radical change in my lifestyle. Little did I know what fate had in store for me.

PART II

# CHAPTER ONE

# NIELS
# ABLE SEAMAN

## STARBOARD WATCH

It was September 1925. I was eighteen and on the beach in Seattle. There was little or no shipping out of the Sailors' Union Hall, and no work to be found on the waterfront. In those days any area north of Seneca Street and above Second Avenue and the Pike Place Market was out of bounds for sailors and prostitutes. Being broke and out of work, this edict did not deter me, and I walked up First Avenue to the Pike Place Market, and inquired at the various food stalls. The third place I asked, I was given a job at two dollars a day wrapping up fish for customers. I found the work at the market new and interesting; meeting and conversing with a family class of people, a rare experience for me.

After working for a few days, and while in the act of wrapping fish, I spotted in *The Seattle Times* a photo of a five-masted sailing ship, together with an article saying the ship was loading in Victoria, B.C. for a voyage to Mauritius, an island in the Indian Ocean. The vessel was named *Forest Dream.* I still had dreams of Joseph Conrad's wooden ships, towering masts, billowing sails and following seas. I knew instantly that come what may, I must be off to British Columbia, where waited the *Forest Dream.*

At the union hall of the Sailors' Union of the Pacific I had made the acquaintance of a sailor by the name of Frank Garlock. Frank was two years older than me, of Polish descent, quiet and reserved. His father, a widower, worked as a janitor in a large New York apartment building. I had loaned Frank several of my Joseph Conrad novels, and together we had mourned the fact that sailing ships were a dream of the past.

We habitually ate dinner together at one of the skid row Japanese restaurants on Washington Street, where a steak dinner with soup, salad, and pie a la mode cost fifty cents. That evening I showed Frank the newspaper clipping, and so after dinner we headed for the downtown City Library to look up the island of Mauritius.

We learned where Mauritius was on the map, along with a brief description of the island. One reference in particular made a deep impression on both of us: "The island is renowned for its beautiful, exotic Creole women." We learned that the island was lingually French and English. It had at one time been a French possession, but was now under British rule. For many years it had been used by the English as a place of exile for recalcitrant Indian Royalty. A number of Rajahs and Maharajahs with their families and retainers resided permanently on the island, living in grand style.

The following day, filled with excitement, we boarded the bus to Victoria and made our way to the ship, whose masts were visible for miles.

With lumps in our throats, we drank in the sights of the towering square-rigged foremast with its tracery of spars and rigging etched against the sky, guarded by its four schooner-rigged masts. On arrival at the ship we called to a man pacing the poop deck aft. He was the first mate. He nodded his head in response to our request for permission to come on board. Once on board, he informed us that there were vacancies in the crew. The *Forest Dream* would first head for the island of Mauritius in the Indian Ocean via Cape Horn at the tip of South America, then pass the Cape of Good Hope at the tip of Africa, and sail on to Mauritius. From Mauritius the ship would load sugar for Singapore, then load hardwood for Vancouver, B.C., circumnavigating the world. Frank and I were dazzled. We were eager to let him know we would like to sign on as able seamen.

The mate went below and returned with the Captain. After some questioning we were told to report to the ship the following Thursday with our passports and sea bags. We did not discover until later that the ship was being boycotted by the Sailors' Union in Vancouver and had been trying to find a crew for several weeks. The reason for the boycott being that a sailing ship of her size and rig normally required a minimum of 12 deck seamen to hoist the heavy yards and booms. The *Forest Dream* was being manned with only six seamen. The *Forest Dream* was a "one time" shipping venture by two Vancouver lumber merchants who had contracted to deliver a cargo of creosote railroad ties for the construction of a railroad on the island of Mauritius. They had contrived successfully to legally circumvent the normal crewing requirements by installing a gasoline hoist to replace the six additional seamen required by the Sailors' Union in Vancouver.

We also discovered later that several crews had been hired, but after finding out that six sailors would constitute the entire deck crew, they had quit. Had we known of such happenings, in all likelihood, it would have made no difference to Frank and me.

It should be borne in mind that finding an experienced crew of officers and sailors with sailing ship experience in the year 1925 posed some difficulties. It was 20 years beyond the time when there were over a dozen sailing ships plying the oceans of the world. In the Pacific Northwest were the four-masted Arctic trading schooner *C.S. Holmes*, the cod-fishing schooners *Wawona, Azalea* and *Sophie Christensen.* The four-masted schooners *Commodore* and *Vigilant,* of Captain Matt Peasley fame, were sailing out of Bellingham, Washington, in the Hawaiian lumber trade. Another was the *E.R. Sterling*, a six-masted barkentine in the Australian lumber trade. Most sailing ship masters and mates had died, retired or carried on in steam vessels. The same condition applied to seamen with sailing ship experience. The only sailors available were alcoholics unable to hold a job in steam ships because of their drinking, or some starry-eyed romantics like Frank and me lured by the stories of tall ships as described by Conrad, Alford Lord Tennyson, and Richard Henry Dana's *Two Years Before the Mast.* To sail on the *Forest Dream* seemed the fulfillment of our dreams. Even the ship's name set bells ringing in our ears. We were blind to reality, and we closed our ears to the dire predictions of certain disaster expressed by passing seamen. What innocents we were.

Frank and I took the bus back to Seattle to make preparations to return to Victoria the following Thursday. Frank was a mature, conservative person, and felt that we should take out some life insurance. He offered to lend me the money to pay the first years' premium for a $3,000 policy with

New York Life Insurance Company (with a double indemnity clause in case of accidental death.) We bought heavy clothes and oil skins for heavy weather. Thursday, we boarded the bus to Victoria and reported on board the *Forest Dream.*

The hold was fully stowed with creosoted railroad ties, and most of the deck load of timber was in place. Later we would be strapping the deck load down with heavy chains and turnbuckles. Truck loads of ships stores were being taken on board and stowed in the storeroom under the poop deck. Louie, one of the sailors, told us that during our absence two hundred cases of Welches grape juice belonging to the captain had come on board. He hoped to sell it at a profit in Mauritius.

It was obvious that this was the owners' first maritime venture, and even we could see from the stores coming on board that it was a real "shoestring operation." There were casks of flour, sacks of beans, casks of corned beef in saltpeter (salt horse) and casks of salt pork in brine. It was as though the ship's owners had reached back two hundred years into the pages of history and revived an English frigate's list of stores.

By the end of the first day, Frank and I had met the rest of the crew. I will describe them as I came to know them by the time the voyage ended in Newcastle, New South Wales, Australia fourteen months later.

## THE CAPTAIN — WALTER H. MYERS

A tall heavy-set Dutch Boer from South Africa, with a florid face and veined, bulbous nose from over-consumption of alcohol. He was in his late fifties and a product of the foc'sle. He had achieved the position of shipmaster by being ruthless and energetic. In earlier times he would have been called a slave driver. He was a cruel, uneducated person, on the downhill path in his personal and professional life, who became violent when drinking. Even I, with my limited education and deprived cultural background, viewed him as a crude individual. At one time in his career, his Master's License had been suspended because of brutality towards his crew. Such a man would be the undisputed master of eleven men on an anticipated four month-long sea voyage, with no contact, not even by radio, with the outside world. The winds of the earth would carry those of us who survived through 20,000 miles of the world's oceans with this man having the power of life and death over us. He answered to no higher earthly authority. His name was Walter H. Myers, and his power over us was as absolute as that of the Holy Roman Emperor, Gaius Julius Caesar over his subjects.

## THE FIRST MATE — LOUIS HUET

The first mate was a fitting companion to the captain with whom he had served on other sailing ships over the years. He was an extraordinary looking person, who resembled and behaved exactly like a Hollywood casting office version of a pirate, except that he was for *real.* Of French descent, he spoke with a heavy accent. He had a short, stocky build, was very bow-legged, and his bare feet were encased in a pair of knee-length, black rubber boots. He was bearded, with long, black, greasy hair to his shoulders. His face seemed wrapped in a perpetual snarl. One-eyed Louie told me that he was a man to be avoided as much as possible, and that on the voyage that Captain Myers had his license suspended, Louis Huet, A.K.A. "French Louie," had been the captain's first mate.

## THE SECOND MATE — JOHN JOHNSON

A Swede about fifty years of age, John Johnson was a quiet, inoffensive man of rather slight build. He was a gentle, pipe-smoking person with ruddy cheeks, who had spent most of his life at sea and had no family connections. He lacked authority in his manner and was no match for the captain or the first mate who belittled him and pushed him about at will. He had the sympathy of all the sailors in his relations with them.

### THE STEWARD — HOOD

This was the fourth member of the afterguard who lived aft with the three officers, sharing a small room with the carpenter under the poop deck. His duties were to tend to the needs of the ship's officers, bringing meals aft from the forward galley to the after cabin. He had the responsibility of issuing ship's stores to the cook from the captain's storeroom, as well as keeping the after cabin spaces clean. He was an Englishman and spoke with a pronounced Cockney accent. Because he lived aft in close contact with the afterguard, none of the crew forward trusted him. People in his position were always suspected of talebearing to the captain and first mate, although he may have been perfectly innocent. The crew forward never discussed any matter of significance in his presence. Actually, I think he was a good enough chap who must have been very lonely. He seldom talked, and life became extremely difficult for him later in the voyage when the captain and the first mate began their voyage-long drunken orgy. His name was Hood, and he was thirty-one years old.

### THE DONKEYMAN — EMIL NELSON

The title of donkeyman is always given to the man whose primary task on board the vessel is the operation and maintenance of any type of machinery. In this case it was the gasoline engine used to hoist the heavy yards and booms when setting sails. He tended the oil lamps, keeping them filled and the wicks trimmed. He was also the ship's carpenter. He was forty-two years old, a Scandinavian named Emil Nelson. Because he, too, lived aft we never felt that he was one of us.

### THE COOK — LARS TIMMERMAN

A chubby round-faced Estonian by the name of Lars Timmerman, I never saw him without a pipe clenched between his broken teeth. He was a pleasant person with a fine sense of humor, always cheerful, he never lost his temper or showed anger. A fine cook with a wealth of experience, and no matter what the weather, or how the ship threw itself about, he was always ready with a cup of coffee and something to eat. He was a real stalwart when things got rough. He was not the cleanest or tidiest cook I ever knew, as I never saw him with a clean apron. He had a love affair with Victoria, a little black stray cat he found on a street in Victoria one rainy night. She helped him retain his sanity. He was forty years old.

### LOUIS GIMEL — ABLE SEAMAN

Louie at fifty-four was the eldest of the seamen. He was from Steilacom, Washington, and had been going to sea in sailing ships since the age of fourteen. He was a gentle, sensitive man with craggy features, and an excellent seaman. He had little or no schooling and had never married. Louie had lost one eye as a small child and was known up and down the Pacific Coast as "One-eyed Louie". He had been a confirmed alcoholic since the age of fifteen. He never drew a sober breath after two hours ashore until his money was gone. No matter how large his payday after a long voyage, he was always broke after a week ashore. He would teach Frank and me the art of seamanship in sail in his friendly, kindly way.

### CHRIS JOHANSEN — ABLE SEAMAN

His given name was Chris, and he was known as a "Black Dane" because of his jet black hair. He rarely spoke; kept entirely to himself, and was an excellent sailor. Thirty-five years old, he was a confirmed alcoholic like One-eyed Louie. He and Hubert shared the starboard foc'sle. We other four sailors shared the port foc'sle.

## MALCOLM CHISHOLM ABLE SEAMAN

A talented artist and intellectually very gifted, Mac was the epitome of a southern gentleman from the nineteenth century. He was twenty-four years old, and from a prominent Mississippi family. He was a genuine idealist. He watched over me, and we became close friends. I idolized him, and by my actions throughout the years, have tried to emulate him. He carried with him a small library of classical literature which he shared with me. At the time he came on board he was immersed in Carlyle's *Sartor Resartus*. He was a natural leader, a fine sailor and unquestionably the most outstanding person on board in character, intelligence and maturity. Eighteen years would elapse before I would learn of his tragic end.

## HUBERT SCHLEE — ABLE SEAMAN

Hubert was German, about thirty-five years old. A tall blond man with a close-cropped Teutonic haircut, he was garrulously argumentative in his views, but a cheerful and good shipmate. He had run away to sea from a deprived home life when he was fourteen years of age; life had not been kind to him. He liked to tell us that his sister was a well-known Wagnerian opera singer in Germany - a statement we accepted with a grain of salt.

## FRANK GARLOCK — ABLE SEAMAN

Frank was twenty-two years old. A short round-faced Polish lad from New York City. Frank's father was a janitor in a large New York apartment building, a widower, and Frank was his only child. I had sought him out and enlisted him to come with me on the *Forest Dream*. Though our friendship was fairly recent, we had much in common, and there was a strong bond between us. Frank was quiet, alert and soft-spoken — a romanticist in search of adventure as promised by the *Forest Dream*. Because of my having seen a newspaper article in a fish market, his life would end in my arms.

## NIELS THOMSEN — ABLE SEAMAN

At eighteen, I was the youngest of the crew; my mind and heart filled with Victorian ideals and romance. I was strangely naive and light-hearted in my approach to life among this mixture of men drawn together on this ship of another time and place. Along with other lessons in life, I would wear deep scars of sorrow before this fateful voyage ended.

Of such stuff was our crew composed. Twelve men of totally different ages, personalities and backgrounds, one who would be buried at sea before three months had elapsed.

On October 18, 1925, the *Forest Dream* was preparing to sail. This was the violent era of prohibition in America, and rum-running was an active, lucrative business between Canada and the United States. On the evening prior to sailing from Victoria, the captain came forward to the foc'sle and said, "Tonight after midnight a truckload of one hundred cases of whiskey belonging to me will be coming down to the ship. I will give each of you twenty-five dollars for moving the sails from the after lazaret, stowing the cases, and putting back the sails." We all agreed to his request, and one hundred cases of White Horse scotch whiskey was taken on board and stowed in the lazaret.

Little did we know how these cases would affect our lives in the coming months. The following morning a tug came alongside. A towline was made fast, the lines let go, and we set out for Cape Flattery and the Northwest Pacific storms. Off Umatilla lightship the tug cast us off, and we scampered aloft to loose the sails, Frank and me to the royal.

For several weeks we had been practicing climbing up the rigging to the various crosstrees and out forty feet to the end of the yards. The second mate and One-eyed Louie always went aloft with us, continuously drilling into us that it was one hand for the ship and one hand for ourselves. That one mistake could be our last. Both Louie and the second mate worried about our safety. To work the sails one had to climb aloft and out onto the yards with one's feet on a wire rope that hung three feet below the yard by wire supports every six feet. Every five feet along the yards were rope loops six or eight inches in diameter through which an arm could be thrust. This arm would hold the sail being hauled in by the free arm. Many times we neglected to make use of this safety loop, finding it a hindrance and a delaying precaution. Louie and the second mate became very provoked whenever they saw us ignoring the safety loop.

At first, going aloft was frightening, but gradually we lost all fear of falling. Soon we were scampering about the rigging, high above the deck, wrapping our legs around the backstays and halyards, and sliding to the deck, 120 feet below. On the evening of the first day we picked up a strong northwesterly wind and sea and sped down the coasts of Washington and Oregon. The next day was bright and clear. We could see the snow-covered peaks of the coastal mountain ranges. We stayed well off the coast until the evening of the eighth day, when we headed in towards the land.

Mac, who was in the first mate's watch told us that the first mate had told him we were planning to rendezvous with a high speed rum-running boat opposite San Pedro for the purpose of delivering the cases of whiskey we had on board. The next morning, shortly after daybreak, we sighted a U.S. Coast Guard cutter leisurely patrolling the twelve mile offshore International Zone Line. On five or six occasions an unidentified speedboat would appear on the horizon.

After drifting about for five or six days, and the speedboat making no attempt to contact us with the Coast Guard vessel always in sight, we headed farther in towards the shore. There the captain hailed a passing launch and requested a boat to tow

us into a dock in the outer harbor of San Pedro. In about one hour we were taken in tow and moored to the dock.

On arrival at the dock we were boarded by customs agents who were told by the captain that we had come to the dock for the purpose of taking on water and supplies for the voyage. We went through the motions of taking on water, topping off the tanks in less than a half hour. We thought this was a strange, meaningless operation, the tanks being full. In the meantime the watch on the vessel by the Custom Officers had doubled, with another shift having relieved the day watch. Of course, there was no shore leave.

At about eleven o'clock on the second day, the captain had several visitors who stayed for an hour in his cabin. As soon as they departed, the captain ordered a tug to tow us out to sea. It was our reasoning that the captain had taken the ship to the dock in the hope that he could discharge his hundred cases of whiskey stored in the lazaret, but had been discouraged from attempting this by the Customs Guards and by his visitors.

On November 10, 1925, the tug dropped us off near Catalina Island. We set sail on a southward course for Cape Horn at the lower tip of South America. After rounding Cape Horn we would have strong steady westerly winds and seas, known as the "Roaring Forties." These were furious, cascading, following seas known to reach heights of up to sixty feet roared out of the west, all the way to the Cape of Good Hope and beyond to Mauritius.

Voyage plans and navigational information were passed to us by the second mate, Mr. Johnson, without the knowledge of the captain or the first mate. It was customary on most sailing ships to treat information of the ship's position as a secret and navigation as a profound art, available only to the captain and the first mate. Traditionally, this was in all probability a precaution carried over from former times as a protection against mutiny by the crew.

Except for some few occasional remarks by the second mate who did have some idea of the ship's position and overheard comments passed between the officers which referred to whether we were in the northwest tradewinds, the southeast tradewinds, in the doldrums, or that we were near the Equator, we had only a general knowledge of the ship's position. For the first four weeks after leaving the California coast all went smoothly and without incident. The winds were fair and on the quarter, and we worked the ship's yards and sails on deck and aloft. No land or ships were sighted.

The two mates stood watch in six hour stretches. The captain would relieve the mates for short periods night and day and during meal hours. Except for Malcolm's special relationship with the first mate, there was little or no conversation between the officers and deck crew, other than passing orders concerning the ship's work. The sailors' quarters were in the bows of the ship under the foc'sle (forecastle) head and were referred to as the port and starboard foc'sle. Each contained six pipe berths, one above the other, secured on the side of the ship's hull.

The mess room was cramped, seating eight persons on two benches with a small square opening into the galley through which food was passed. A tiny oil lamp hung from the overhead. Attached to the galley was a small room containing a berth for the cook. Inside each foc'sle sliding door was a half barrel which was used to store whatever fresh water was left from our daily water ration. Each Sunday the crew drew lots for their turn at using the water for washing clothes. Sometimes, in case the water was very dirty when it came to your turn, we would wash our clothes in salt water. This clothes washing routine was often a source of minor dissatisfaction and arguments amongst us.

The basic diet was beef cured in saltpeter, a curative used since time immemorial to suppress libido in prisons and on sailing ships when on long voyages. It was referred to as "salt horse." The other meat course was salt pork in brine, which, because it came in 200 pound wooden casks, was usually rancid by the time it was half empty. The only way we could stomach it was if it was highly spiced. Timmerman was a master at disguising unpalatable dishes. We had sacks of rice, dried beans, dried peas and hard sea biscuits. There were no canned goods, except one gallon cans of cheap, mushy, pear and peach pie filling — awful stuff. The list of provisions today sounds most austere, but I do not recall that we did any appreciable complaining about the food. We knew there was no other food available on board, except the captain's private stock, and we knew we were not about to be invited to consume any of that. One day the steward reported that a porthole in the storeroom had leaked seawater into the area in the after storeroom where the flour was stowed. An inspection revealed that seventy-five percent of our flour was wet and mouldy, a calamity. Having no source of replacement, we had to make use of it, without regard to it's condition.

On leaving Victoria we had on board three live sheep and two live hogs which we slaughtered sometime during the first two months into the voyage. A dozen laying hens provided eggs for the captain's table, as well as for anyone intrepid enough to risk his life if caught in the chicken pen. It was stowed aft on the main deck under the ever watchful eye of the captain and the mates. I had an occasional egg or two which had to be eaten raw, there being no way I could have cooked it surreptitiously.

CHAPTER TWO

# MALCOLM ABLE SEAMAN

*PORT WATCH*

November 10, 1925: Abreast of the San Pedro breakwater we let go the lines of the tugboat on our port quarter, played out our towline on the winch head for a long lead, and stood by to hoist and set our sails. Beyond the breakwater the sea lay smooth, with a cheerful smiling sun overhead, the gulls wheeling and following. Because of the light winds near the shore, the smaller diesel tugboat continued out to sea after her larger mate had dropped astern. For several miles she towed us seaward while we set sail, hoping for an offshore breeze. Halyards were laid for hoisting. Main, mizzen and jigger sails were soon set and drawing. The square sails hung in the buntlines. It was but the work of a minute to loose the bunt gaskets and sing out, "sheet home" to the men on deck. Topgallant sail and foresails were set with a will, the little royal soon after. From a lofty perch, a colorful panorama of San Pedro and the coast lay stretched out in softened tones of distance. A luminous haze hung over the sea and gave the air a tingling coolness like alcohol drying on the skin. The soft snoring of the surf along Point Fermin sounded clear and subdued from our quiet height. A most auspicious departure.

With the setting of the main staysail, the ship soon had way on her, making an estimated six knots. The tug at our head let go the towline, tooted a shrill farewell, and headed back to San Pedro. Haste was made to set gaff topsails and spanker so that we might make the most of the favorable offshore breeze. The wind held fresh from the northeast until sundown when the fun began. Gaff topsails were clewed up, jibs lowered; then followed a succession of bracing yards and tacking ship as many as four or five times in a watch - a wearisome trial for our scanty crew of only three men in a watch.

At times our becalmed ship would set in toward Catalina Island as though she was determined to go ashore. It was then that we worked feverishly to take advantage of the slightest breeze in order to lay an offshore course and clear the menacing island. Daylight found us still becalmed with flapping sails and groaning blocks. Towards sunset, catspaws began to etch the glassy surface of the sea and grow into fitful breezes. The wind soon steadied, however. At eight bells we were logging eight knots, and the California Coast was sinking behind us.

In the spanking breeze that pushed us southward, there was just a hint of the northeast trade winds. With every sail drawing slow and aloft, the ship was a symphony of curves, lifting and bowing into the clear blue sea like a thing alive, showing the buoyancy and grace that are the inner qualities of a wooden ship. I knew why I was here.

The *Forest Dream* was one of four sister ships built in Grays Harbor, Washington, in 1920. They were the *Forest Dream, Forest Friend, Forest Pride* and *Forest King*. A wooden vessel through–out, possessing graceful lines and staunch sea–worthiness that does honor to her builders. Her rig is that of a barkentine, square-rigged on the foremast, fore-and-aft rigged on the main, mizzen, jigger and spanker, five masts in all. She carries three head sails, that is jibs — inner, outer and flying jib, two stay sails, main and main topgallant staysails. The latter are often called "napkins" by some of the older men on board. On the foremast, the fore course begins at the base of the white pyramid, just above are the topsails, upper and lower. The top-gallant sails also come in a set of two, followed by the tiny royal which crowns this tower with a queenly grace. In the days of clipper ships, loftier sails were carried, such as skysails and moonsails. But with the reduction of crews and the passing of first rank packets, they have been abandoned. With the mainmast, the schooner sails begin, presenting a broad, unbroken curve, that seen from forward, possesses the classic lines of a Grecian vase. These three sails carry topsails on their gaff, giving a greater spread of canvas. The spanker is distinctive in that it is of a shape known as a-leg-o-mutton or triangular, carrying no gaff. There is a topsail however, sometimes called a "ring-tail." The reason for such a name will soon be made clear to anyone who has to set or clew up this outlandish sail for it is certainly a piece of monkey-business to handle.

The ship has a small steam boiler forward of the mainmast which is used in heaving up the anchor and working cargo. Besides this, there is a small gasoline motor connected by gears to gypsy heads on deck for hoisting sails and other heavy work. It is only by such mechanical "extras" as this, that so small a crew could ever undertake to sail a vessel of this size, over 1700 tons.

Forward, is the raised type of ship's forecastle, so dubbed by another generation of sailors. The poop is the same raised construction, thus giving the ship an extra seaworthiness and greater safety of height. Under the forecastlehead, the sailors, the crew, have their quarters — the cook too, most precious one, has his home here. His room is alongside the galley, or kitchen as it is known on land. The carpenter shop, just outside our forecastle (room) is also the meat locker for the casks of salt pork and salt beef, space for cargo gear, bos'n's (boatswain's) paint and lamp lockers, potato bins, a room for two men, and a tiny mess room, all crowded under this small deck where we eat, sleep and sail the days away. The crew are twelve all told: the captain, mate, second mate, cabin boy and carpenter make up the afterguard, that is, those who live aft. Forward in the foc'sle, we six men "before the mast" live like a lost tribe — a very small tribe, most everyone will agree. For it is generally learned with surprise and astonishment that only a half-dozen men do the actual handling of the ship. I would like to make it clear that this is no boast, but an admission, for the helplessness of seamen today who possess no organized power, coupled with American law, or lack of law which permits a ship to put to sea so manned, makes it so.

Until some misanthrope proved it could be done with less, ships of this size and rig carried ten to twelve men in the forecastle. The newspapers have referred to the ship as having a "skeleton crew," grimly enough. To round out the muster, let us not forget the cook and his foundling cat which he loves with a love that passeth all understanding.

Watches are divided into four hours each, beginning the day at noon. The port watch, let us say, come on deck at 12:30 P.M. and the starboard watch go below for dinner, or lunch as it is known ashore. Frequently it is only "lunch." Our watch (port) then goes about the work on deck, patching sails, over-hauling rigging or the like; as well as taking the usual wheel watches, until four in the afternoon, when we are relieved by the starboard watch again. The following four hours are divided into two hours each, these being called dog watches. So, at six P.M. we turn to again, keep the deck until eight P.M. (eight bells) to be relieved by the starboard watch who carry on until midnight. After tumbling out of our snug bunks, we stand another watch of four hours, to be relieved at four A.M. Now, at 7:30 A.M. we are called again, have breakfast, and take the deck watch at 8:00 A.M. and keep it until 12:30 P.M., when the cycle is completed, and begins its rounds again. Thus, with the watch and watch of the ship's routine, Jack never gets more than four hours sleep, frequently less in bad weather, or when both watches are kept on deck in handling sails.

But with the clean sea air, the simple food and manly work, we hardly notice the broken hours of sleep. We are certainly never troubled with insomnia. It is difficult at first to become accustomed to lookout watches of two hours length. I often fell asleep standing on my feet, only to awake with a violent lurch, hands extended wildly in an instinctive effort to clutch at some support. There is always the danger of tumbling overboard as well. The railing along the forecastle head is only a foot high, however, the long reflector of the running lights affords a sort of a guard beside the breadth of the light towers.

After being laid up for two years, idle and uncared for, the *Forest Dream* was in a badly neglected state. Below the cabin deck, piled pell-mell and damp, sails lay in unmarked disorder. Now that we were in summer weather, warm and dry, all spare sails were hauled out upon the deck and exposed to the sun to be thoroughly dried and patched. Following this, they were rolled into very tight bundles like long white snakes, labeled with canvas tags, and stowed below in well-planned order. It was surprising how much sail could be

stowed in so small a space, using every nook and cranny. On the sea, economy of space is an art. Many of the sails were secondhand from the four corners of the earth. There were several staysails and topsails that were taken from a big German ship interned in Canada during the war. In the corners could be seen the name of the sail neatly lettered in black with the date 1914 — sails that were never made use of, perhaps before the vessel was seized.

Most of these foreign sails were made of hemp, much lighter than cotton and easier to furl when wet. That is important to a sailor when fighting with slatting sails on a dark and squally night on a yardarm eighty feet above the ship's deck. I have noticed that hempen sails have the peculiar quality of turning a dark brown when wet.

It was almost a certainty that we should go around Cape Horn, across the South Atlantic and Africa, Cape of Good Hope and on to the Indian Ocean and Mauritius. But the continual heaving up of the rudder post and the hollow pounding of the rudder post shaftway caused the captain so much alarm that he decided on the south of Australia route, not normally used because of prevailing head winds.

This rumor drifted about, as it is ship's style to "permit things to be known," never to announce a thing, point blank. But nobody wanted this — to offset the cold weather off the Horn; and something of the same, but in a lesser degree, off the Cape of Good Hope, in exchange for the head winds that would be waiting for us south of Australia. By the Cape Horn route we could at least have looked forward to strong fair winds.

It was so decreed, and the course was gradually altered south of Australia. We accepted the knowledge that we were destined to face a great deal of contrary winds, together with much hauling around of braces. Our one atlas was consulted, and our probable course laid out: south through the middle of the South Sea Islands to the Australian coast, sailing between New Zealand and the continent. Bass Strait, to the northward of Tasmania, was expected to be our first trouble-maker.

Beyond Bass Strait lay the Indian Ocean with all her whims and hurricanes. After clearing the south coast of Australia, there would be a long stretch of landless sea, until we lifted the tiny island of Mauritius, 500 miles east of Madagascar.

In this interval of fair weather and steady sailing, it will not be amiss to tell something of the men who sail the ship, the men who make up our little world on the sea.

**The uncrowned King is, of course, the captain;** so, following custom and tradition, let us look at him first. He is about fifty years of age, standing five feet nine and of stout build. Blond, with a full, pink face, lined with blue veins about the cheeks and jowls from an over-indulgence of alcohol. Ships worries, he says, have caused him to lose most of his hair, although anyone would have reason to believe that he sleeps with his hat on, so much is it a part of him.

At night in the warm southern latitudes, he appears on deck clad in a faded old dressing gown, looking like a tonsured monk in the dusky light of the stars; but there the resemblance ends, for he certainly is no ascetic. At this time of the day he feels in a genial and expansive mood, and he and the mate have long talks together as they pace the weather side of the poop deck. He has known the sea and ships from early boyhood, coming originally from the Transvaal, a Dutch Boer they say which explains his decided Anglophobia. On the other hand he champions things American and shows it in many of his actions. A passion for cleanliness is one of his characteristics, any dirt or laxness about the ship cannot last long. It is by his orders that everything forward is given a thorough scrubbing each Saturday.

**The mate, the Lord High Chamberlain**, is the very opposite in appearance and character, the most original and distinctive individual I have ever seen. He is short, wiry, lean and broad of shoulder. He has the most marvelous hands of any man on land or sea. They are twice as large as the ordinary hand, with great, flat tips and nails that seem to be made for the purpose of digging caves in stone. There are tattoo marks in faded blue on the backs of his hands, almost covered with thick, wiry, black hair -- "every hair a rope yarn, every finger a marlin spike," to quote him. Almost fifty years old, he has the outlook of a youth, and in energy and strength, he puts the younger sailors to shame. His hair is thick and graying. A beard covers his cheek like frost and is mowed off every two weeks, blow high, blow low. In all the ports on the Pacific Coast, wherever men of the sea foregather, he is known as "French Louie" — a seaman to his fingertips and a hail fellow. His dress is no less original than his personality: a green or red woolen shirt, khaki trousers, no belt, his heavy trench shoes (which he never laces) and the white crown of a officer's cap without the visor. "The kind I wear when I am chief officer of a steamboat," he explains with a grin.

He always has a story to tell or a joke to amuse the crew. He is a man with the gift of a storyteller, and he never tells the same story twice — which makes him a genius. He was born on the Isle of Jersey in the English Channel, but came to America when only six months old. It is a saying of his that he has been going to sea for forty-nine and a half years. I cannot keep from smiling at the thought of him furling topsails at six months of age, still in triangular trousers.

**The second mate** is from Sweden, tall, thin, with large protruding ears and a mustache. His manner is quiet and reserved, seldom raising his voice. He is not at all like the first mate who roars away at the braces and halyards like a young bull. In the evening dogwatch he always comes on deck with the heavy scent of lilac toilet soap hanging around him; the odor of lilacs, a thousand miles out at sea, and from a tanned and weather beaten old veteran of the sea! He glories in ten suits of clothes and, "a pair of suspenders for each of his trousers, too," he adds with pride.

**Chips, the carpenter**, also hails from the land of the Vikings and might easily be mistaken for a brother of the second mate. He has the same spare figure, long nose and quiet way. In the way of dress, there is the same eternal cap and the baggy suit of khaki overalls. No matter what weather, Chips is garbed the same. If it is cold, he adds more overalls; if the thermometer rises, he simply peels. His duties include the care of the pumps and the donkey boiler, the gasoline engine, the lamps, the lights, blocks, and repairs to woodwork about the ship. His pleasures are simple, an ardent devotion to the card game of pinochle. He claims to have played no less than fifteen hundred games in his day.

**Whenever we read or hear of a cabin boy** we visualize a round-faced, apple-cheeked youth, but our cabin boy is well over thirty with drooping eyelids and the worldly-wise keenness of a Parisian boulevardier. Small, slender, and dark, Earnest is the dapper man of the world with graying temples and a soft-spoken manner.

Plainly he is not aboard the ship merely in support of a living, but he is a man who makes no confidences. He piques another's curiosity, only to leave it unsatisfied, for I could learn only that he is from Montreal, Canada, and is of French extraction. These are the five men who live aft. "Those who live in the high places," as Jack London was so fond of calling it.

**Holding the place of honor "before the mast," the cook is King.** He is everything a good cook should be, plump and pink, rounded beaming face and a mane of yellow hair crowning all.

Good old Timmerman hails from the Baltic lands, having been born on a small island in the Gulf of Finland. He sailed as a fisherman in his youth, only to discover his talents as a cook to his profit and our delight. There is a cat, of course, his bosom friend. She's a ragged little thing that he picked up one night in Victoria, B.C. during a rain shower, and as there is room for all the world in this man's heart, he brought the bedraggled little waif on board and gave it a home. He has a portable phonograph in his room, with fifty good records, so we have music to while away the long hours at sea. We are four in the port forecastle, the forecastle proper.

**Louis is the acknowledged father of the flock.** Of middle age, tall and sunbrowned, he is a fine type of American seaman, one of the remaining few. Louis Gimel spent his boyhood in Tacoma, Washington, but took to sea after being expelled from school for some boyish prank. What a trifling thing to shape a man's life.

He is kindhearted, like most sailors, showing a fine patience with the younger men: teaching us knots and splicing of wire and rope, the making of sennit slippers, the care of clothes, and a hundred little things that make for comfort and safety on board ship. He has thick, black hair which curls, a fine keen face, the rugged face of a pioneer. Although he lost his left eye when ten years old, his sight is as keen as a hawk's. He is known to sailors in Northwest ports by the name of "One-Eyed Louie."

**The most interesting of the younger men is Frank,** a sailor from Baltimore and New York. He is one of the finest shipmates a man could wish -- a lover of books, an observer of things, quiet and unobtrusive. He came on board with his friend, Niels. Frank is of sturdy build, even stocky, with a head of curly brown hair and perfect teeth. He has the most unusual eyes of gray, flecked with brown, green and blue in a mosaic of marvelous variety. The stars have a great attraction for him; like close friends in his eyes, to be pointed out familiarly on the clear unclouded nights of these southern latitudes. While he knows practically all the principal constellations and planets, I have the pleasure of telling him the stories of mythology concerning them, so that we never tire of looking up to the great purple sea-roof and searching out the little Pleiades, Orion, Scorpio, and all their attendant train. One of Frank's hobbies was reading the dictionary with as much interest as most people read a novel. I have seen him sit for hours with his eyes glued to my battered old Webster, lost in a treasure of words.

**The youngest of the crew is an eighteen year old Dane,** who has spent most of his youth in Fresno, California. He is known to us as Niels. Slender and of medium height, he is a fine example of the fair Northman. His hair is as yellow as gold, light blue eyes and rosy cheeks that any girl would prize. He originally came from a small town by the sea in Denmark where he played in the shadows of an ancient castle, digging in the moat for old tankards and platters.

**These three men, Louis, Niels and Frank, make up the starboard watch,** so that, with them on deck, I spend my watch below in solitary silence like a hermit. There is the little cubby hole of a room over on the starboard side of the ship where my two watchmates live: a big blond German, and Chris, a dark, gloomy Dane. Although Hubert Schlee was born in Hamburg, he left home at fourteen and spent so much of his youth on the coast of Chile that he looks upon that far country as the home of his heart. He is a brawny two hundred pounds and comes in handy at the braces. All these years in knocking about the world have not dulled his interest in

things, on the contrary they have served to widen his views. The persecution and ill-treatment that he has endured through the accident of his birth have been enough to embitter him for life. When squaring yards, Hubert always has a song to make the work lighter and to put us in a swinging chorus. On the sea since he was fourteen, he is now nearly thirty. Ships are just chapters in his life.

This day came in with rounded cheeks, a fair wind blowing in our wake. The mate talked of nothing but fast ships and famous passages, the captain "sang" in a most unusual manner, the carpenter, often paused, saw in hand, to dance a little jig, while the cook, just to show how he felt about it, played "Mother Machree" on his portable phonograph all during the day, and men sang snatches of chanteys. Even the cat came out of hiding with its right eye closed from the effects of a love spat the night before leaving port.

Coming on deck at midnight we found that the wind had increased a great deal. On taking the wheel I soon saw that I would have my hands full with no time for dreaming. After two hours of wrestling with the wheel, my ankles, knees, and wrists ached with the downthrust and kick of the weather helm. The flat muscles of my shoulders felt as if they had been pummeled with a maul. Still, I enjoyed every minute of it to the fullest.

With the beginning of lookout, the wind sang through the rigging in a high-pitched, reedy note, jib sheets and halyards, topsail sheets and braces were now as tight as harp strings to the touch. Aloft, the billowing square sails curved out until hosts of glittering stars could be seen dancing between their arcs.

The following seas climbed along her weather side like black hounds in chase. Ahead of her she threw a shining carpet of white, foaming seas, then trampled it underfoot. The deck of the foc'sle head was so steep that pacing was difficult. I leaned against the light tower and watched the phosphorescent sea flow by the ship's side a foot above the rail, rushing aft like shining marble dust. She was logging twelve knots with an effort that can never be appreciated by one who has traveled only in steamers where there is no feeling of sinewy life.

For many days now our rudder has kept up a continual pounding that sends a shock through the ship causing the captain so much concern that he often comes on deck in the small hours of the night, unable to sleep because of the booming noise, worry over the threatening condition, and trying to devise a remedy. Heavy tackles have been rigged on the tiller to absorb some of the shock and to ease the wheel, but the rudderhead began to lift and plunge in an alarming manner. The captain and the mate examined it for the purpose of rigging another checking tackle, but nothing could be added. With the relieving tackle on the tiller, the wheel was harder to turn, even in a light breeze. We were forced to go on the lee side and climb up the wheel with our feet in order to keep the ship from running up into the wind.

The pounding of the rudder must have started some of the ship's seams aft. The pumps began to bring up more water, even after long spells of pumping.

In the afternoon, the carpenter attempted to start the smaller gasoline pump intended for use in pumping out the ship's bilge, but with no success. After many tries, it was found useless, so we turned to on the hand pumps. We pumped for two hours, deep down in an eight foot by eight foot hole in the lumber deck load which had been created so we could have access to the pumps. This compartment is twelve feet deep. A rickety ladder leads to the two heavy wheeled pumps, with a little light and air filters through a three foot square opening at the top.

The iron wheels are monstrous, exuding a quality of malignancy. This is where we labor day and night, a part of every watch, keeping the water level below the danger point. During the intervals of calm, while the ship is on an even keel, we often pump for two hours out of four, to be relieved by the other watch, who carry on until the pumps are sucking, no matter how long it takes. These two massive main pumps, besides being too heavy for two men to turn, are located too far forward to catch all the water.

Sunday is supposed to be the day we wash and mend our clothes; when we are allowed to read on our lookout watch on deck, with no work to do except handling the sails. Of course there are wheel watches to stand, the decks to wash down, and pumping out the ship, still, it is called a day of rest by the captain and the mate. We do not wholeheartedly consider it a day of joy and relaxation. On some of the larger vessels, the captain holds church services on Sundays. Some give the crew Saturday afternoon off, or they may have Sunday all to themselves.

In the morning the men aboard the *Forest Dream* bring buckets up on the forecastle head, sit in the shadow of the foresail and wash the dirty clothes they have accumulated during the week. A line is stretched from the forestay to the fore rigging. By eight o'clock our dungarees and singlets, bandannas and hickory shirts are flapping in the breeze, while the owners stretch out in the shade and read.

At noon, the Sunday dinner graces the clean fresh pine boards of our little mess room. There is thick creamy pea soup, canned roast beef and potatoes, string beans and a heavy black pudding made of flour and molasses, sprinkled with raisins (the famous plum duff). Last of all, tea, of a sort. This order of fare is as fixed as the laws of nature. The pillars of heaven may fall, but we will have plum duff on Sunday.

We have an advantage in this, for like the man who had fried pork seven days a week,"once we git our mouf fixed for duff, we don't have to unfix it again."

Since we were well out to sea, Chips began to be made the subject of an intensive training program, as the executives style it. With the engine's breakdown, the carpenter fell into disrepute; besides this, the captain and the mate continually found fault with his carpentry. He was referred to as that Wood Butcher, the Swedish Prince, etcetera, until poor Chips was flying about the decks, fumbling his work, and working himself into such a nervous state that he hardly knew whether he was coming or going.

His true nature came to his rescue. He adopted a passive resistance. To every order, criticism and insult he only replied, "Yes Sir, Captain. Yes Sir." The powers found that there was little sport in kicking a wet pillow and left him in peace soon after. He was thus reduced to servility and made into putty, as was the captain's and mate's plan.

The second mate too, became a part of this program. Fault was found with the way he left the braces. They were too slack, or they were too tight, or his men did not do enough work during their watch on deck. One watch was pitted against the other, an effort was made to breed jealousy and dislike in our little clan. But we talked it over and decided that, no matter how much the afterguard might war amongst themselves, we would steer clear of it all.

There was a weak link in our armor, as we found out the next day when work was resumed on the sails. This time the object of attack was the big German. It was the first example of hazing I had ever seen, and I hope it is the last. Several of the hemp sails from the locker were hauled on deck to be made over. One was marked "Mittel Kluver" or middle jib, a sail from a German ship. The mate had decided it was to be cut down and made into a main staysail. This was the occasion for the unpleasant incident that followed.

Undoubtedly, the best seaman in the crew was Chris. He was the first to make his topsail fast, the first to finish a job of splicing, the handiest and most thorough man in the rigging. In short, he was the stellar able seaman. He was held up as an example to the rest of us who continually were told that they did only half as much as Chris. On the contrary, Hubert the German was slow, methodical and painstaking, so his work on sails suffered by comparison. The mate, being of a bustling, hurrying nature, resented this, and it seemed suspected Hubert of intentionally loafing at his work.

He often stood over the big, slow fellow with a sardonic grin on his face, criticizing his work and his plodding ways, until Hubert's watch began to be four hours of misery. Besides, he often took up work next to the harassed man, and by sewing rapidly, overtook him, then berated him for holding up the completion of the sail. There was never an answer from Hubert, only scowls and mutterings for days on end. He went about his work with a broken spirit and sullen frown. In the evenings he no longer sang "The Miller's Song," or the "Rose of the Heather" folk songs. All were forgotten in his abject misery.

This suffering went on for a week until the sail was finished. We were watchmates, so later we talked it over; a kind of a "tropic choler," he called it. He had seen it in other ships, he said, but had never been abused as a result of it before. There was no wisdom in fighting such a treatment; silence was the best weapon. He had little spirit left, he said. He had been driven from place to place as an exile because of ethnic hatred brought on by World War I and being a German.

We younger ones did not escape altogether. There was much talk of reducing our wages and working on our watch below. But as we were willing, and took it all in good spirit, things soon settled down to an even tenor.

These days of fair winds and smart sailing soon brought us to the Doldrums or Horse Latitudes, so-called from the days when ships carried live horses from England to the West Indies. When becalmed for long periods, they were forced to throw a great many horses overboard due to a shortage of water and fodder. The trade winds deserted us, followed by days of calm, light baffling winds and squalls, and constant bracing of the yards.

We took advantage of the least pocket full of wind, while the ship continued to make a tour of the compass. At times the ship's head was pointed north, as if it wished to be homeward bound. Although the decks were wet down morning and night since leaving port, the ship's seams had not become tight and closed. Our forecastle was in a miserable state: water lying in pools on the floor, dripping down into our bunks making them damp and chill. Our clothes were soggy from the lengthy periods of rain. The air was damp and nothing would dry. We wore our oilskins and southwesters, but the short spells of hot sunshine made it so uncomfortable that we ended by stripping to dungarees and a singlet, forgoing such non-essentials as shoes, hats and shirts.

The palms of our hands became wrinkled as if we had been swimming too long. The softened condition of the skin, together with the constant hauling on braces and halyards, caused fingers and palms to split open with deep wounds like knife slits. There was no remedy for this for they were continually opening with the least bit of strain. During these showers we collected rainwater in barrels to be used for washing purposes. Our water tanks were insufficient and we expected little rain after passing south of the line (Equator).

Thus, through squall and calm, sunshine and shower, we finally won through to encounter light favorable winds. On December 5, 1925, we crossed the Equator at four in the morning under the pressure of a smart breeze. There was none of the traditional ceremony in this crossing of the line, no initiation of the landlubbers passing the brown jug.

Our crew was too small, and there was too much work to do.

We heard popping of corks and loud merriment coming up from a little party the captain and the mate were having in the after cabin. That lasted for twenty-four hours.

After passing the line we still experienced squalls, light and harmless, during which time all the masts and booms were oiled with linseed oil. The carpenter had fashioned several scrapers from pieces of bandsaw blades, set them in short oak handles and sharpened them to a razor-like edge. The rain softened the surface of the spars, making the scraping much easier. We swung aloft in bos'n's chairs, starting from the top and working our way down the mast to the deck, clambering with feet and hands clasped about the big sticks.

During the frequent rain showers, the mate was never at a loss for finding something for us to do. We turned to on the spars no matter how hard it rained, the same hurry-up practice continuing, making drudgery of what could have been agreeable work. As soon as the masts were scraped, they were slushed down with a mixture of tallow and linseed oil, deepening the rich tone of the pine, as well as serving to waterproof the wood.

Several days of tradewind sailing followed. It was broken only by a lively squall in which we shortened sail, taking in topgallant sails and gaff-topsails along with losing one of our washports.

CHAPTER THREE

# NIELS
# ABLE SEAMAN

*STARBOARD WATCH*

My life on board ship was brightened by the presence of Malcolm Chisholm. From the day I came on board the ship, he had watched over me like an older brother. I idolized him. He was an extremely talented and cultured individual, an artist and a graduate in journalism from the University of Alabama. He kept a diary, which he would read to me from time to time. He was building a ship model, persuading me to do the same, and assisting me with the building of it.

Our quiet and peaceful four weeks came to an end as we entered the doldrums, a six hundred mile belt of light, variable winds and calms lying between two tradewind belts on either side of the Equator. The winds died completely, and we faced four hundred miles of listless airs and flat calm seas. Sails and booms slammed from side to side, day and night, with the ship rolling wildly from the excessively high deck load of lumber.

To make matters worse, the gasoline engine intended to replace six "absent" seaman in hoisting the heavy booms and yards could not be started. Whenever hoisting of booms and spars was required, it was "all hands on deck" including the captain and the first mate. It came to light that the

carpenter who had been selected particularly because of his stated mechanical qualifications, had not the slightest knowledge of the workings of a gasoline engine. Naturally, he became the scapegoat from then on, to be abused not only by the afterguard but by the sailors as well.

This was when the captain and the first mate began their serious drinking. We saw very little of them, and the second mate stood more than his share of deck watches, napping whenever Mac had the wheel watch. Their drinking became a daily fact of life following tragic, bizarre, and sometimes comic patterns. They would have alternate periods of quarreling and friendliness. One week they would be bitter antagonists, quarreling like two fishwives, and the next week they behaved like a honeymoon couple. All of us forward were delighted with their periods of disagreement, when individually they would alternate coming forward to the foc'sle to malign one another. The first mate would tell us that the captain was an incapable, dishonest drunkard, who had used the ship's money to buy the cases of whiskey and grape juice which he planned to sell at a profit when we arrived in Mauritius. He would say that the captain was unfit to be a shipmaster; that he intended to report him to the authorities when we reached port. We would agree with all his declarations concerning the unfitness of the captain and pledge him our loyalty.

No sooner would the mate have left, when the captain would appear at the foc'sle door to ask, "Has that drunken mate been up here telling lies about me?" We replied in the affirmative, inventing a few extra derogatory remarks that the mate had said about him that we felt the mate might have forgotten to mention.

The captain would say that the mate was a mutinous rascal, and that as soon as we reached port he would have him arrested for drunkenness and stealing whiskey from the cargo. It would be in our best interests to stand by him in case he had any difficulties with the mate.

We aggressively encouraged these differences between the mate and the captain. At every opportunity we fueled their animosity towards each other. Their periods of dissention sometimes lasted two weeks. Both would compete for our goodwill, and we were required to do only necessary ship's work. We lounged about in the sun, worked on hobbies, fished over the side, and enjoyed the extra food delicacies handed out by the captain from his private storeroom under the poop deck.

But you may be sure that during their friendly periods we paid dearly for our two weeks of wallowing in a fool's paradise. They took turns thinking up ways to make our lives miserable with meaningless tasks.. We were sent aloft to tie up buntlines that were already tied. They called us on deck during our watch below until we grew hollow-eyed from lack of sleep. The rations were reduced to a bare minimum. They had one hundred cases of prime Scotch whiskey (White Horse), and we could see no end to their drunken spree. In retrospect, these events seem unreal, but the ship had become the only world we knew. We had been through so much, that everything seemed normal. I think that some wall of psychic defense mercifully developed

in each of us so we could retain our sanity, but this was only the beginning. There was much more to come.

One day, while the ship was rolling from rail to rail in a dead calm, the captain noticed a great many barnacles on the ship's hull below the water line. Twelve to fifteen feet were exposed each time the ship rolled. He decided this would be a good time to scrape off the barnacles by putting our ten foot boat over the side, and with hand scrapers and brushes remove the barnacles, as well as clean the sides of the hull below the water line as the ship rolled. When he broached the proposed project to the sailors and to Mr Johnson, the second mate, he received surprised looks and a negative response. He pointed to me, saying, "I will do it myself, and take Thomsen the Dane with me in the boat."

The small boat that hung from the two davits at the ship's stern was lowered and pulled alongside for the captain and me to board. Mac pulled me to one side and said, "Niels, you don't have to go in the boat if you are afraid. We can stop him." I told him that I would go. Two long-handled scrapers and brushes were placed in the boat which was up to the rail one minute and twenty feet below the rail the next minute. I hesitated for a few minutes in jumping and finally, the captain pushed me off the rail. By some miracle I landed unhurt.

The captain took about fifteen minutes before he made up his mind to jump. It was a ridiculous, dangerous, and futile exercise. Besides concern about being drowned in a boat submerged to the gunwales, I was thinking about the large, white sharks we had seen swimming about the ship on previous days.

After a half hour of accomplishing exactly nothing, the captain sobered up enough to call off the project. The boat was pulled around to the stern. To hoist the boat a man had to be at each end of the boat to hook on the boat tackle, so the captain took the stern tackle and I the bow. The captain failed to get his tackle hooked, and the boat was pulled vertically out of the water, tossing the captain, brushes, and scrapers overboard. I hung on to my boat fall and managed to get the captain into the boat. It was pulled alongside of the ship, and we were hauled on board with ropes. Blocks and tackles were rigged from the shrouds and the boat hoisted on board, with the now completely sober and water-soaked captain blaming me for the loss of the ship's scrapers and brushes. I was just glad to be alive.

Later in the day a great white shark about twenty feet in length came alongside to rub off his barnacles. He stayed with the ship for more than a week, eating everything we threw overboard, even tin cans and cartons. We were all relieved when he departed.

The captain and the mate continued their drinking as we sailed in the direction of Cape Horn. One day, after having been at sea for several months as I was chipping rust on some iron braces in the chain locker, I thought of the cases of grape juice stored in the forward cargo hold adjacent to the chain locker.

An investigation revealed a plank that came loose with a little urging from my scraper. From then on, almost every night, I crept into the hold to bring up a bottle of grape juice for each of the sailors and the cook. A plan was worked out for every empty bottle to be placed under my mattress, so I could drop them overboard during the night. I justified my action with the theory that the grape juice would prevent us from getting scurvy. The disappearance of the grape juice was never mentioned when the holds were opened in Mauritius. The captain may have thought that it had been taken by longshoremen in Victoria where the ship was loaded.

The captain had his own special supply of canned, pickled and preserved foods for his exclusive consumption. Occasionally, one of the sailors would be selected to assist the steward in arranging boxes and casks in the storeroom underneath the quarterdeck. It had two portholes opening out to the after main deck.

While assisting the steward one day, I spotted a cask of salted butter which I managed to maneuver under one of the portholes. While the steward was busy in another part of the storeroom, I loosened the dogs on the porthole. After midnight I crept aft, and on my knees, reached my arm through the porthole and came up with four two-pound blocks of salted butter. This acquisitive action of mine was again motivated by my concern for the health of my shipmates.

It had been several months since we had tasted butter so by dawn it had been consumed. Nothing was said about this incident by the afterguard but that should have alerted me.

Two weeks later I was again asked to help the steward in the storeroom, and again I maneuvered a barrel into position. At two o'clock in the morning when I reached through the porthole into the storeroom, my arm was grasped firmly by the steward. He shouted for the captain, who dashed on deck and began kicking me until I was half conscious, my arm firmly held in the porthole.

It was a week before I could move about normally, at which time the "Captain's Mast" was held. It was like a scene out of *Mutiny on the Bounty*. All hands were present on the main deck facing aft. The captain and mates stood on the quarterdeck facing forward. The captain came on deck wearing his full shipmaster's uniform with four gold stripes. It was the first time any of us had seen him so attired.

Holding the logbook in his hand, he took a stance like Captain Bligh. He began to read "Niels Peter Thomsen, a Dane." It had never occurred to me that I was not an American citizen, nor would I become one until I was twenty-one, and then only if Chris had become a citizen by that time. The captain read out my crime, calling it theft on the high seas, and with the second mate and steward as witnesses, entered it in the log book. I was fined the sum of twenty five dollars, a month's wages.

The fine never bothered me, I had half expected to be flogged. That night, in defiance, I increased my shipmates' ration of the captain's store of Welch's grape juice by an extra bottle. I later learned that the captain had been married to a Danish woman and was paying alimony. In some small way this may have accounted for the special attention I always seemed to be getting from him.

The ship's rudder had been damaged by the pounding of the heavy swells we had encountered in the doldrums, and although we had rigged heavy tackles to lessen the strain on the rudder pintles, there was no improvement. Rumors were floating about the ship that the captain and the first mate had been overheard discussing another route to Mauritius by going south of Australia, and then westward. One-Eyed Louie, Mac, and the second mate talked about the steady head winds, and high seas we would run into if we took such a route.

Several days later a change in course was made. Mac said we were now heading for the eastern tip of Australia. We spent a week in heavy southerly weather before the winds moderated. We began slowly but made steady progress towards the Antipodes, tacking back and forth (zigzagging).

It was very cold. Fortunately, we had heavy underwear from the ship's slopchest. They were of one-quarter inch-thick wool, and we wore them in and out of bed. The ones I had were a very large size, and I wore them outside my clothing.

Since the onset of the latest storm, the captain and the first mate had been sober most of the time. We concluded that in heavy seas their stomachs could not handle heavy drinking, which we estimated was two or three bottles of scotch whiskey each day.

There was no heat on the ship except in the galley stove. Only by sawing up extra ship's spars and booms would we be able to provide fuel for the galley in the months ahead, inasmuch as the lumber cargo was mainly creosoted railroad ties unsuitable for firewood.

We made extra bedcovers out of layers of cardboard and paper sacks from grocery containers obtained from the storeroom aft. The only sea life we noticed were Stormy Petrels, also called "Mother Cary's Chickens," that hovered a few inches above the water between the waves. Now and then a lonely albatross with a six foot wing-spread would swoop and glide to and fro across the ship's wake close astern. These were trying days for all of us, especially for the captain, who had resumed his daily pilgrimage to the sail locker where one hundred cases of whiskey were stowed. The mate, temporarily at least, seemed to be off the bottle.

Then came the first act of violence towards a crew member. It took place during a severe storm, pitch black, raining heavily, and in the second mate's watch. I was at the helm, bundled up in oilskins. The wind was so strong that it was almost impossible to prevent the ship from running up into the wind, keep the topsail from shaking, and the ship on course. There should have been two men at the five foot diameter wheel. The captain came on deck, looked into the compass, and at the sails, and said, "God damn you Thomsen, stop shaking the foresail!"

I was struggling with the helm, my arms aching as though they were being pulled from their sockets, and in tears of pain, I muttered, "A team of horses couldn't steer this damn ship!"

The captain, who had been drinking, grabbed me by the front of my oilskins, and shouted, "Don't you curse my ship!" He struck me on the shoulder with such force that I slid flat on my face across the deck to the starboard railing. The second mate grabbed hold of the wheel and the captain went below. Mr. Johnson sent for one of my watchmates to help with the steering.

I duly entered this incident in full detail on the blank pages of my Bowdich logbook where I kept a full account of the captain's sins. A word is due describing the relationship that existed between the captain and me. Almost every ship I have known has a person on board who has invited the role of scapegoat. One or another of the individuals in authority can vent their frustrations upon this designee. My future fifty years as a shipmaster will attest to this as a fact of life. On the *Forest Dream* I qualified for this unenviable status for a number of reasons. The captain was an exceedingly brutal man for whom I had no respect, and I lacked the experience and wisdom to conceal these feelings. I was the youngest on board, slight of build, and the bane of all shipmasters — a sea lawyer. I was always on guard against any infringement upon the rights of oppressed seamen. I was ready to challenge authority if I felt it to be unjust. Until Port Adelaide where Archie Horka joined the ship, no one else in our crew challenged the captain's rule. Later, in my military and civilian careers, I was able to discard this sometimes self-destructive character trait, but during the war years it was a decidedly advantageous asset.

Fortunately, months before the captain's serious drinking had begun he had designated the daily winding of the ship's chronometers to Mr. Johnson. Before ships were equipped with wireless, in order to navigate with precision by using celestial navigation, every oceangoing sailing ship carried three chronometers. These were usually kept at a watchmaker's establishment whenever the ship was in port. The rate of loss or gain would be accurately calculated and recorded. The chronometers were brought on board on sailing day with a certificate indicating the daily loss or gain in fractions of seconds, to be recorded in the ship's chronometer log. All three chronometers had to be wound at exactly the same time each day, usually at eight in the morning. When making observations for determining longitude, the time used in calculations would be the mean of the average corrected time of the three chronometers.

For over two months no ship was ever as alone on any ocean as the *Forest Dream*. We had the entire lower Pacific Ocean from latitude forty south to the Antarctic to ourselves. We were a thousand miles from the closest steamer or sailing ship route. The crew also had a gnawing concern that the captain and the mate might not actually know the ship's position. The mate's abstinence had lasted only two weeks, before they were both back to their former three bottle ration, retrieved daily from the lazaret.

The heavy linseed-soaked oilskins we wore constantly became stiff with salt and cold weather. Where they touched our wrists and neck was a ring of raw, cracked flesh, and at each inside joint of our fingers were deep, split-open sores from the hauling of ropes and the gripping of ratlines when going aloft. Coming off watch we would urinate in our cupped hands, bathing our faces, necks and wrists with our warm urine, which seemed to have a soothing effect. I have since been told that urine contains tannic acid, a beneficial ingredient. Sometimes one even resorted to using urine from others when it was in short personal supply, regarding it as a medicine. All this now seems insane, but that is exactly as I remember it.

After one especially violent storm, the ship started to take on water from straining of the ship's planks. It became necessary to pump bilges one hour out of every four. The pump had two large, heavy, iron wheels about five feet in diameter, equipped with two long handles. To operate, it required two men on each side facing one another. This meant coming on watch one half hour earlier and remaining on watch one-half hour longer. In a twenty-four hour period, this meant sixteen hours on watch and eight hours off watch, plus being called out to hoist sails.

Day after day we were faced with heavy seas and strong head winds. Most of the time we were unable to "tack ship," and of necessity resorted to "wearing ship," a much more laborious and dangerous procedure in high wind and seas. Because of our rudder problems, much time and work were required re-adjusting the tackles in place on the steering apparatus. Life became more and more miserable. We never bothered to remove our clothes, but just threw ourselves into our bunks when we went below. Cook Timmerman was a jewel, always on hand with hot coffee, and a cheerful word. The coffee was terrible but always welcome.

Our small messroom, lit by a tiny oil lamp, was taken over entirely by cockroaches. The table was covered with a light-colored piece of oilcloth and if one entered the room in the dark and hit the table with a cup, the table would appear as if by magic. I could never figure out what they lived on.

One pitch black night, with the ship racing through the water, powered by sails that any prudent shipmaster would have furled hours before, the captain, who had been drinking, came on deck. He ordered the second mate to call all hands to shorten sail, while he took over the helm.

With the ship rolling and pitching and the decks awash, we clambered aloft. One-Eyed Louie, Frank and I were out on the upper topsail yard in the act of furling the sail, when the captain allowed the ship to veer off before the wind. The sail then ballooned out of control, flinging Frank and me backwards.

I was at the outer end of the yard with my legs wrapped around the footrope extension, which saved me from falling. Louie was inboard next to the mast. Dear Frank was not so fortunate, and he was thrown off the yard, plunging in darkness eighty feet to the deck below. Mr. Johnson and Louie came to help me furl the sail. As soon as the task was finished, I hurried down the rigging.

Mac and the mate had brought Frank into the foc'sle where the water was almost level with the lower berths. Frank had been laid in my upper berth. He was badly hurt but conscious. Mac told me that he had landed on his knees, which were crushed, and that his pelvis was also smashed. His head was badly battered, swollen and bleeding.

The fury of the storm was increasing. Whole seas were pouring over the bows of the ship and splashing into the foc'sle where a foot or two of water was sloshing about. All hands except Mac and I were on deck struggling to take off sail to prevent the ship from foundering. Mac left to stand his wheel watch.

The captain and the mate were running about the deck shouting orders, several times appearing at the door of the foc'sle door to ask about Frank. I was in Frank's berth, kneeling over him, and he kept asking to sit up. I had my arms around him, but whenever I lifted him up, blood would spurt from his mouth and cover my neck and chest. I held him in my arms for almost two hours. I prayed for him to die quickly. Finally, with a sigh, he asked me to hold him tight, which I did. And so he died. Inconsolable, I laid down beside him, bereaved, exhausted and crying.

Mr. Johnson came into the forecastle and took me from my berth, where I lay alongside of Frank. I was dazed, and felt as though my world had ended. I felt I would never be able to laugh or smile again, or be glad to be alive.

I was obsessed by the knowledge that I was the one who had brought Frank to this tragic end, by enlisting him to join me in signing on the *Forest Dream*. I grieved so that Mac and One-Eyed Louie took care of me as though I were a small child.

Frank was sewn into canvas, lashed to anchor chain, and buried at noon. The crew had assembled on deck. Mac committed Frank to the ocean with a verse from his New Testament. I was too distraught to leave my berth.

Several weeks later, according to custom, we distributed all Frank's clothing, except for his watch, among his shipmates. At Frank's insistence, before we left Seattle, we had both taken out a three thousand dollar life insurance policy with New York Life, with double indemnity clauses in case of accidental death. Frank had loaned me the money for my policy. Twelve months later, I delivered his policy and pocket watch to his father, a janitor in a New York apartment building.

As I relive the voyage of the *Forest Dream*, I sometimes wonder whether the one hundred cases of whiskey were a curse or a blessing, as these two men who controlled our lives were evil and completely devoid of basic principles. How might they have behaved without the oblivion of alcohol to separate them from the half year of nightmarish existence the rest of the crew endured.

We sailed into the outer harbor of Port Adelaide, south of Australia, having been at sea for almost four months. On arrival, the captain announced that there would be no shore leave. Obviously, he did not want us ashore with tales of happenings on the voyage, but also, it would have been difficult to obtain a crew to replace us. Divers came out to the ship and made an inspection of the rudder, after which arrangements were made to move to the inner harbor for repairs.

Mac and I were assigned to assist the diver on his barge, helping him by pumping air and manning the air hose. This was interesting as it gave us an opportunity to converse with someone other than the ship's crew. In less than ten days the rudder was repaired, and a new crew member, Archie Horka, came on board to take Frank's place. One of his duties would be to operate the gas engine, which had been repaired.

We were allowed one supervised trip ashore by the Immigration Authorities for the purpose of purchasing some clothing. While we were unhappy over not having some unsupervised shore leave,

along with money to spend, we were so occupied with enjoying fresh meat, fruit and vegetables, we did not complain. We had planned to go ashore to register complaints with the American Consul about the lack of adequate, decent food and general shipboard conditions, the tyrannical behavior of the captain, and his and the mate's drinking, but nothing came of it.

One of the reasons may have been that ten days before arrival in Adelaide, the captain and mate went out of their way to figuratively pat each one of us on the head, saying what fine seamen we were, and all of us having endured so much hardship together, we should band together to see that the *Forest Dream* made it safely to Mauritius. We swallowed the flattery, which may give the impression that we were naive and without spirit, which was not the case. It was mainly that we were physically and mentally exhausted, and needed a time of healing.

The trip from Port Adelaide was uneventful, the winds were fair, mostly on the beam, brisk and steady. We quickly dropped into a fairweather routine except that now we had a good supply of edible food. The salt horse and the salt pork in brine, a barrel of each which had come on board in Port Adelaide were of fair quality. We had a good supply of potatoes, beans, rice and flour, as well as other staples. The captain and the mate returned to their regular alcoholic diet, though seemingly modified, and the days passed quickly. We were able to catch fish almost every day by skipping a white rag on a hook through the water, either over the stern, or from the end of the bowsprit. Our catch was mostly dolphins, two or three feet long, with shining spade-shaped heads, gleaming and shimmering in the sunlight.

These fish were true dolphins, not porpoises, measuring up to three feet in length, and like the albatross, as any real sailor knows, are protected from harm by tradition and superstition. I believe that since the death of Frank, when things seemed to be getting out of hand, there grew an unspoken pact among the crew forward. If we were to overcome the threat to our common welfare (which in our eyes the captain and mate represented), we must maintain complete solidarity never to show any kinks in our armor.

Nearing the second half of the voyage, we believed that the captain and mate were beginning to have concerns of possible dire consequences to them. They feared we would go in a body to the American Embassy with the story of their conduct on the voyage.

With each gust of wind and forward surge of the vessel to the eastward, the crew's spirits rose in anticipation that just over the horizon lay Mauritius, the Nirvana of our dreams. There awaited "beautiful, exotic, Creole women," as described in the archives of the Seattle Public Library. If only Frank could have been here with us, was the thought uppermost in the mind and heart of Mac and I.

Having no intimate experiences with women, I listened with great interest to Hubert, the man of the world. He described in graphic detail his days and nights spent in the brothels of Berlin, Amsterdam and Paris, and the pleasures that lay in store for us in Port Louis.

The voyage to Port Louis took fifty-four days. When five miles from the island, we were met by two small tugboats, named *Paul* and *Virginia* after a local legend of two star-crossed island lovers — an appropriate welcome for a ship of love-starved sailors. We had been sighted far at sea by a lookout on the highest peak on the island, namely Le Pouce (the thumb). An hour or more later we were at anchor in the inner harbor of Port Louis.

Now that we were safely moored in the harbor, with hundreds of dollars in wages due us, we thought that our troubles were at an end. But they had just begun. By law, half of the crew's wages were now payable, but the captain informed us that he could not reach the charterers' bankers. He offered us each the sum of fifty rupees, the equivalent of five dollars, scarcely sufficient for two rounds of drinks for six thirsty sailors.

Next to our anchorage in the harbor lay a small bark. At first we thought would be the *Favell*, but it had turned out to be the *Gwyder Castle*, a small local sailing vessel. The *Favell* had come and gone, on her way to South Africa.

The capital city of Port Louis lay in a long narrow valley facing the harbor. High on the lush, green-carpeted hillsides were many luxurious homes, inhabited by the upper class English and French whose family histories in Mauritius spanned six generations. In the valley, the city of Port Louis housed several hundred thousand East Indian and Asian immigrants, almost all living in extreme poverty. The streets were filthy, with open sewers paralleling them, and where giant rats and cockroaches scurried about in broad daylight.

When the captain returned from his first trip ashore, he was accompanied by a man named McNiel with a strong Scottish accent. The owners had appointed him their agent and representative while the *Forest Dream* was in Mauritius. The owners had returned to Canada, after waiting for two months for the ship to arrive. Mac told me that he had overheard the mate saying that the ship had been presumed to be lost at sea, and that the assignees of the cargo had ordered lumber elsewhere. They were now refusing to accept our cargo. The captain passed word down to the crew that owing to this development the charterers were short of funds. That would mean a delay in our receiving any sizeable advances on wages which were now due to us. This was discouraging news.

CHAPTER FOUR

# MALCOLM
# ABLE SEAMAN

*PORT WATCH*

*Saturday, December 19, 1925*: Palmerston Island lay abeam, twelve miles distant. We were in the heart of the South Sea Islands. The men suggested that we beach this good ship on one of these utopian islands and lead a life of palm-shaded ease; no more pumping, no more salt beef or sleepy-eyed wheel watches in the wee small hours, a dusky maid to catch the fish and serve the palm wine. All such options were discussed, with heavy joking, in the dog watch, for a sailor has his illusions, no less than a homebound landsman. However idyllic may be the life of a beachcomber in these motion picture islands, I am at least certain that the beauty of the sea and sky are unequaled anywhere in the world. Any description that I could undertake could only appear florid. The colors and tones are enough to make an artist tear out his hair. Days followed in such a succession of unbroken monotony that Sunday became the unit of time for us. The routine of the days were broken on Saturdays, when the wheel watches were changed.

Days passed in the following way: At four in the morning, the coffee watch, Chris, Hubert and I come on deck a few minutes before eight bells (4:00 A.M.). We talk for a little while with the sleepy-eyed pair in the starboard watch who have been on deck since midnight, standing the graveyard watch. At

eight bells, Chris takes the wheel. After one of us has called the cook out of the land of dreams, Hubert and I pace the forecastlehead, athwartships, from light tower to light tower. Then a dull amber glow from the galley oil lamp springs out of the galley porthole, followed by a rattle of stove lids and poker.

The pungent tang of wood smoke wafts from the galley. A little while later the cook sticks his tousled yellow head out of the galley door and calls, "coffee," the magic word. Hubert goes aft and relieves Chris at the wheel for ten or fifteen minutes. The slight form of the cabin boy comes out of the gloom, outlined against the white of the after bulkhead, the cup bearer to the gods of the afterguard, coming for the mate's coffee. Chris has returned to the wheel, and Hubert and I stretch our legs in the little messroom, pour the divine poison, brown and smoking, while we talk of ships and sugar cane, poetry, and the ship models that Niels and I are building. At four bells (six o'clock) I take the wheel while the rosy-fingered dawn comes up from the east. The wetting down of the deck is done by my two watchmates, Chris forward, Hubert aft, with the mate to give him a hand.

With the hot coffee under our belts and a genial sun to warm us, the heavy "longshore wit" flies from man to man. The mate comes in now and then with one of his priceless stories concerning some old sea captain, or what the Irishman said to the Scotsman. There is no brass button dignity here. The mate is respected because he has served his time under the most severe and unrelenting of taskmasters, the sea, and because in fair weather or foul, he is the man for the job, as he has proved to be.

With a few small jobs around the decks to be done, serving or reeving new gear, or the like, the three men are engaged until seven bells, seven-twenty A.M., when the watch is called Chris and Hubert descend into the "pumphole" the pit left in the deck load, and soon the sluggish sound of the pumps is heard, like the groaning of some giant from the inner depths of the twelve foot high, deck cargo.

The cabin boy goes forward to the galley, basket in hand, fetching the cabin breakfast. Chips (carpenter) climbs about the rigging with a tomato can full of oil hung around his neck, oiling the blocks aloft. The old man (captain) goes his rounds of the deck, and eight bells is struck.

The starboard watch takes the deck, to patch sails or overhaul rigging, while we go below for breakfast and sleep. From twelve-thirty till four we are on deck again, then follows the dog watch from four till six, four bells. We come on deck again at six P.M., wet the decks, pump ship, and are relieved at eight, to sleep until midnight. Then we are roused out again to stand watch until 4:00 A.M., and so it goes, day after day.

### December 23, 1925

Today we passed Eoa Island, high, rocky, barren, a desolate mountain peak rising in the sea. But it is land, and for that reason the center of attraction and conversation until we sank it astern the same night.

### December 25, 1925

Christmas Day at sea. The day was broiling hot, decks steaming from passing showers, no work was done, and something extra was added to the dinner. The cook made a three-story cake, with frosting and all. On the top in letters of pink sugar was scrawled "Mary Xmas." We wished each other a "Merry Christmas and a Happy New Year," with the guilty feeling of people who should be spending the day of cheer, "At home with the folks."

### December 26, 1925

Today we crossed the International Date Line, losing a day. Since the twenty sixth was a Saturday and was skipped in keeping with the custom, Sunday fell the day after Christmas, and we had two days of leisure.

Holding a general southwesterly course, our next sight of land was Norfolk Island. Once used by the English as a penal colony, now it serves as a cable station. On the chart it has the appearance of a spider in the middle of a web: the cable from Brisbane makes an axis of the island and swings northeast to the Fijis, while another line swings down to the northern point of New Zealand, thus linking the three by invisible threads like a gigantic nerve center.

Since nearing the Australian coast, there has been much talk of "Southerly Busters" a kind of sudden, fierce squall. These squalls are characterized by a rapid drop from summer heat to near freezing. The nights were dewy and I noticed the mate feeling the surface of the glass skylight now and then during the watch. He said that a sudden drying of the moisture is one of the best ways of foretelling these fierce storms.

While lying becalmed this morning, the nearest thing to a humorous but potentially tragic happening took place. The ship had collected a few barnacles and some seaweed on her passage from the north, which attracted the captain's attention one forenoon during a period of calm weather with a giant swell running. Deciding to take some action, he ordered the carpenter to construct an enormous scraper with a twenty-foot handle and a broad blade of sheet iron. To weight this formidable looking tool (contraption), the heaviest sledge on the ship was lashed to the head of the scraper. A stage was then hung over the ship's side on which a man stood, guiding the blade, while other men on deck hauled the unwieldy device up and down the ship's side, crushing a barnacle at every third stroke. The heavy ground swell was coming up to the waist of the man on the stage, also, there were several large white sharks cruising about the ship. The only man who volunteered for the stage assignment was Chris. After about thirty minutes, the captain decided to abandon this particular scheme.

For some reason, probably having something to do with the fact that he had been drinking steadily for a number of days, the captain had a fixation about the barnacles. He announced that we would tackle the barnacles by lowering the small boat hanging in the stern davits, and go after the barnacles with some small scrapers.

The boat falls were made ready; the boat filled with scrapers and brushes, and with some difficulty it was lowered into the water, the stern of the ship rising and falling in twenty-foot arcs. When the boat was hauled alongside, the captain asked for volunteers. There was no response, not even from the toady Chris, the mate's stellar seaman.

"I will go in the boat and take Thomsen the Dane with me," the captain announced. Niels looked at me, and I shook my head sideways saying, "Niels, you don't have to go," but the captain and Niels sat down on the taffrail, with their legs hanging over the rail, preparing to jump into the boat.

There was a dilemma. How to get into the boat without breaking your leg or losing your life. The boat was on the port side, and when the ship rolled to port the small boat would be even with the rail. When it rolled to starboard, the boat would be fifteen feet below the rail. So there they both sat, side by side on the rail, each waiting for the other to jump. At last the old man said, "Thomsen, why don't you jump?"

Niels replied, "Why don't you jump?" The next time the boat came up, the captain pushed Niels off the rail, and he fell about five feet into the boat, unhurt. After about ten more rolls of the ship, the captain jumped into the boat.

This was during a period when the captain and the mate were not on speaking terms. All through this scenario the mate stood by, saying nothing, just looking on with a gleeful, sardonic trace of a smile on his face, as though he savored the incident.

Lines on deck were made fast to stem and stern of the boat, so it could be moved along the side of the ship. The captain and Niels commenced making war on the barnacles, but they had problems. With every passing ground swell the ship's side rose and fell, tossing the boat away from the ship. The boat filled up with water, and every now and then the fins of two or three large sharks broke the surface of the water about fifty yards distant. After mangling a few defenseless barnacles in this manner, the captain decided that the day was not favorable. The boat was hauled astern, boat falls lowered, and the crew stood by to haul away on the falls. The stern of the ship was rising and falling fifteen to twenty feet.

Niels managed to hook on the bow, but the captain did not get the stern hooked fast. The boat hung in the air, bow up, spilling the two men in a tangle into the water, showered by tools, bailer, oars and whatever. It was a case of each man for himself, the captain scrambling for the nearest boatfall. Except for a few bruises, cuts and scratches, both adventurers were hauled on board in a boat full of seawater. The barnacles were left in peace, and the captain sobered.

*January 7, 1926*
At 10:30 P.M., we were saluted by a heavenly

reception committee with a long roll of thunder and blinding flashes of lightning, while a heavy, coal black curtain raced over the starry sky, shrouding the night in inky gloom, broken only by zig-zag lightning streaks like wounds against the sky. Hot, heavy rain fell. The captain was called. Hardly had his head cleared the companionway, before he shouted, "Clew up the royal, the topsails, fore and afters, the top-gallant sails," all in one breath. Then he took the wheel and, with the mate standing by to sing out the word to belay, our mighty watch of three men clewed up the square sails and made them fast, first taking care of the gaff topsails in a fashion. To set a seal on this, the mainsail was lowered and furled. Shortened sail was carried until the following morning when the weather cleared.

All the sails were set again at eight bells, including topsails. All hands and the cook tailed on, the halyards being snatch-blocked on deck, and with a raucous chantey from the mate, the canvas was stretched. All help from the gasoline engine hoist was abandoned. Everyone who could hold a wrench had tried his hand at repairing it, without success. This was the "miracle machine" designed to replace six men.

Good weather held throughout the day, favored by a fair wind. In the evening we saw our first vessel since leaving San Pedro, a large passenger steamer, tearing along towards the west. With his binoculars, the captain made out her name to be the *Nakura*. Our flag was hoisted and dipped, she returning our courtesy, and we soon lost sight of her in the twilight. Presumably, she was bound for Sydney, Australia.

### January 24, 1926

At 4:30 A.M. a violent squall struck the ship, heeling her over, ripping the spanker topsail by the sudden blast. All topsails, royal and topgallant sails were clewed up and made fast. We had barely finished furling them when the wind changed to the opposite quarter. We tacked ship, standing in towards the coast, with yards braced sharp up in an effort to keep offshore as much as possible.

The halcyon days were over, head winds set in, cold rain poured down, nights were shrouded in mist. High seas rolled up from the southward. At times we gained a few miles, beating to windward, only to lose it on the next tack. Providentially, after five days a fair wind set in, and with everything set, we made way towards Bass Straits. After eighteen days of dogged fighting, we sighted Green Cape, the southeast corner of New South Wales. The blur of the shore loomed out of the rain and mist, and we lost no time in tacking ship, and bearing off. Both sea and wind conspired to hold us back, and we gained less than ten miles in forty-eight hours, the hardest ten miles we ever worked for.

As if to propitiate the Gods of the Sea, the mate began to feed albatrosses that soared about the ship. He threw handfuls of fat pork upon the water, and the great, lovely birds came down to pick up these morsels floating there, like chunks of bread. "Big chickens," he called them, standing for a whole watch by the taffrail, admiring their mastery of the air.

### January 26, 1926

This morning a light fair wind sprang up and gradually increased as the day wore on, the ship reaching ten knots through the water. When night fell, the usual mist began to gather, dripping from rigging and sails, making the decks damp and slippery. The mate grew cautious, and we made all the light sails fast. A hot blast of wind dried everything, rigging, sails and deck in just ten minutes. This was a sure sign of a "Southerly Buster."

Hubert was making the fore-royal (the lightest and highest sail on the ship) fast when the ship was taken aback by a sudden shift of wind. Everything aloft shook as if masts, yards and sails would all come down on us in a heap. While the captain relieved the wheel, we took in the topgallant sails, and when the ship was taken aback again, the jibs were furled. At eight bells, the foresail was furled, the spanker, main and mizzen made fast, and the jigger was lowered and reefed.

The mate told us that we were in for a heavy, dangerous storm of gale force. On the twenty seventh we pooped a heavy sea, flooding the after companionway and running into the captain's cabin. The force of the water against the poop wire-reinforced deck skylights was so great that they were cracked. In the afternoon the outer jib tack carried away.

The sheet block on the lee side hammered about so violently that it was knocked clear out of the eye, but was repaired immediately, the mate and I straddling the bowsprit and making the jib tack fast again. Seas rose to our knees with the plunging of the ship down to the level of the water.

The next day brought no change for the better. We were headed northwest, the opposite direction of our planned course, under lower topsail, reefed mizzen and jigger. At noon, the starboard watch attempted to set the mainsail, but a six foot tear appeared near the leach of the sail, making it imperative to lower the sail for repair. As soon as we came on deck at twelve-thirty, our four hours turned out to be a watch of patching sail. The sail was kept wet by continual boarding seas, drenching our work, making our sewing very hard for wet canvas is stiff and unyielding.

The longed-for fair wind came on the thirtieth, and all the reefs were taken out. The ship was once again dressed fore and aft in all her sails, and we began to forge ahead at four knots, no mind that every bunk and square inch of the foc'sle was soaking wet.

At night porpoises played about the silent ship, making long comets of light in the phosphorescent sea. All was well once more. Under the slightest whisper of a breeze, we crept southward, the news

drifting about during the day that we were twenty-three miles off Deal Island, the most important of the islands that dot the entrance to Bass Strait.

*January 29, 1926*
At noon, a steamer was observed coming up astern, directly in our wake, which was feeble, as we were only making about three knots. She soon overhauled us, changing her course a point or two, and came within hailing distance. The spanker topsail was lowered, and the stars and stripes run up the truck. From the port wing of the little steamer's bridge, their mate hailed us, "Where are you bound?" coming in clearly and distinctly over the water.

The captain raised his megaphone and shouted simply, "Mauritius," without giving out any information concerning the number of days out or the port of sailing. He added in a plaintive voice, "Please report me."

The steamer's mate, who appeared to be an Englishman, waved a reassuring hand, gave the engine room telegraph a turn, and rapidly drew ahead. On her stern, we read the name, *Koranui* of Sydney. She was ungraceful and dirty with coal smoke, but to us she represented the "Whole World", a link to civilization. We looked on her with half-longing eyes as she sped away, dipping her Australian flag in salute which we answered in kind.

The new month of February came in like a lion, roaring up from the southeast in a gale, and taking away our fair wind in a mouthful. The head wind created the same wearisome routine: royal furled, topgallant sails, topsails all, reefed mizzen and jigger, main and spanker furled, high seas, a flooded forecastle, hove-to at daylight, meals in silence, long hours of pumping, short tempers, all the followers of bad weather.

*February 2, 1926*
A great day for us, the day we entered Bass Straits, after thirty days of touch and go. At mid-day

the wind came up light and fair, all sails were set, and a southwest course was laid. In the evening Flinders Island reared its blue bulk against the western sky. We went about ship at eight bells, the Sisters Islands on the beam with the amber glow of the fishermen's fires glancing along the shores. Then, just at midnight, we crept past Deal Island, with its lone lighthouse flashing from the summit. Thus, the Straits were won, our Scylla and Charybdis passed, or as the mate expressed it, we were "around the corner."

But our real troubles had just begun. Land lay on either hand, the Strait was thick with rocks and fog. Haze blanketed the sky, with rain squalls following one another steadily throughout the days and nights. Pyramid Rocks was cleared, a keen lookout was kept for Judgment Rock, and we put that safely behind us after many weary tacks. Sail Rock too, lay in our path, but was finally weathered by night.

With the head winds from the west and high seas from the same quarter, attempts to tack the ship met with no success. Both watches were kept on deck, and we had to wear ship instead of tack, with all hands on the braces at the critical moment, the sails filling and bringing her around. This continued for several days, often losing in a few hours all we had gained for days.

### February 6, 1926

A sudden lull of the wind left us wallowing in seas from the west with not enough wind to keep the sails full. Booms and gaffs banged to and fro in lifeless heaviness, sheet blocks shrieked, parcels groaned. The ship's bell tolled with the drunken rolling of the ship while we braced around the whole watch through, hanging on every puff of wind.

### February 7, 1926

The wind hauled fair. A west by north course was laid, bringing us abeam of King Island by nightfall. We were through the Straits at last and the Indian Ocean lay due west. We did not expect a change in the weather. It would be steady beating to windward all the way until we could move into a higher latitude. We could only pray for the boon of a few days of fair winds.

The mate said he had warned the captain earlier of the head winds which we were certain to encounter in the latitudes south of Australia, and that he should have followed the traditional route by sailing east to Mauritius. All this was of course water over the dam; our only choice now was to continue westward towards Mauritius.

During all this time, the captain took direct charge of the starboard watch, so far had the second mate fallen from grace. We in the port watch felt compassion for the men of the starboard watch, now to be continually supervised by this brutal, ill-tempered man. Often, in my watch below I was awakened by the high, strident voice of the captain as he screamed orders about the deck when tacking ship or taking in sail. Commands were always interspersed with lurid threats and violent outbursts of temper; driving the poor second mate almost out of his wits, groaning, "Oh Lord, Oh Lord!"

My shipmates in the starboard watch went about in dull silence. No one talked or sang at the halyards. Frank fell into a deep despondency for days. It seemed anachronistic that to the endless pumping, bracing, making and taking in sail, reefing and hauling there should be added enmity and tyranny.

For that matter, things were no better in our watch, although the mate was never bothered by the captain's interference. He was too able a man to allow any such thing. The drab prospect of two or three months of beating westward to Cape Leeuwin against cold, stormy head winds with hatred forever sneaking about the ship, the drinking water gone bad, the bilge pump jamming, all served to cast a cloud of gloom over us. We were glad to retreat to our watch below, throw ourselves on our bunk and forget it all in sleep.

Chris had not spoken a word at meals for fully three months. He objected to having a light in the messroom, even on the darkest days, and showed all signs of a man on the verge of madness. This state of things continued for days, many times there were only five or six hours between all sails set, being hove-to under lower topsail and reefed jigger. The calms were of such short duration that the heavy seas had no time to subside before it was blowing a gale again. Even the fair wind from the east, light and shifting, was more to be likened to the short breathing spells of a puffing monster — a kind of intake of breath preceding the outburst.

On the eighth, while wearing ship, the inner jib was ripped down its length from head to clew. It was unbent from the stay to be patched at once.

As we bore away from the coast, the albatrosses returned, soaring about the ship, sleeping on the water at night, and begging fat pork during the day.

### February 9, 1926

During the morning, Niels, the youngest of the crew, came forward to the foc'sle with a look of abject misery on his face. I could see that something was wrong for he had been one of the most cheerful of the crew up to this time. I asked, "Why are you so downhearted?" He answered that he had had some trouble with the captain.

It seems that Niels, Frank, and the captain were hauling on the spanker sheet when it became fouled in the block. While Niels was attempting to clear it, the captain leaped forward and struck at him but Niels, light and agile, quickly dodged the blow by jumping clear. The captain vented his wrath with a stream of curses, shouting wild threats of putting him on bread and water, a reduction in rating and fines. From this time on, Niels seemed to lose all spirit. His cheerful manner dropped from him, and in spite of all the comfort I could offer, he lost all interest in the voyage.

### Wednesday, February 10, 1926

A few hours of fair wind, with all sails drawing, we managed to lay a west southwest course, but we were forced to tack in the evening to avoid getting under the land. Heavy squalls were frequent with occasional hailstorms. Having elected to take this westward route south of Australia, we have to skirt the coast in search of variable winds as further south lies the belt of strong and steady head winds known as the Westerlies. At about five o'clock in the evening we sighted a large four-masted bark, hull down to the southward. She was tearing east under full sail and was, of course, too far off to be spoken. We supposed her to be a Norwegian bound from Capetown.

She moved like a phantom ship, "the Flying Dutchman" through mist and rain, running fair before the wind. It was the first sailing ship we had seen since leaving San Pedro. Head wind followed, a living gale. We stripped down to fore-topsail and reefed jigger, and hove her to on the starboard tack for there was nothing else to do. Headway could not be made against such a gale, and to run before it would mean the loss of all that we had gained for weeks. The kicking of the wheel became worse. The rudder post lifted and plunged in a fearful manner, so that the mate, as a last resort, rigged a new tackle. It was a great ponderous rig of sheet blocks and four inch line of many parts, so that the steering gear looked like an ancient catapult of the Middle Ages. To steer, we were obliged to drag all this machinery around with every motion of the wheel, but there could be no complaining, it was for the safety of the ship.

During the middle watch, on the night of the eleventh, Niels had the wheel from ten until midnight. All hands, except the captain were forward taking in sail. In conning the ship, that is, in directing the steering, the captain stood right behind Niels, giving the usual orders, such as, "Ease the wheel" or "Keep her off," according to the variations of the gale. There was no one to give the young fellow a hand at turning the wheel and the captain was not deigning to do so. He shouted, "What's the matter, why don't you put up the wheel?!"

Niels replied, "It is very hard sir. It would take a team of mules to steer this damn ship!"

The captain shouted, "Don't you curse my ship!" and struck Niels while he stood at the wheel.

The only thing that kept Niels from retaliating was the knowledge that there were men aloft on the yards, and the wheel could not be deserted at such a time. This was the last straw! Niels swore that he would even things up as soon as he had the chance, but he lost all heart, never smiling or talking, not even reading or working with me on our ship models, just throwing himself in his bunk at every opportunity in an effort to sleep off his wretched state of mind.

### February 12, 1926

Ever since we crossed the Equator the starboard after bilge pump had been out of order, and the port after bilge pump had been used exclusively. Now the remaining pump began to groan and jam at times, so hard that we could not move the lever with the weight of two men. There was no way of lifting the pump shaft out to make repairs. Just before dawn on this date, the pump gave up the ghost, the shaft breaking off and the lever falling uselessly to the deck.

We then turned to on the forward main pumps with their great, heavy iron wheels, four feet in diameter. These were intended to be driven by the engine, which was broken down. We improvised by doubling the length of the handles and pumped by hand. It took four men, three at least, to operate the pump, and the mates had to relieve the helm so the third seaman in the watch could assist with the pumping. While the ship was hove-to against the violent head winds, albatrosses gathered about the stern, riding the great seas with as much unconcern as if they were in a pond.

The mate decided to catch one of the big chickens, as he called them. A five inch triangle was made out of a piece of sheet tin and a piece of salt fat pork was fixed within the triangle. It was towed by a long line strung out behind the ship.

As the triangle drifted astern, the line was paid out so there was no drag on the snare. The dignified old albatross swooped down, thrust his beak into the triangle in an effort to seize the pork and was trapped without being injured. The beak of the albatross had an enlargement on the end that it jammed into the lower corner of the triangle. The astonished old fellow was drawn on board, flapping and protesting, but once on deck he was helpless as a chick.

He settled down quickly on the poop deck, his legs tucked under him, awaiting the mate's pleasure. He allowed the mate to stroke his head and stretch his wings while I photographed him. They can be eaten, but we were not starving, so with the best of blessings, we tossed him into the air. He resumed soaring about the vessel. Sailors will make tobacco pouches out of their webbed feet and pipe stems from the hollow wing bones, but we had endured enough bad luck without killing this bird and sharing the fate of the "Ancient Mariner". At least this was the unanimous feeling of the crew forward.

Saturday was a day of light, fair wind in which all sails were set. Sunday, a day that might have meant a day of rest, turned out to be another depressing day of head wind, high seas and a howling gale. The ship skinned down to lower topsail, reefed mizzen and jigger sails. In our search for fair winds from the east, we had been driven south into the Roaring Forties. The west winds grew cold, the seas higher and rougher, often climbing over the ship's side, and drenching us as we sought scanty shelter in the lee of the lifeboat.

Oil skins and southwesters were worn day and night. Our hands, faces and arms were whitened with the salt seascurf. Our skin grew scaly and leprous like. Where the bowsprit enters the ship, the caulking had loosened so that with every dive she made, water entered the seams, flowed aft, and streamed into the foc'sle in rivulets. Overhead, the deck, long neglected, leaked rain and boarding seas into our bunks. There was no heat forward, except the galley. Only the after cabin had warmth. Why we did not succumb to pneumonia, I will never understand. Now and then, we could hear a terrific clatter coming from the galley. The poor cook had his hands full.

At night the sea was lit up with great sheets of phosphorus as far as the eye could see. Strange lights of the shape and size of cucumbers lay on the surface of the sea in thousands — a kind of a jellyfish, perhaps, but appearing weird and ghostly at night. Little stormy petrels hovered about the ship, seeming to walk on water, a trait they have of dabbling their feet in the sea while on the wing. These tiny birds are also known as "Mother Carey's Chickens."

*February 15, 1926*
Hove-to, strong hail storms all day long, heavy winds and seas. No let up.

*February 16, 1926*
At dawn, the westerly gale subsided and a fair faint breeze came from the east. The reefs were shaken out of all the fore and afters, the upper topsail and foresail were set after long, weary hauling. We made a few miles of westward progress when the wind hauled to the west again, bringing with it another gale. At eight P.M. we began taking in sail.

The upper topsail yard was lowered, both watches clewing up as the yard came down. The starboard watch, still on deck, were ordered aloft to lay out on the weather side and furl the sail while

Chris, Hubert and I scrambled out on the lee side of the yard to haul up the bunt and work in towards the mast. While we were passing the gaskets we heard someone shout, "Man overboard!"

Instantly, I thought of Frank and Niels — tried to get by Chris who was calmly making a gasket fast — so I could be one of the first in the boat hanging in the davits on the afterdeck. Hubert shouted in my ear, "It's Frank." We slid and sprawled down the backstays and reached the deck where men were running about in confusion.

It was pitch black, and the ship was throwing itself from railside to railside. Then the voice of the carpenter, "Here he is." A flashlight cut a wedge out of the black night, and there on the drenched forecastlehead I saw a sight that took the heart right out of me.

Frank my shipmate, lay stretched out with his head lying in a pool of blood. He was groaning softly. I knelt by his head and spoke to him, but he could only whisper, "Oh, God, this is awful," over and over again. I felt his chest and legs which were twisted and wrenched. Even in the short, quick examination I made I could see that my poor friend was broken so badly, there was little hope for his survival. We passed a blanket under him, stretched it tight, and carried him below to our forecastle.

As he lay there on deck, oilskins, shoes and trousers were cut from him, causing him untold pain, which he bore manfully. There was over a foot of water sloshing about on the deck of the forecastle.

The captain was standing in the doorway of the forecastle, when the mate shouted from the deck outside, "Shall I take in the foresail, Sir?"

The captain turned on him fiercely, "I don't care what you do! Let her sink for all I care!"

"What do you mean, Sir?" the mate replied.

"That's what I mean! I am sick of this God Damn ship! She is driving me crazy!" was the captain's response. It was like a nightmare. Frank broken and bleeding, mate and captain shouting at the top of their voices, the ship pitching and rolling, seas coming over the bulwarks and washing into the forecastle. It came all at once, a maddening climax to all our days of misery.

Sails were made fast somehow. The captain brought splints and disinfectant, but to what avail? Both Frank's thighs were fractured, the bones protruding from the wounds, his jaw was broken at the chin, there was a great soft spot on his head, his eyes were closed, purple and swollen.

Because of the water in the forecastle, we put Frank in Niels's top bunk, wedging him in with pillows and blankets as securely as we could. We agonized over the knowledge that there was no possibility of any medical help or hospital care. At 10:00 P.M. it was my turn at the wheel. Hubert graciously offered to stand it for me, but I wanted to get out in the open air.

There was nothing more to be done. Niels was attending to Frank, kneeling across him in his bunk, and after the crude attention to Frank, I felt weak and tired. Standing at the wheel, easing the pitching vessel, thoughts crowded one upon the other. Frank, my closest friend, sacrificed to the American Skeleton Crew System, the practice of hurry-up.

There were only three men on the weather yard, Niels. Frank and Louie at the time of Frank's fall. The carpenter should have been on the weather yard with them, but being loath to go aloft even in fine weather, he was skulking in the galley. The captain, drinking, had come on deck and taken over the wheel. Instead of keeping the ship up into the wind and spilling wind from the sails, he had allowed it to veer off, and the sail had ballooned, throwing Frank off the yard.

Louie told me later what happened aloft. Niels was far out on the end of the yard taking in sail with his leg wrapped around the stirrup of the foot-rope. Frank was at the center of the starboard yard between Niels and Louie when the sail ballooned out over their heads. Louie said he had just cautioned Frank to be careful with "one hand for the ship, and one for yourself." A moment later, following a violent toss of the sail, he saw Frank disappearing into the darkness as the ship heeled to port, so that he landed on the forecastlehead. It would have been far more merciful had the ship been heeled to starboard, and he had landed in the sea, instead of his fair form being broken on the deck.

I was relieved of the helm at midnight and hurried below, finding the forecastle door closed. Opening it as softly as I could, a glance within was enough to tell me that Frank was gone. Niels sat huddled in six inches of water at the far end of the forecastle, with tears streaming down his face. His shirt and arms were covered with blood, and he had drawn a sheet over Frank's still form with just the top of his curly head showing. I tried to be the comforter, the older one, but I felt just as Niels did, and we sat there for a long time, until he told me, in snatches how Frank had asked for water, and said he felt very tired. Then, just at eight bells (midnight), he asked Niels to hold him in his arms, and died. Frank had gone on his long watch, with never a topsail to furl again, nor a long lookout to stand. There was no sleep for us that night.

*February 17, 1926*

All day we hove-to, riding out the worst gale and high seas we had ever experienced. When the bow dove into the waves the jib-boom cut the waves like a great blunt knife and rose up streaming with water pouring from the furled jibs. In the afternoon the second mate came forward with a bundle of old canvas and some sewing gear. This was to be Frank's burial shroud. We lifted him from the bunk and gently laid him in the middle of the old sail. The corners were folded inward and sewed along the folds. We all wanted to take part, so we took turns sewing, dully, without speaking a word, the rude covering taking the form of an Egyptian mummy.

Towards evening, the rain squalls became less frequent, and the high wind and sea subsided. Frank's shrouded form lay on a wide plank. We gathered round, and moved slowly aft, our hearts heavy with sorrow. The burial plank was carried to the lee taffrail, one end resting on a slant, one on the rail. All hands stood alongside, southwesters were removed, the flag was spread over his still form after two great iron shackles and an iron band were tied to the foot, and I read a short prayer for our dear shipmate. The captain had asked me to do this, I don't know why, except that he knew Frank and I were such close friends. I added a few words we all felt, and his body plunged into the seas. A thin line of bubbles streamed up to the light, and Frank left us.

Words can never tell how we missed Frank. Little things were always reminding us of his presence — his pipe, his knife, his clean white seabag, his book of navigation, some reminder at every turn. All his papers were carried aft to the captain, later to be turned over to the Shipping Commissioner. His clothes and personal belongings were put away in his locker. One of us later would be selected to bring them to Frank's relatives. His bunk was made up and left untouched until his last shipmate had left the vessel, according to custom.

### February 18, 1926

The sea continued running high, but we tacked ship and headed northwest, going back! There was reason to feel a resurge of spirit; there was scant hope of finding easterly wind at forty-three degrees latitude, even the sailors in the foc'sle knew that. A little more to the south lay the drift ice. The farther we drove south, the harder blew the westerly winds, and the higher rose the seas. This scenario had been predicted by the mate from the very beginning of the captain's mad decision to route the ship to Mauritius by heading west. But the captain had been and was still adamant in his fixed plan to continue westward.

All of us forward could not but note that the captain had for some time been in the habit of using alcohol to excess, and that his frequent appetency for this nourishment was a fixed habit. Fair wind lay along the southern coast of Australia, we knew, but could the mate prevail upon the captain to agree with him? It was plain that the captain was shy of the proximity of the coast, and reason enough, after the mate told us that the captain had lost a schooner in these waters ten years earlier.

The mate painted a gloomy picture for us, and our confidence in the captain was faltering. There was talk of beating to windward for two or three months in order to "make" Cape Leeuwin, the southwesterly corner of Australia. When we went "about ship "and pointed her head northward, is it any wonder that we managed a chanty at the braces?

### February 20, 1926

Until this time, there had been no friction amongst the crew forward; all seemed to realize that there was enough to contend within our series of misfortunes without letting personal differences arise. But this could not last and peace flew out the porthole.

The trouble began when the carpenter complained to the captain that the men burned the lights too much during the day. This was so trifling a thing, there being only one oil lamp in each of the two forecastles, each required some sort of light in order to read.

This action started a seed of discord to grow, for a tale-bearer is the most detestable of all men on board a ship. Several scuffles followed, often when we were at the pumps, but no real fights developed. The carpenter was so frail and wasted that we dared not give him a good pummeling, only a shaking. He sometimes held his axe by his side while he defied one or the other of us. The problem finally ended with the carpenter being shunned as an outcast, the most fitting punishment.

With our northbound progress, the days became warm and pleasant. We fell in with a fine fair wind, squared the yards and bore away for Cape Leeuwin.

### February 23, 1926

In the first dogwatch, the captain abruptly called the mate into his cabin for an important announcement. They reappeared a few moments later, the yards were braced up sharp on the backstays, and we learned that we were bound for Port Adelaide, Australia, for rudder repairs. There was great excitement, and much yo-ho-ing at the braces brought on by the prospect of soon being in port. However, it was too soon after Frank's death for Niels and I to feel joyful or enthusiastic about any change in our situation.

The following day brought light, variable winds, which steadied in the afternoon, and at sunset we sighted Kangaroo Island. Finding ourselves close under the land at nightfall, we shortened sail and hove-to until daybreak. Fortune smiled with a fair wind, and we bowled along through Investigator Strait at a nine knot clip. St. Vincent's Gulf lay white-capped and smiling, the air was clear and cool, a perfect day for entering.

Later in the afternoon, church towers and ships' masts stood out against the background of hills. On nearing Semaphore, the signal station for all ships entering or clearing, we began clewing up, and lowering sails. The anchors were made ready for letting go, and just at one-thirty P.M., with a hoarse roar from the starboard hawsepipe, we came to anchor, 130 days from Victoria, British Columbia, Canada.

The anchor had hardly touched bottom before a small launch was alongside with three men dressed in white linen dusters, sitting in the stern sheets. These were agents of the ship chandlers,

"Providers" as they call themselves, suppliers of food and ship's tackle.

We laid aloft and furled the square sails, rolling them neatly along the yards, using for the first time the fancy bunt gaskets designed by the mate. They were gay things with red stars on yellow skies. A little steam tug, the *Edith*, came alongside puffing as if she were out of breath. Officers of the Customs and Quarantine Service came on board. All hands were mustered amidships, passports were collected, and the ship was entered.

Our first impressions of South Australians were very favorable. They were most friendly and genial. A deckhand aboard the *Edith* gave us some newspapers and magazines and stopped for a brief chat. In the early afternoon five of the remaining sailors turned to on the main pumps. We whirled the old man-killers around like a spinning wheel and soon brought up the foam.

After setting anchor watches by drawing lots, we were knocked off for the day, all hands sitting on the forecastlehead and gazing at the shore. There were letters to be written, go-ashore togs to be hauled out and brushed off, and without being conscious of it, we whistled and sang. Great talk flew about the supper table, rumors and conjectures as to the length of our stay, how long we would lie at anchor, and would we receive any wages.

At eight bells P.M., I went on deck to stand the first two-hour anchor watch. The bay lay calm and unruffled, the stars holding a carnival overhead. Two miles distant, the lights of the little town of Semaphore blinked and danced in the clear air. Along the beach, scores of midway booths gave out an amber glow, a lofty ferris wheel stood out against the dark hills.

With the rise and fall of the offshore breeze, faint music could be heard coming from the concert band in the little diamond set pavilion. A small harbor steamer passed along side, her decks crowded with boys and girls who called and waved their hands to me. After they passed, the air was heavy with the scent of the wind. At ten o'clock I was relieved and went below for the first night of unbroken sleep since leaving San Pedro almost four months ago.

### February 26, 1926

This morning a small tug made fast to our port quarter. A diver with all his gear, pump hose and suit, and a Lloyds's Surveyor Insurance Underwriter were on board. Two men from the ship were sent down to the tug to act as air pumpers. The diver made an examination of the rudder and found the bearings in the gudgeons were worn so badly that the rudder had a play of several inches. That accounted for the terrible pounding of the rudder post for the past four months. An important conference followed, but no decision could be made for several days. The diver returned ashore, and we continued to swing on the hook.

Sunday dawned clear and warm. Yachts circled the ship with mild curiosity; sharks played about the anchor chain, bathers swarmed along the beach, and we sought scanty shade on the forecastlehead to wash our clothes. In the afternoon, Hubert gathered enough courage to ask the mate for the use of the small boat, but the mate refused with a curt, "Hell no!" A few days later, under the care of two powerful sea-going tugs, the *Wate* and the *Woonda*, we entered the outer harbor channel and made fast to a long pier where several mail steamers were berthed.

Here was quiet water where the divers could work on the rudder, safe from dangerous currents in the bay. The next three or four days we spent our working hours in the usual ship's fashion, patching sails, touching up paint work here and there, overhauling the rigging and the like. After the day's work, our evenings were spent in the simple pleasure of walking along the pier where we could study the little wheat ketches, the yachts and steamers, or talk with the people who, for some unknown reason, are always found sitting or strolling along the wharves. During these days, Niels and I were loaned to the diver, helping him rig and don his gear and pumping air for him when he dived.

We learned much about divers, their difficulties and risks, how the heavy dress was put on, the signals to the diver and we enjoyed working with such a likeable man. Stewy Dunbar he was called, and he had been diving since a young man. By accepting us as companions, he won our friendship completely, although he was twice our age. After the shipwrights dismantled the steering gear, the diver removed the woodlock. The rudder was then lifted clear of the gudgeons with tackles and dropped astern. The contractors for this work, the McFarlane Brothers (seven of them) were a canny clan. By keeping in the background and allowing the mate to handle all the rigging of gear, unshipping and heaving the rudder on deck, the job was done with dispatch and less expense to them.

There was little to be seen of the captain during these days. He was rumored to be ensconced with a woman at one of the better hotels in the town. He came on board each morning about ten, staying for less than an hour, and then disappeared until the next day. Naturally, we kept a sharp lookout for him. We wanted money of some sort as there was not the price of a postage stamp between us. It finally dawned on us that he was purposely avoiding us. Together, we hashed over the subject of money and the fact that we all had four months wages due us. In our contract it stated that on arriving at Mauritius we would be entitled to one-half of our wages. Added to our concern was that the captain had not even offered to take our mail ashore to the post office.

On Saturday, just when we had reached the point where we had decided to send a delegation to ask the captain about money, word was passed by the mate that the men could come aft and that one pound (five dollars) would be allowed each man. We were all thunderstruck and protested to the captain. We received the response that the ship's charterers were having financial difficulties, and we must be content with the one pound. Out of the fullness of his heart in a spirit of noble unselfishness, he, the captain had arranged with a local clothier for the crew to purchase any necessary clothing.

We were not fooled, this was the old "percentage game," thinly disguised. We each took our pound and a letter of credit, dressed, and hurried to town. The afternoon was our own, and although most of the men left in the early afternoon, it was agreed that all hands would meet at six o'clock in front of the little store where the captain had arranged for us to make our purchases.

Accordingly at five, I set out with Niels, the beloved carpenter and the second mate. A short tram ride brought us to Port Adelaide. At the first saloon, Miss Rose McGuiness, Proprietor, beers were in order, each of us standing a round. The carpenter was avoiding payment for his by a sudden interest in a wall photograph of a horse. Then we were off for Bowler and Shaw, Fashionable Tailors, Mercers and Outfitters. As four bells drew near, the crew began to gather, and it was a jolly reunion.

Everyone was pleasantly jingled and a great shaking of hands took place, with inquiries after one another's health, as though we had been separated for years. A bustling young man came up to us and asked that we follow him as quietly as possibly, this being Saturday, when all Australian shops must by law be closed. To be caught selling goods on this day appeared to be a capital offense. He led the way around the corner, down the alley to a rear entrance to the shop. We strung out in a straggling line, some of the crew having a little trouble weathering the corners, but Niels and I took them in tow. Finally we were all gathered in a hushed knot at the counter of Messrs. Bowler and Shaw.

There followed a burlesque of buying, most of the men hardly knowing what they held in their hands, and after all the buying was over, we each apologetically asked for a pound of cash, or a little beer or two. This from men who had brought a ship halfway around the world through storms and calm, even death, men who had thirty times this much owing them in wages.

To top off the evening's good cheer, Mr. Shaw, after a good deal of whispering over the telephone, went out, returning a few minutes later with sixteen bottles of beer. This worked out to two bottles for each of us, so we were another hour in the store toasting each other and Mr. Shaw.

Bronze bearings were cast and fitted into the rudder gudgeons or sockets. Other repairs were made to the rudder and work went steadily on in leisurely Australian fashion. One after another, the crew approached the captain and asked to be paid off. One after another, the captain parried and half promised until they were silenced with excuses that the United States Consul would not permit any of the crew to be paid off. Besides, he said, "The company is bankrupt, and there is no money to be had to pay off the crew."

There were five sailing vessels in port: the American six-masted barkentine *E.R. Sterling*, whose crew ran away as soon as the ship arrived in Australia; the *Pamelia*, a small bark flying the Norwegian flag; two German four-masted barks, the *Gustav* and *Elizabeth* (the latter lying at anchor in the roadstead off Semaphore), and our good ship. While uptown we often met men from these ships. The crew of the *Sterling* in their anxiety to get clear of the vessel had left without their wages. Two men, an American and a Chileno, were sticking it out in the hope that the vessel would be sold, and they would get their wages.

To take the place of Frank, another sailor shipped through the Consulate. From the moment he stepped on board, we could see that our new man was a good seaman and a likeable person. He gave his name as Archie, and I later learned he hailed from Passaic, New Jersey. We exchanged books, talked ships for hours, and showed each other our sketches.

Among the books in his seabag were two or three volumes of English poetry, a history of the sea, Byron's complete works and a biography. Besides these, he also carried several volumes of navigational works. This man was so much like Frank in his orderly habits and keen intelligence that all the men noted the similarity.

Fresh food came on board and for the first time in 110 days, we tasted green vegetables, a welcome change from the eternal dried fish, boiled potatoes, salt pork and salt horse. After a few deft turns, the mechanics repaired our hoisting and pumping engines, finding only a minor fault with the ignition, so they said. But what weary toil it had caused our handful of men. With the shipping of the rudder and assembling of the repaired steering gear, we were ready for sea once more.

Rumors of all sorts crept about the ship and whispered in the corners: the deck load was to be sold in Port Adelaide; Lloyds's men had taken measurements of the ship and she was to be sold to fly the English flag; the charterers were coming by steamer to arrange a sale of the cargo; we would never see Mauritius. But we had reached a point where we did not care what happened as long as *something* happened. Harbor Officials informed the captain that the port was in need of dock space. After a brief "Pow-Wow" with him, we were shifted further out to the sea-end of the pier until, with the rudder repaired, we lay with our stern only to the pier. After our one and only shopping trip in town, except for the pier, we were never again permitted ashore. While we had no solid proof, we were convinced that there was an understanding between the captain and the American Consul to keep us restricted to the ship so we could not desert.

*March 17, 1926*

This morning the two sister tugs, *Woto* and *Wonda*, took us in tow down the channel and out into the by to anchor off Semaphore, our old anchoring ground. The *Lisbeth* lay some distance away, anchor hove short. It was late afternoon, almost twilight, when the offshore wind came up, the wind she had been waiting for. Through Archie's glasses we could see them setting topsails, heaving in on the anchor, and swinging slowly around so as to bring the wind on her port quarter. Sail after sail followed, her deep topgallants, and then royals. At last, she stood out, a towering column of white against the purpling sky, bound away for the Pacific Northwest.

The snug little *Pamelia*, a few ship lengths away, kept us company, but only for a day. During the night a light fair wind crept out of the hills, and so silent was her going that not until morning did we know that she had sailed bound for Callao, Peru, and the Guano Islands.

On the night of our entrance into St. Vincent's Gulf, a great sugar refinery had burned. Water from the fire hoses had washed tons of burned sugar into the Murray River, killing thousands of fish, and through some chemical action it turned the white paint on all the ships in the harbor to a dirty, dark grey. Steamers coming out of port looked as if they had passed through a fire. Our ship, lying miles from the infected area, did not escape the effect of the fumes, and we were kept at work for several days, washing the blackened paint work while we lay in the offing. All the woodwork on the poop, maindeck, and forecastlehead, was "soogied" and then painted a fine light gray, after the good taste of the mate.

For nine days we swung on the hook, living on rumors and gossip. Anchor watches went their rounds; we grew restless not knowing what would happen next. Then, on the evening of the twenty-fourth, the little tug *Edith* came alongside with the captain, and we learned that tomorrow would be sailing day.

### March 25, 1926

This morning at daylight, the mate roared into the forecastle, shouting, "All hands on deck!" In ten minutes we were on the yards: gaskets were taken off the square sails, halyards laid out for hoisting, the anchor heaving short, fore and afters hoisted, square topsails set, anchor broken out, and we stood away — for the beach! The captain was maneuvering the ship, as became a captain, and in spite of everything he tried to do, he could not get the ship around and headed seaward.

After several attempts to bring her around, things reached a state where the mate was shouting advice to the captain from amidships. The captain called the mate aft, and after talking for a minute the captain threw up his hands and went below to his bottle of scotch, and the mate took charge. Orders flew right and left. The ship was tacked in a few minutes, and we headed for Investigator Strait with a fair breeze coming over the fantail. We were at last bound for the fabled and enchanted island of Mauritius.

On nearing the entrance to Investigator Strait, the mate kept close under Kangaroo Island which lay to windward in order to weather the islands on our lee. But the captain, coming on deck at noon, kept shouting, "Keep her off, keep her off," that is, steer away from the land to windward.

Consequently, later in the evening, it was nip and tuck whether we would be able to weather (avoid) Althorp Island which lay to leeward. The captain fumed about the deck, the sails were too full, the sails were not full enough. With some skill but mostly luck, the island was cleared. The wind held strong, and late that evening we began to feel the rise and fall of the Indian Ocean, having covered one hundred miles in twelve hours. Wedge Island and Neptune Island, with their little winking lights were put astern, the yards were squared, and it was Westward Ho! Our old friendships with the albatrosses were renewed, Catastrophe Cape was put astern, and we sailed into the Great Australian bight.

### March 26, 1926

Noonday sights found us halfway to Cape Leeuwin, our nemesis, and logging ten to twelve knots with a glorious breeze astern. The steering wheel worked easily with half the effort of the old days. The spanker topsail, the infernal ringtail, gave us some trouble, making the steering difficult, and needing patches at every setting. In the afternoon, we learned that the ship's chronometer was out of order. The captain had brought it on board in a small boat the night before sailing from Adelaide, during a long rolling swell. The mate conjectured that since the boat and the captain were not too steady, it probably had been jarred.

Until this time Victoria, the ship's cat, had been sprightly and full of life, but an in-port diet of meat and excessive nocturnal adventuring had been too much for him. His hind legs gave out, his eyes filmed over, and every man on the ship had a pet remedy. The cook nursed him tenderly, worrying over him like an only child, but Vic continued to languish. When I asked for some copperas (ferrous sulphate), the captain replied, "A dose of strychnine was best for the damn cat", not because he hated the cat but because he disliked the cook, a man who refused to allow the captain to aggravate him.

April the first came in with the usual trail of fools' jokes. We were expecting to sight land almost any day, our position being doubtful owing to the damaged chronometer. Deep sea soundings with the lead were taken with no bottom at 140 fathoms. On Saturday the captain sighted a group of islands on the starboard side which he believed to be West Cape Howe. These were anxious days for the captain. He spent hours in the rigging, glasses in hand, sweeping the horizon for signs of land. The mate even suggested that we rig an old beef barrel on the foremast, provided with a few comforts so that the tedious business of constantly searching for land could be done in comfort and safety.

*April 4, 1926*

Main and mizzen topsails ripped today. We celebrated Easter Sunday by hauling sails from the locker in the after lazaret, unbending the damaged rags and bending the spare sails. Still no sighting of any land.

Head winds came up in the afternoon and we took in all topsails, both topgallant sails, and reefed the fore and afters. The contrary wind held until Tuesday, when it hauled to the east, blowing fair and steady. It was clear that there was dirty weather to the south, for an enormous ground swell was rolling up from the southwest throwing the wind from the sails, banging the hoops, rattling blocks, and clanking chain sheets, so that it sounded like a Chinese laundry, as the captain expressed it.

The captain spent most of his waking hours, and no doubt part of his sleeping hours, talking about the chronometer, but since it would take more than words to find our longitude for us, he called the mate into consultation, something that pained him to do. They put their heads together and our course was altered so we headed up the west coast of Australia. At this juncture, the powers came to a deadlock. The mate proposed heading in towards the shore, picking up a landmark or any prominent shape. By keeping within its latitude for a few days and by checking each day by sights the error in the chronometer, he would adjust the precious instrument accordingly and proceed to Mauritius with confidence. The captain replied that any such course of action was madness and that the mate was ready for an old folks home.

We proceeded up the coast, gradually hauling to the northwest in order to fall in with the latitude of Mauritius. After bearing away from the coast, we encountered the southeast trades and bowled along at a great rate, sometimes making twelve and fourteen knots an hour. Fine weather prevailed as trade wind clouds moved across the clear sky in magnificent pageantry.

The mate continued to chafe under the rebuffs of the captain, but no matter how resentful he felt, the mate's remarks always took a humorous turn. "Most ships take the great circle route," he said, "but we take the great square," a reference to our having sailed around three sides of Australia. For the first time on our voyage, a dolphin was caught. The mate sighted a few over the bow early Friday morning. The way he ran aft for his fishing line would have made a stone man laugh.

In catching dolphins and bonitos, no bait is needed, only a strong hook with a white rag attached so that it looks like a flying fish. This is dangled off the jib-boom and skipped along the surface of the water. A flash of white, blue, and green follows, the dolphin often leaping clear of the water in its eagerness. His powerful jaws clamp about the hook, and he is hauled on board.

Poor Vic, the weather-prophet cat who had been dragging himself around for the past two weeks, recovered immediately when he caught sight of the big fish floundering about on deck. He did very little running about that night.

Before sailing from Port Adelaide, we learned that a Russian-Finn bark, the *Favell*, had sailed from Melbourne, Australia, twelve days ahead of us. This was a great topic of discussion at meal times: the prospect of beating her to Port Louis; what route she took, perhaps a more southern route, or perhaps a northern route via Timor straits above Australia.

Chris never took part in any of this table talk. He always kept a gloomy silence, hunched in his corner, so he might as well have been a stuffed dummy for all the notice he took of us or us of him.

During the first two months of the voyage, my feelings towards him had changed from resentment of his attitude, to revulsion. By the time we passed Cape Leeuwin, I accepted his presence at the table, on deck, and everywhere with the same feeling that I took notice of a stanchion or a deck fitting. This arrangement suited us all, and we got along fine. He never talked to anyone except the carpenter, and then only to recount some orgy in Skipper Street or the Boca — famous brothels.

With fine weather and smart sailing, we set to work cleaning and painting the ship, literally but not quite from truck to keelson. We painted over the side, touching up the white stripes along her bow and sides with the waves drenching us and filling up our paint pots with water. This was really dangerous work, for if a man lost his footing, it would be too late to recover him with the ship going at a ten knot clip and only a small crew to work the ship around. During this time, there was not one single life ring or line handy on the poop deck. It was interesting to see how the men who had risked their lives aloft in squalls and in the dark recoiled from the danger of working over the bows on a staging (plank).

Louis, who was a man of spirit, refused point blank to work in such a place, but the second mate, in fear of the captain, went through with it. When it came time for our watch to take the deck, Chris clambered over the side onto the stage, looked at me with a dare in his eyes, and I followed. Since the bugaboo of Cape Leeuwin was passed Niels made up a list of names, and opposite their names the men wrote the date they predicted we would arrive in Port Louis. It was posted and we called it a sweepstakes.

We have been blessed with continual fair wind. The mate says that by dead reckoning, that is, estimating the courses steered and the miles recorded on the ship's log trailing astern, we should be 300 miles eastward of the Island of Rodriguez, which is again 300 miles east of Mauritius or 600 miles in all from Mauritius.

By sighting Rodriguez, he expected to get some idea of our longitude. Our latitude we knew by daily readings of the altitude of the sun at its zenith (greatest height). In his lordly way, the captain allowed it to be known that he would give five dollars to the first man to sight land. The mate dared to say to me that the captain would be glad to give several hundred dollars to the man who could find it for him. If we missed Rodriguez entirely, our next chance was Mauritius itself.

Beyond that, a thousand miles further lay Madagascar and beyond that, Africa. Unlike Columbus, we at least have the knowledge that we will not sail on and on until we drop off the end of the earth.

There has been a decided break between the captain and the mate. The ship's politics have taken a most singular twist. The second mate and carpenter who have both been slinking about the decks in servility were now taken under the wing of the captain as confidants.

The mate allied himself with the men before the mast, and the feud was on. In the evening the captain would come on the poop deck with a forced air of unconcern. He and the mate would then pace back and forth on opposite sides of the poop deck, avoiding each others eyes, speaking never a word, and never looking at the same thing at the same time.

The disaffection of the captain and the mate for one another was much to our liking. There was no unpleasantness during our watches on deck; the work went leisurely on without the captain's interference. For the mate was an able man, and besides, any interference on the captain's part would have necessitated his talking to the mate. He was not about to do that. We might have thought their behavior to be humorous except for the disquieting knowledge that we were in dangerous waters, and if the combined knowledge of these two men was ever needed, now was the time. But no, their bitterness lessened not one bit, if anything it increased. Often, while standing at the wheel at noontime, I could hear their voices raised in argument coming up through the cabin skylight which as every sailor knows, is better than a sewing circle for picking up gossip.

*May 3, 1926*

This morning at six o'clock, Archie, the new sailor, sighted land — a dark, blue smudge on the horizon. There was a great craning of necks and men clambering aloft. The captain agreed it was land, but made no acknowledgement to Archie. On drawing nearer, under a light breeze, further to leeward, the island of Mauritius could be made out, its sharp, jagged peaks losing themselves in the clouds. It soon became known that the first island sighted was Round Island. Later a small rock called Serpent Island appeared, making a kind of crouching camel outline in conjunction with Round Island. The breeze, light as it was, deserted us, and with our goal almost won, we lay becalmed, wallowing in flapping sails in the long, oily ground swells.

For four days we beat and tacked about against a head wind, and sometimes no wind at all, always within sight of land or lights. A little barkentine came up from leeward and joined us in an effort to make port, but it had worse luck than we had, often disappearing below the horizon with only topsails showing.

The captain's efforts to get the ship around the distant point where he believed Port Louis lay, almost drove the mate to madness. We tacked ship, we wore ship, we lowered the spanker, hoisted the spanker, and braced the yards dozens of times, until we thought we would drop in our tracks. Then, when I took the wheel at eight bells on Thursday evening, the mate motioned over his shoulder, grinned, and said, "There is Port Louis." We had passed the place a dozen times while trying to weather a point where no town existed. I learned that the mate had been trying for days to persuade the captain to accept his opinion of where the town lay but to no avail. The captain believed that Port Louis was around another point and held on to that belief until he saw the city lights that evening.

The next morning, Friday, as we crept closer to the shore, the captain suddenly tacked ship saying, "I saw white water and reefs ahead!" Later on, the mate headed in again towards Port Louis, like a man cautiously approaching a mule. Through the glasses, steamers and sailing vessels could be made out. A white bark lay at anchor, surely the *Favell*, our rival.

Houses resolved themselves from the haze of distance, little stretches of white beach peeped up with every lift of the ship's bows. The Stars and Stripes with the ship's name in code flags were run up the spanker truck, the pilot flag bent to the fore, and we sat down and waited.

*Forest Dream*, November 1925

# The von Buchholdts
The Danish Branch
1593 –

NIELS PETER VON BUCHHOLDT THOMSEN
1907 – Present

### *Paternal*

| | | |
|---|---|---|
| Father | Hans Christian von Buchholdt | 1883–1937 |
| Grandfather | Peter von Buchholdt | |
| Great Grandfather | Count Henry Leopold von Buchholdt | |
| Great Grandmother | Claudia Sophia Lund von Buchholdt | |
| Great Uncle | Hendrick Lund | 1811–1905 |

*Beginning with King Frederick VII he held the post of valet at the Royal Palace of Denmark to four Danish Kings.*

Jenny          Hans Christian

### *Maternal*

| | | |
|---|---|---|
| Mother | Jenny Katrina Johanne Andersen | 1887–1976 |

*born in Nykobing on the Island of Mors, Northern Jylland, Denmark*

| | | |
|---|---|---|
| Grandfather | Jens Andersen | 1862–1934 |
| Grandmother | Karen Jensen Andersen | 1865–1897 |
| Great Grandfather | Anders Nielsen | 1827–1896 |
| Great Great Grandmother | Anna Maria Guldstrom | |
| Great Great Grandfather | Niels Anders Rytter | 1793–1857 |

Niels

Jenny — Age 19

Hans Christian — Father — Age 50

Hans Christian
Age 20

Estate          Peter von Buchholdt

Above: Mr. and Mrs. Aaron Joseph Guldstrom and
Anna Marie Guldstrom
*Aaron Joseph Guldstrom, Estate manager for the
Duke of Gram, Grams, Denmark.*
Top Right: Hans von Buchholdt, Niels' father.
Bottom Right: Hans Christian and Jenny von
Buchholdt

Left: Niels, age seven, with Chris and Adelhaid Thomsen; Above: Adelheid and Niels, age 13.

Below left: His childhood home; Below Niels age 12.

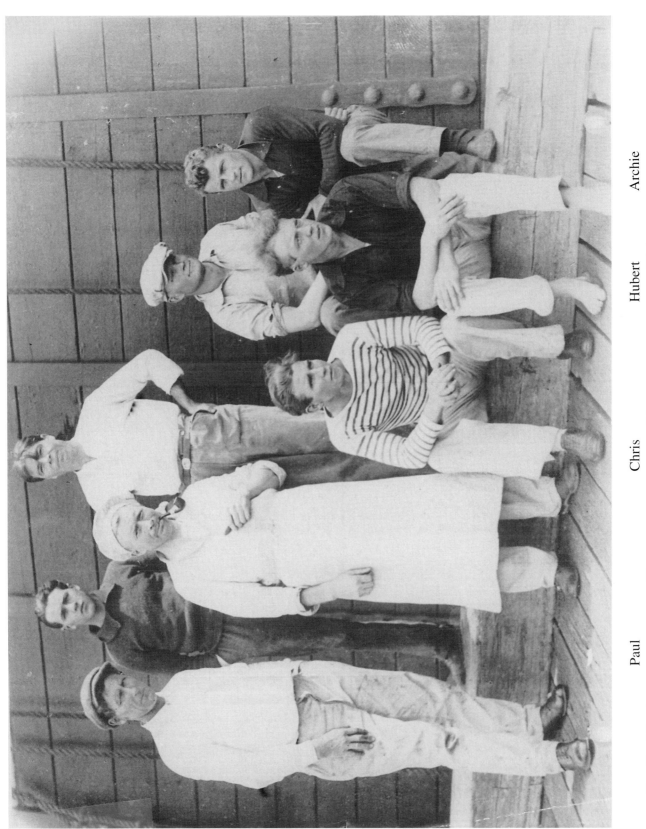

One-Eyed Louie        Paul        Timmerman        Chris        Mac        Hubert        Niels        Archie

Barkentine *Forest Dream* — Australia 1926

Upper left: Paul
Gueho in
Mauritius, 1956;
Below left: Paul
Gueho, 1926;
Top: Mac, Archie
and Niels in
Mauritius, 1926;
Above: The
*Forest Dream*;
Left: Niels, aged
20.

Niels — Seattle, age 18.

*Forest Dream* (near foreground) and *Forest Pride* (beyond), Lake Union, Seattle about 1923.

Cross-Dale Photo Co.

*H.F. Alexander*

Fur trading schooner *C.S. Holmes.*

Captain John Backland, Jr.

Sled dogs aboard the Arctic schooner
*C.S. Holmes*.

Niels Thomsen aboard *C.S. Holmes*, c. 1929.

Niels

Joe Bone

# Requiem for a Sailor

I know not
What lies beyond
Or in whose care
I'll be —
But it must end
As it began —
This wedding
With the sea.
My course is laid
My sails unfurled
And my heart
Is light and free —
So scatter me
Over the ocean wide
When the helm
Is hard-a-lee.
My dust will mingle
With each curling wave
And perhaps
I'll a merman be
And there'll be
Singing and dancing
With sea horses prancing —
And a harem
Of mermaids
All trembling for me —
When I am laid
To rest in the sea.

NIELS THOMSEN

# CHAPTER FIVE

# NIELS
# ABLE SEAMAN

*STARBOARD WATCH*

The charterers of the ship, after waiting six weeks in Port Louis for our arrival, had returned to Vancouver leaving behind a Scotsman by the name of McNeil to act as their agent should the *Forest Dream* ever arrive. As far as the charterers and owners of the ship were concerned, our belated arrival was not good news, the assignees of the cargo having been able due to the two months delay in delivery, to cancel their contract to purchase the cargo. The ship had been assumed lost and insurers so advised.

We were unwelcome seafarers. They would all have been happier if we had perished at sea. The agent for the charterers, Mr. McNeil, came to the ship daily to confer with the captain. It was apparent to us that his mission, more or less, was to monitor the activities of the captain. We arrived at this conclusion because no purchases could be made by the cook without McNeil's approval. That irritated the captain. The captain informed us that only limited funds were available for advances on our wages.

On the following day, the captain and McNeil were able to obtain credit with a local Chinese shipchandler for provisions and a few thousand rupees. A fifteen pound order of meat and vegetables were delivered to the ship for consumption by those living aft. The captain doled out 150 rupees ($30) to each of us. The ship's credit being limited, we continued on our regular diet of salt pork and salt beef, interspersed with a few local vegetables.

We had permission to go ashore. Unable to afford transportation, we used the ship's boat which accommodated only four persons, one of which had to row the boat back to the ship. It was very awkward arrangement.

After seventy years, memories of Port Louis have dimmed, but I recall that the port area was blacked out at night without street lights. The only "exotic, beautiful, Creole women" we ever saw were either unattainable or too expensive for sailors of our financial status. Even Hubert voiced his disappointment.

Two weeks after our arrival, I came down with a severe attack of malaria and was placed in the local hospital. I lay ill with fever and chills. The hospital was quite primitive, and not having any personal funds, I occupied a bed in the large dormitory paupers' section. The toilet facilities consisted of ten holes in a tiled floor in one large open room, where one not only stood in a waiting line, but made use of a water faucet in lieu of toilet paper. Also in the hospital several beds from me was our cabin boy, Hood, suffering from delirium tremens after a two week period of heavy drinking.

It was the custom in Port Louis for upper class English and French ladies whose opulent residences lay with acres of lawns on the hills above the city of Port Louis, to make weekly visits to the hospital passing out books and gifts to patients in the paupers' ward.

After two weeks in the hospital, Mrs. Gueho stopped by my bedside while passing out books and spent some time talking with me. The following day the doctor came to tell me that a carriage had arrived to take me to the Gueho home.

The family consisted of Mr. and Mrs. Gueho, two sons — Jean, two years older than me and Paul, who was my age, and two daughters ten and twelve years old. My stay with them created one of the warmest memories in my life.

I will never forget attending the opera as a guest of the family Gueho in their private box at the theater. Each year an opera company from Saigon, French Indochina, came to Port Louis for a series of performances. The opera for the evening was Verdi's *Aida*. This was the most important social event of the year, and all English and French families attended, as did the exiled Indian maharajahs and rajahs.

The opera house was a large conical-shaped structure resembling a beehive with rows of seats and private boxes. The most impressive were the ones filled with the Indian Royal families — the princes with their jeweled headdresses and the princesses in beautiful saris dripping with pearls, diamonds, rubies and emeralds — a stunning display.

I was treated as one of the Gueho family. Proper attire was never a problem, I could wear all of Jean's clothing. I wore his extra evening clothes to the opera, and his casual clothes on the tennis court. This particular Mauritian episode was and will always be, one of the most treasured experiences in my life. I stayed with the Gueho family for approximately six weeks, after which I reported back to the ship to be met with frowns by the captain and first mate and envy from the sailors (Hubert especially) whom I regaled with richly embroidered accounts of my life as a member of the island's elite.

The next few days I listened to all that had transpired on the ship in my absence. The most dramatic news was the battle between the captain and the mate on the deck of the ship one night. The second mate had been absent ashore drinking for over two weeks.

Soon after my return, the captain called us aft and informed us that we would soon set sail for New Guinea to load a cargo of gold ore for Australia. Then two weeks later he said the sailing orders had been changed, we would proceed to Newcastle, New South Wales, Australia, to load a cargo of coal for delivery to the port of Callao, Peru. There was a possibility, he said, that we might from there load a cargo of guano (bat dung) for a port in France, all very exciting to contemplate.

Paul Gueho and I had forged a strong friendship. He had some seagoing experience on a local sailing vessel and wanted to see more of the world. We discussed this with his parents, the outcome being that I would smuggle him on board the ship when we left for Australia. The night before sailing I hid Paul in the forward hold where the grape juice was stored by removing a loose plank in the chain locker.

In the forenoon a tugboat towed us five miles out. We hoisted our sails and set off for Endeavor Straits and Australia. That evening in the pink backdrop of the setting sun, we saw the peak of Le Pouce for the last time. I brought food and water to Paul the first four days. On the fifth day he came on deck and was taken aft to the captain who was pleased to have an extra unpaid hand on board. The sailors were happy to have another watchstander.

While in Port Louis almost all of the thirty cases of whiskey, the balance of the hundred cases loaded in Victoria (the private property of the captain and mate) were taken ashore one dark night. They had been sold to the Chinese shipchandler. A barrel of rum was brought aboard and stowed away in the captain's cabin in the dead of night, so as to escape the watchful eye of Ship Agent McNiel. For once we gave the captain credit for some imagination.

The voyage from Port Louis to Newcastle was made in forty-two days. Although the wind was abaft the beam most of the time, it was a rough and stormy voyage for we had sailed far to the south after leaving Mauritius, seeking the "Roaring Forties" with its gale force winds and gigantic seas.

Life was miserable for Paul and me in the Second Mate's starboard watch, as the captain had taken complete control of the watch from the second mate.

There was scarcely a day that the captain did not have his beak in the barrel of rum brought on board in Port Louis. Louie and I had become accustomed to his abuse, but it was difficult to absorb the vile treatment he heaped on the second mate who was a kindly person and of whom we were fond.

I rebelled on a number of occasions. In one incident where he struck me, I retaliated verbally. The consequences were another of the captain's *Mutiny on the Bounty* pet scenarios. I was called to the cabin for the reading of the ship's log; charged with being a "Bolsheviki", and then received another fine.

I added more particulars on the spare empty sheets in my Bowditch where I chronicled all the captain's sins. I looked forward to the day when I would have him brought to justice. I was determined that in some way he would pay for his derelict drunken action at the wheel which cost my dear friend Frank his life.

# CHAPTER SIX

# MALCOLM
# ABLE SEAMAN

*PORT WATCH*

 It was almost twelve o'clock when two gray-painted tugs could be seen coming out to meet us. As they drew nearer, we saw the pilot in white clothing and a cork helmet, the *Forest Dream* charterer representative who had come all the way from Canada, and a score of small dark-skinned men in white shorts and sailor hats of the type that young boys wear. The two tugs were named *Paul* and *Virginia*, after the legendary lovers in Bernadine du Pierre's novel of the same name.

When within shouting distance, the pilot called to the captain to clew up the square sails. McNeil, the charterer's agent, asked after the captain's health, but received a non-committal reply from the man. After the sails were clewed up, the fore and afters were lowered, lines were hauled up from the forepeak, and everything was made ready for entering port. After towing us for a few miles and breaking several hawsers, the tugs moored alongside, and we continued towards Port Louis.

We entered a horse-shoe shaped harbor with a noble range of peaks in the background overlooking the little port. Several steamers lay anchored with sterns moored to buoys. The little bark was not the *Favell*, but the *Gwyder Castle*, owned in the island. The *Favell* had gone on to Durban, South Africa.

Customs officials made the usual rounds looking for contraband, and a number of boatmen came alongside selling fruit and vegetables which, having no money, we could not buy.

We all heaved a sigh of relief and prepared to settle down to an easy life in port, after a fine passage of forty-four days from Port Adelaide, and seven months from Victoria, four months overdue on the voyage.

With our ship safely moored in the harbor, we thought our troubles were over, that we could now enjoy the fruits of our labor, but in truth, our troubles had just begun.

In accordance with the shipping articles, the crew was now entitled to one-half of their wages, and the average amount due each man was at least a few hundred dollars. After a reasonable wait of several days, we approached the captain for money, for after all, that is what makes the mare go or takes Jack ashore. True, we could borrow from the boatmen, but these fellows, Indians all, were "usurers" of the most objectional sort. Most of us preferred to wait until word was received from South Africa, the nearest banker of the charterers, according to our captain.

We spent an impatient week rigging cargo gear and making the ship snug for a lengthy stay in port, two months at least, or so we thought. At the end of the week, we were called aft. The captain gave each man 150 rupees ($30).

Here was the same almsgiving we experienced in Australia. We all voiced our displeasure at the scanty sum, but there was no one to whom we could appeal, the nearest U.S. consulate was 2,000 miles away. Furthermore, the captain was claiming that his interpretation of the ship's articles were that the wages were not due until the start of the discharging of the ship's cargo, a convenient argument.

There was nothing we could do, so we accepted the 150 rupees to take the edge off our appetites, each man according to his lights. Some bottles of red wine were smuggled aboard by the boatmen, healths were drunk, but there was no glowing bowl and no sliding under the table. The supply was too scanty.

A few of the men went ashore that evening, returning around midnight with some great tales. Port Louis they said, was a patch-quilt of colors and languages, French being predominant. Clothes and most other items were found to be dirt cheap. The streets were poorly lighted, and there was not a white woman out after dark. They found everyone very friendly, and they felt that we were all going to like the place. They also dramatically recounted more intimate adventures ashore, the likes of which are given in forecastles, barracks and men's clubs the world over, but which convention forbids retelling.

From the time of our arrival, I was made ship's watchman. In the evening, there were two anchor lights to be hung out — one on the forestay and the other hoisted up on the spanker halyards aft. All about the harbor I could see the watchmen of the other ships going about a similar task; a glow from the fore-castlehead while the lamp was being lit, then the gleam crawling up the stay as the lamp was being hoisted.

Hardly a stone's throw away on our port beam lay an old hulk of a torpedoed steamer patched up with a cement bottom. A very old Indian, thin, stooped and wearing a bright red shirt, was her watchman. At sundown, lamp lighting time, we saluted each other very gravely as we went about our work. I had to wet down the poop deck and the forecastlehead with the help of an old tattered canvas bucket every morning and night to prevent cracking of the deck seams. After these duties, I was free to roam about the ship as I pleased.

This was the best part of the day. The cool of the evening had come on, sounds came clearer from the shore, a stray stretch of song, a dog barking, or the honking of an automobile.

The little lateen-rigged pinnaces of the reef fishermen passed close under our bow each evening after sunset, their light sails curving to the light offshore breeze. At times these small fishing boats would come too close together so that the weather pinnace would take the wind out of the sails of the other. A hot argument would follow with lurid threats, insults and name calling. But neither would bear off. The boats would creep along, side by side, as far as the outer reef, the uproar continuing far out of earshot with the fishermen waving their arms in silhouette against the sun. There is nothing that a Mauritian Creole loves as much as a lively argument.

It was but a turn of the head from such amusing things as this to the beauty of Ursa Major hanging just above the northern horizon, casting its seven-starred reflection in the lagoon of Mer Rouge, over beyond the long stone jetty. It was enough to be here at the hard-earned goal, and at anchor, without a wanting for the doubtful pleasures of being ashore.

Once or twice the captain called, wanting some minor thing done, but if the truth were told, only to see if I was awake.

A few nights later, a rowboat glided up to the gangway in perfect silence, only the feeble spark of an oil lamp on the bottom of the boat giving any sign of its approach. I met a young Indian boat boy at the head of the gangway. "Is that you, Mr. Mac?" he whispered.

I replied,"Yes. What do you want?"

"I have some girls for the captain and the mate," he answered. As two well-fed Creole girls came up the gangway in a glory of pink and yellow finery, I reflected that the requirements of a good watchman depended as much on what he shut his eyes to, as to what he saw.

After that night, no one bothered me to see if I was the perfect sentinel. Anyone who has ever been a watchman can easily guess that I learned the art of napping with one eye open. For two weeks we lay at anchor with the chain lashings still around our weather-beaten deck load of timbers. All kinds of rumors flew about. The ship was to be sold to British interests, why else was Lloyd's surveyor measuring her in Adelaide? The crew was to be paid off and sent home as passengers; the deck load was unsold; the Mauritian government was demanding its cross railroad ties deep in the hold of the ship, or the Company was bankrupt. On and on the tales spread. The crew forward consoled one another with a bit of vino, but there was no neglect of work on the ship, however little there was to be done.

The first cloud appeared on the horizon one evening when we were gathered on the forecastle-head, talking quietly amongst ourselves. The captain suddenly appeared out of the dark and called for the watchman. I came up to him, and he asked for a light, saying he wanted to read the forecastle card (a list of government regulations required by law to be posted in the forecastle). He wanted it in a hurry. I was fifteen minutes finding a box of matches in my left breast pocket. After a brief examination of the card tacked on the bulkhead, he pointed to the clause which prohibited bringing liquor on board an American ship. He said that the men had better read that paragraph in the morning when he intended to have a talk with all the crew forward. This! From the number one liquor smuggler?

This incident was treated lightly by the crew, but there was still a feeling of apprehension, of doubt, and all during the next day the men went about their work in an ill humor. Near sunset, when the captain was taking his evening walk along the deck load. Archie, the American sailor who had joined the ship in Port Adelaide, approached him and began to talk in a very earnest manner. Their conversation lasted almost an hour, and when it ended, Archie told me he had asked the captain how he intended to interpret the liquor clause in the ship's articles. The captain had backed and filled for a time, but they came to an understanding, Archie being a gifted negotiator.

He had pointed out to the captain that no one in the crew had neglected their work as a result of a few bottles of wine. In addition, it had served to keep the crew more or less content.

He also pointed out that, as to the question of prohibition laws on American ships, could the pot call the kettle black, and was not sauce for the gander equally sauce for the goose? Archie's cool logic carried the day. The captain blustered for a while when asked why this matter seemed to concern him so much. But the matter was settled, and there was not another problem about wine coming on board. The captain made a point to search for hard liquor in the baskets of the bumboatmen who brought fruits and vegetables to the ship, but after a few days he gave it up.

The representative of the ship's charterers, Mr. McNeil, a tall, angular Scotsman, spent a great deal of time on board the ship. This caused the captain so much irritation that when they sat side by side on the poop deck for hours, they never spoke to one another. McNeil's presence on board ship served to reduce the quality of our meals for he watched every little expense with the eyes of a hawk. By the same token, he monitored all expenses charged to the ship which served to drastically curtail the captain's life style afloat and ashore. This he deeply resented!

There were many days when we had no fresh vegetables with our meals, only meat and potatoes. The meat grinder in the galley worked overtime converting mixed scraps of food into spiced meat loafs. We were still being served salt horse and salt pork three days a week, a practice unheard of in an American ship in port.

On arrival of the ship in Port Louis, the captain had ordered fourteen pounds of fresh beef, nothing more. It was used to serve those who ate in the after cabin, over the objections of the crew forward. Neils, Archie and I, the younger men particularly, were always challenging the captain and getting into difficulties.

Timmerman the cook took things into his own hands and ordered fresh fruit, fish, and vegetables. This brought about a great uproar in the galley the next day when the captain made it known that he, and he only, would do the ordering for the ship. Out of our own pockets we bought bananas from the Indian peddlers.

A keg of mackerel which had been opened out at sea had driven us out of the foc'sle with its smell. I was still kept stored under the hawsepipe, awaiting the accounting of Mr. McNeil. When it was re-opened for his inspection, the contents were alive with worms. With reluctance and much sadness, the frugal Scotsman McNeil reluctantly gave permission to dump the keg overboard. It was rushed to the rail by willing hands.

Although we heard all kinds of tales concerning the disposal of the cargo, no move had been made for unloading, even after ten days lying in port. McNeil flitted from ship to shore in his efforts to find a market for the deck load of timbers, which was now unlashed and awaiting longshoremen's hooks. One afternoon, we saw him rowing ashore in the small ship's boat with a railroad tie at his feet. One-Eyed Louie, who was full of humor, remarked that McNeil was going to peddle the cargo from door to door, and that he was going to try to figure out the number of years we would have to stay in Port Louis if we could sell five ties per day.

Money being scarce, in fact *non-existent,* it occurred to Archie that the time was ripe for him to claim his five dollar reward for being the first to sight land, which the captain had promised. This had come about during the anxious days of looking for Rodriguez Island which had been passed unsighted. Archie had been the first to sight the dome of Round Island, an outpost of Mauritius proper. But when Archie presented himself before the captain with a gentle reminder of the five dollars, he was told that only Rodriguez Island was meant. Since he had not sighted that particular island, he was not eligible for the reward. A real sportsman, our captain.

At the time of our arrival in Mauritius, the danger of malaria was on the wane, but we were warned by the people in the town and the harbor against sleeping in the open without coverage by mosquito netting. Niels, the youngest of the crew, was the first to be attacked. His face and neck turned a fiery red as if sunburned, and he complained of pains in the back and chest. After three days of suffering, he was given the address of a doctor in Port Louis, and the Captain sent him ashore for treatment.

When Niels returned to the ship with an armful of medicine bottles and capsules, he astounded the mate with a note from the doctor that he was not to do any work. This was such a blow to the mate, that he forgot all about his usual boasting of his own excellent health at the age of fifty whenever anyone reported an illness to him.

Our Canadian cabin boy Hood was the next to enter the hospital with fever and delirium-tremens. This man who had been such a quiet, taciturn person during all his months on board ship had gone ashore with part of his wages and gone wild. He had been holed up ashore in a hovel with two dusky sirens. Several times we had made attempts to force him back to the ship, without success. He was sick of the ship and the captain and wanted only to be left in peace. Finally, he was found wandering along the waterfront by a local person at 2:00 A.M. and was taken to the hospital. He was treated for a high fever and shattered nerves.

The next day he was joined by Niels who had completely collapsed from the fever. Up to this time Niels had made several attempts to gain admission to the hospital but was repeatedly put off by the captain. He worried about the expense this entailed.

Niels appealed to the doctor who had been treating him. While he lay for an entire day on a lounge in the waiting room the doctor made repeated requests to the ship's agent for a letter of credit to guarantee hospital expenses. After lengthy dickering over costs with the captain and McNeil, Niels was rushed to the hospital to be treated for advanced malaria fever.

Around about this time, it was given out that a market had been found for our deck load with discharging to begin the following day. Best of all, the crew would now be able to draw on one half of their earned wages. True to the rumor, a swarm of Creole longshoremen clambered on board the next morning. Large, staunch, wooden lighters were tied up along each side of the vessel, and the unloading of our weathered timbers commenced. On seeing the first layer of sun-browned fir peeled off the deck load, we all heaved a sigh of relief as the last of our doubts were dispelled. Since most of us had asked for the entire half of our wages due us, our interest in the unloading can easily be imagined. We were now free to demand payment.

Two days later, the captain and McNeil were standing on the deck load watching the unloading when Louie and Chris, the two oldest of the seamen forward, approached the captain for money. McNeil replied, "Money is a pretty scarce article." But this time, we were not to be put off. We pressed that as the discharging had begun, we wanted half

of our wages. A few minutes later the captain and McNeil went ashore together.

The day after, we were doled out another thirty dollars (150 rupees), a fraction of what we legally were entitled to draw. After this, whenever the money list was made up and presented to the captain, he would shake his head doubtfully, and say, "I will see what I can do." In addition to reducing the amounts requested by fifty to eighty per cent, he would always adopt an attitude of charity and alms-giving.

Archie and I, in one of our pleasant out-of-the-way strolls, passed by the La Flor Oriental, a strange sort of restaurant run by an ancient Chinese. One of us suggested a dinner of chicken curry and rice with a liter or two of wine. Upstairs we found Chris, two sheets in the wind as the saying goes, with the strangest drinking partner east of Capetown.

He sat across the table with a handful of greasy cards spread fan-wise in his long supple fingers. He was a tall, stooped Englishman with lank, black hair, and wearing small, steel-rimmed spectacles. I judged him to be about thirty-five. His soiled brown suit hung in loose folds upon his body and showed careless patches in the places where clothes are usually mended. As he talked, his breath whistled through black spaces where several teeth had been knocked out.

He was in the act of going through a card trick when we came in, and with easy presence, he asked us to have a seat and look on. When he had finished, Chris rang a silver rupee upon the table. We followed suit for we wanted to see more of this seedy-looking magician. There was no knowing how many rupees he had conjured out of Chris before we came in, but that was none of our business. As we listened to the usual stock phrases of the medicine show trickster, we learned his story.

Since a boy of ten, he had practiced the handling of cards and handkerchiefs, kneading his bony fingers to make them supple and facile. Most of his bag of tricks he had learned unaided for a conjurer will rarely teach another person his stunts. When he was forced to earn his own living, he became a coal passer on a British tramp steamer, and finally found his way to Mauritius. There he contrived to be paid off the ship, bought a cheap costume to imitate an Egyptian King, took on the imposing name of Rameses the Great and set about making his fortune.

For a while he prospered, gathering in rupees right and left from the awe-struck local inhabitants. But he took to drinking up all his earnings. From a traveling performer, giving his shows in vacant stores, he sank to a street corner fakir with the curbstone for his stage, his sole possessions being the clothes he stood and slept in. He had finally run afoul of the police for contacting English-speaking sailors when they came ashore, getting them drunk, and going through their pockets. All this he told us unabashedly without shame.

Second mate Mr. Johnson was the next man to join the mad whirl ashore. Since his first night ashore with the roll of rupees he had received, he kept himself in a continuous stupor from red wine. For ten days he kept clear of the ship sending his dusky paramour to the gangway now and then with a message that the second mate needed more money. Naturally, the Creole was given none by the captain. We all knew that it was only a matter of waiting until his money was exhausted, when he would be thrown out of his lover's home and be forced to return to the ship.

Of course there was a reason for both the second mate and the cabin boy's debauchery. They had been living aft with the captain for seven months, and they were so disgusted and beaten down by the captain's cruel abuse and vile attitude, that they had to seek some form of deliverance from their pain. Late one evening, when the captain was ashore, one of the Creole women came on board with a note requesting the delivery of the second mate's gold watch. The mate gently escorted her from the ship and put the second mate's watch in safe-keeping.

The second mate returned, dirty, footsore and weary, looking like a ghost. He said nothing, went to bed, slept the clock around and returned to the patching of the royal. He never, ever, mentioned his shoreside experiences to anyone, and no one ever asked. Each man had now had his fling, and we hoped for a period of quiet after these hectic two weeks.

But the peace was shattered altogether with the coming on board of more women. The cook was such a cavalier that one of the captain's chocolate-colored Circes came forward one night and asked to hear his phonograph. The captain came forward to the galley, ostensibly to protect the morals of the cook, but in reality under the urge of a more primitive instinct. He protested that he could not allow women to come on board after dark, it was not right in spite of the fact that he had been carrying on nightly saturnalias in his cabin with this same and other women.

Chris too, was in the room listening to the phonograph. With the help of a bottle of red wine, he was in a genial mood, a rare condition. Quite drunk, he said to the captain, "Be a decent man for once in your life. People in glass houses shouldn't throw stones." This confused the captain, so that he retreated in haste, leaving the cook, Chris, and the Creole woman to their own affairs. When he reached the mainmast, he met the mate, and demanded of him why he did not come forward and run the woman off the ship. The mate replied that he would see what he could do, but it was plain that he had little desire to interfere. The captain glared at him and shouted that he could lick any man in the ship.

The mate replied, "You might as well start on me," and the fight was on. The captain struck and drew first blood. The mate rushed in, they clinched and fell, rolling about on the rough timbers of the deck load. Lurid oaths colored the night as the two fifty year old salts belabored each other with the liveliness of school boys.

All hands gathered round, cheering. I rushed into the forecastle to call Archie, and between us we attempted to separate them. The captain shouted to us, "Stand clear, this is my fight!" There was nothing to prevent them from failing overboard, and at times they threatened to roll into the pump pits where space had been left for the deck winches, a dangerous fall. So we turned to and separated them, bloody and tattered. They were no sooner apart than the mate flew at the captain like a bantam rooster and gave him such a blow on the jaw that he was sent reeling backwards to fall and hit the back of his head on the deck load. There was such a fearful crack that we thought the captain's skull was fractured.

He lay unconscious while one of the men ran into the galley for a bucket of water. Archie bathed his head, but just as the captain was regaining consciousness the mate grabbed the bucket of water and dashed it in the captain's face. "Now see what the French Eagle has done to the British pig," shouted the mate, "I'll fix him so he'll never fight again!"

We supported the captain, while he shambled aft to his cabin. He sat down on the medicine chest with his head in his hands, dismissing us and saying he was all right.

On the poop, sniffling now and then, stood a Creole girl, mumbling supplications in the French patois of the island to the various saints. I put her into a small bumboat that lay alongside and had her taken ashore. Enough excitement for one night.

Luckily there was a strong offshore wind at the time so the noise of combat carried out to sea. The ships anchored about us were none the wiser, and there was no interference by the water police. About two o'clock in the morning the captain and mate met on the poop and argued loudly until daylight. The storm had passed. All was calm.

Our Sundays were usually spent strolling about the town into the byways and side streets where we could see all the interesting modes of living and learn the customs of the many-tongued population. But the most interesting were the visits we made to other ships in the harbor, even to the hulks of ships.

The most imposing was a one-time English bark, the *Gwyder Castle*, owned in Mauritius and lying at moorings with all her topgallants hanging down in a tangle. Her topgallant masts were to be sent down while she waited for the end of the hurricane season. This rigging down was an added precaution against the danger of breaking her moorings and being blown onto the beach. Only a few men were standing by her, a Japanese watchman, an Indian cook, and a Mauritian sailor. The captain, a Dane, came from his home in the countryside each day and returned home in the evening.

The vessel was very old with heavy decks and ancient running gear. Her only hope of continuing in trade lay in picking up a charter now and then for hardwoods from Australia and Singapore or carrying ponies from the Malay Islands to Mauritius. There were many quaint features about her rigging and gear, the most interesting being a head of Neptune with open mouth at the spill of her hand pumps.

Alongside the *Gwyder Castle* lay an American schooner called the *Gardener Williams*, a high-pooped wooden vessel, war-built and owned in Port Louis. Besides two hulks being stripped of masts and teak decks, there were two small barkentines — the *St. Geran*, a former paddlewheel tug, and a graceful island trader of two hundred tons and the *Union La Digue*. This last we found the most interesting of all.

She was originally a Norwegian schooner of 210 tons, but after her sale in Port Louis, she was rigged as a smart little barkentine. Her crew was made up of all kinds of islanders: Seychelleans, men of Diego Garcia, of Bourbon, of Reunion, even a kinky-headed lad from Madagascar showing his grinning face over the rail.

During our Sunday visits on board her, the young sailors showed us the primitive rice mortar that was used by deck passengers in making rice cakes. Compared to our vessel, everything seemed to be in miniature, the tiny royal yard, a knee-high capstan, and braces no longer than our gaff-topsail halyards. Before we left the gangway, these friendly fellows gave us coconuts, seashells from the islands and a basket of fruit.

Our deckload was now gone, hatches were uncovered, and the Creole longshoremen commenced unloading the railroad ties from the hold. There was a little work to be done about the ship, the square sails were unbent while the yards were being painted, some sail work. Sailmaking and repairing was carried out on deck beneath the forecastle awning in shade.

Later on some of us worked from a float, scraping the barnacles and green whiskers from the ship's side. After a fresh coat of black paint and trimming her copper paint on the waterline, we could say the *Forest Dream* was the smartest looking vessel in the port.

There was the usual variety of vessels in the harbor: coal carriers from Durban, a British ship from Calcutta and Bombay, obsolete tramp steamers with rice and coolies for the sugar plantations, an occasional French mail steamer with a war hero's name, and two or three inter-island coal burners no larger than tugboats.

After we had been in the harbor for over five weeks, we read from signals at the summit of Le Pouce that a large square-rigger was cruising offshore, visible only from the top of the mountain. Two days later, soon after daybreak, I made out a handsome bark standing in for the harbor buoy with a fine leading wind in her favor. She was carrying everything but the royals, the perfect ship in a perfect setting. Coming to anchor just outside the reef, she lay awaiting customs practice while a swarm of men furled her sails. The two government

tugs, *Paul* and *Virginia* soon had her in tow and headed for the harbor moorings. We learned that she was the *Favell*, the Finnish training ship. Reunion was her last port, having sailed from that island seven days before. Her decks were alive with husky young men who waved to us as they passed, greeting us in English in a most friendly manner.

A few nights later, Archie and I visited their ship and found her to be clean and comfortable, with an enormous crew. Thereafter during our stay in port, we exchanged many visits, and arranged swimming parties and hikes into the country, making many warm friendships.

With the cabin boy Hood in the hospital, I often visited him, bringing cigarettes from the crew. Hood was showing no improvement. He seemed to be wasting, his arms and legs pitifully thin. Niels had been taken from the hospital into the home of a prominent French family.

I visited Hood at the hospital and hardly recognized him. He was very weak, with his cheeks hollow and sunken. His arms and hands had fallen away so that the cords stood out. I sat on the iron cot beside him and we had a long talk, the native patients eyeing us with friendly curiosity. He told me he was suffering from gonorrhea, the result of his ten day spree in the red light district. Complications had set in, and the doctors had told him that an operation was necessary, something he dreaded. There was no alternative as something had to be done quickly, so the poor fellow turned to me for reassurance which I tried to give him. When I left him that evening he followed me with his eyes as I crossed the court, waving a feeble hand at the last turn, as if saying goodbye to the world. In trying to find a few hours of forgetfulness, he paid a terrible price — fever, delirium tremens and a case of neglected venereal disease.

The *Forest Dream* left Port Louis several days after this visit, and though we made inquires, we were unable to find out whatever became of Hood.

The Creole longshoremen made a good job of unloading, even though this was the first cargo of heavy timbers they had ever handled. It was a relief to finish with the large timbers and get to the ties in the hold. With the last of our cargo gone, our stay in Mauritius was coming to a close. There was talk of taking a full cargo of sugar to British Columbia, or that we would sail light to Singapore and load hardwoods for Victoria or Vancouver. But the mate felt that in the end, we most likely would receive orders to Newcastle, New South Wales, for a cargo of coal.

Among the visitors on board the ship, one of the most interesting and best liked was a brisk little Frenchman called La Giroday, of an old Mauritian family. He had great plans for establishing a regular trade between British Columbia and Mauritius with Canadian flour and Mauritian sugar as the main cargoes. His hopes centered on the Forest Line's three barkentines. Mauritius was full of young people who thirsted for greener pastures, and La Giroday was promoting immigration of Mauritians to Canada as a pasture land. By painting the charms and opportunities of Canada, another British commonwealth, he had created such an enthusiasm among the youth of the land that a colonization scheme was promoted.

The government appropriated a considerable amount of money in support of the plan. Wealthy planters contributed, and before we sailed from Port Louis, we learned that a number of families, mostly younger people, had expressed a desire to settle in Canada and take up farming. For a people to leave their tropical home where their families had lived for generations and venture into a strange country of the North, where customs, climate and prospects were unknown to them, requires a great deal of courage. They deserved much credit and respect.

For two or three weeks, while Hood was in the hospital, we had a young Indian lad working on board ship as cabin boy. The shipmaster had a local drinking buddy, the captain of the *St. Geran*, a Mauritian barkentine, whose nephew had a desire to work his way to Australia, so he discharged the young Indian lad. Going aft to the poop one evening on my rounds of the ship, I found the young fellow standing near the aft cabin companionway, crying as if his heart would break. The boy was well liked by all hands forward, so I asked him why he was so upset. He replied that the captain had given him only half of his promised wages and had roughly told him to, "Clear out." The noise attracted the captain. He came up the companionway saying, "What's that? What did he say?" Turning to me he began to explain, but I had no heart or desire to listen to him, and I went about my rounds.

The boy continued to cry as he shouldered his bundle of clothing after a suspicious search by the captain, and walked dispiritedly down the gangway, still in tears.

A number of sample logs of ebony came on board, perhaps for Canadian importers, along with a few scanty stores. Among these was a large keg marked "Pickles" but it actually contained rum. Its stowage was personally supervised by the captain who hurried it aft to his cabin. This was one little Port Louis transaction of the captain that escaped the watchful eye of the Scotsman McNeil. For once, we gave the captain credit for showing some courage and imagination.

One day, we were told that the ship was scheduled for sailing on Monday for Newcastle, New South Wales, Australia. The following morning at eight bells all hands turned to, singling up mooring lines, loosing the sails and heaving short the anchors. McNeil, the charterer's agent, stood on the poop and watched all the proceedings with the air and stance of an admiral. This irritated the captain beyond measure for McNeil's monitoring presence on board ship during all of our four months stay in Port Louis had served as a nagging daily check on the captain's conduct and activities. To toe the mark was something he was not in the habit of doing.

The pilot came on board at noon. A few minutes later the *Paul* and *Virginia* were tied up alongside, and our mooring lines to the buoys were cast off. With their ship lying just behind us, the crew of the bark *Favell* gathered on their stern, watching us get underway. When all was clear, we gave the *Favell* three lusty cheers. They were returned by all hands on board the *Favell*, the hills ringing with the mighty shouts of over thirty men. We replied with a last single cheer and wished our friends the best of luck as the ships drew apart.

Even with the fair wind blowing from the mountains, we experienced some trouble in clearing the narrow harbor entrance. The two tugs were too small to handle the ship well, but with the setting of the lower topsail, the ship steadied. The tugs were let go abreast of the vine-covered ancient fort that guarded the harbor entrance on our starboard beam.

The captain gave the pilot and McNeil a hurried handshake, and set about shouting up the sail. Homeward bound at last, or so we naively believed, having lain in the harbor of Port Louis, Mauritius for four months.

The second mate was down on the foredeck seemingly in a wine fog, paying no attention to the shouts of the captain from the poop deck. He had his back to the poop, watching the hoisting of the mainsail. Finding no notice was taken of his whooping and hollering, the captain scuttled down the poop ladder to the main deck. He ran up behind the second mate and gave him such a jab in the ribs that poor Johnson thought he had been harpooned. Except for this little incident, everything went well. The breeze blew fair, a brilliant sunshine glistened upon the spars, the white sails curved, and southward we bowled along.

*"The ship was cheered,*
*The harbor cleared*
*Merrily did we drop*
*Below the kirk, below the hill*
*Below the lighthouse top."*

There were a few half-hearted shouts of "homeward bound," but Newcastle for orders could mean anything. We had seen enough of the jinx that was riding on this ship to know that the future might hold as many delays and trouble as we had already experienced. We were still hostages wrapped in the mantle of power held by the captain of the *Forest Dream*. Still, we were headed back around the world and that should mean something.

Steering a south by east course, we expected to soon fall in with the strong westerly winds in the "Roaring Forties," and run the Easting down. Cold, hail and rain were expected. We had overhauled our oilskins and cold weather gear against the day. Nothing happened to break the steady sailing until the fourth day when the wind hauled unfavorably. In an attempt to tack ship, the captain got out of temper as usual, and ended by clewing up the fore royal and upper top gallant sail, as well as wearing ship.

On the morning of the fifth day after leaving Port Louis, a stowaway came out of the forward hold. His name was Paul Gueho. His people were of an old Mauritian family. He was a well-mannered young man about the age of Niels, in whose company I had seen him on several occasions while ashore, but we made no mention of this for obvious reasons. He was taken aft to the mate, who called the captain. Rather than being annoyed, as we had anticipated, the captain and the mate were pleased to have an extra hand, whom the captain informed would be working for his passage, and could expect no financial remuneration. I found out from Niels that Paul was the son of the family he had stayed with during part of his stay ashore while in the hospital.

The cook, who had shown no signs of fever during our stay in port now began to lose weight, and complained of sharp pains in his back. Although it was plain that he was suffering, there was no word said about the cook being given an extra hand in the galley. The mate chose to keep Paul on deck cleaning deck seams or making up sennit and baggy-wrinkle for sail chafing gear. Both Archie and Chris were also taken down with some stomach disorder, but it was almost impossible for them to "lay up," as it is called on board ship. They carried on with their regular watches as a skeleton crew is expected to do — sick or well.

The beef (salt horse)that we had brought from Victoria began to smell to the heavens, maggots crawled on the floor of the meat locker and even into the passageway to the messroom. We called the captain's attention to this rotting mess, but he did nothing about it.

*Sunday, July 4, 1926*

A holiday for us, with the weather growing cool and nippy. At night the captain fired off half a dozen rockets, each one bursting in a golden plume against the black sky, giving a fine effect. He was in a liquid, holiday mood. On Tuesday we learned that we were in the latitude of Durban, Africa. The sea lost its brilliant glitter along with the dulling of the skies. We were nearing the grey latitudes, but no westerly wind favored us.

The captain, bored, took up his bear-baiting of the cook. They had two or three rows which led to the promise to the cook that he would get paid off in Newcastle. This was likely in any event for he had grown so thin and weak that he could hardly get about in the galley. The two young men from Mauritius, Paul Gueho, the stowaway, and Thatcher, the new cabin boy, were told by the captain that they would be put on the payroll at wages of $40.00 a month. None of us believed that this would ever happen. It was only a maneuver by the captain to get the maximum amount of work out of them. By now we knew most of the captain's tricks, large and small.

Long grey-bearded seas rolled up from the southwest along with freezing rain and hail. We were put to work scraping deck seams of the pitch which had boiled out in the tropical latitudes. Although the decks were wet with spray and rain throughout the day, work went on with the loose pitch blowing about the deck and getting into our eyes. The captain mentioned the island of New Amsterdam to the mate and remarked that he should like to sight it in two days.

*July 13, 1926*

Just the day to have the upper top-gallant sail rip along the weather foot. Chris and I were sent aloft to unbend and send down the sail, finishing just at the change of the watch. It fell to the starboard watch to drag the new sail on deck and bend it in the cold driving rain. Sails were ripping every single day. Fore and afters were lowered and patched from the deck while the square sails were clewed up and "given a stitch and a promise" from the yard.

*July 18, 1926*

The westerly wind has found us at last. We are tearing along eastward and south with all the light sails furled. In the afternoon main and jigger sails were reefed with all hands on the job. Now making fourteen knots in a glorious fashion. A few days later our sails began to show signs of weakening under heavy pressure; the fore-upper top-gallant sail ripped along the weather leach. It had to be taken in before it was reduced to rags. The flying jib was the next to go, followed by the mizzensail, ripped from gaff to boom. At eight bells on a cold drizzly night, we discovered that the rotator was gone from the taffrail log, probably bitten off by some hungry shark, which often happens.

The following watch we lost the outer jib, saving only the boltropes and a few ribbons of canvas. Sunday came in with cold, driving rain and intervals of hail. A new outer jib was hauled up from the sail locker. We began preparations for bending the head sail at the first crack of dawn. The mate supervised the work as usual, he and I working on the bowsprit with wind tears streaming from our eyes and drops of clear water blowing from our nostrils.

A cold piercing wind was blowing with heavy squalls at five minute intervals. Working unhampered by oilskins, it was one of the most unpleasant tasks imaginable. I shall never forget this incident on the bowsprit with the mate, for it gave rise to a remark by him, that in spite of his surface hardness and amusing vanity, showed his real nature. Working with blue, numb-fingered hands, he looked at me after a short laugh and said, "I have to laugh at my own misery."

Except for a reefed main-sail, and occasionally the jigger, the fore and afters were used but little. With squared yards, we ran before the great, towering seas that seemed just on the point of crashing down on the ship's poop deck and tearing the helmsman from the wheel, but always at the final moment, they passed under the stern, giving the vessel the same swift gliding motion of a surf board. For one who has exhausted all the thrills of life, let him "run the Easting down," in a sailing ship.

One evening after the sun had spent itself, the mate dropped a remark about the man at the wheel, "bundled up with so much clothing." Hearing this, the captain asked the mate if he himself was not heavily padded, too. The mate lost his temper and declared that he could stand cold more than any man on the ship.

Thereafter he paced the poop deck clad only in trousers, sea boots and a lumberjack shirt. The white top of a uniform cap completed the picture. It was a special pleasure of the captain to come on deck wrapped in a great sheepskin coat with a high fur collar, woolen gloves and a heavy winter cap. This irritated the mate so much, that he paced on the opposite side of the poop deck, avoiding the captain, and growling under his breath. With light squalls passing over — a dozen in a watch — the mate disdained using oilskins. He shuffled up and down the heaving poop, wet and miserable, snuffling with a cold. By day the cook crawled about the galley, haggard, unshaven and pale, his clothes hanging on his thin form. At night, tossing in his bunk with chills and fever, he kept every crack and cranny of his galley closed tight in an effort to warm his shivering body. He told me he counted the bells of the lookout watch, heard the watches change, and dozed off every few minutes, only to awake again, cold and shivering. The least bit of food gave him intense pain in his stomach, so he ate only enough to keep alive. Besides these miseries, he discovered he had contracted the same venereal disease (gonorrhea) which had taken Hood to the hospital. The captain had advised him to drive the eruption back with applications of iodine, which he did. But he weakened faster than ever, so that after two weeks he was only a shadow of his former self, having dropped from two hundred and ten pounds to one hundred and sixty pounds.

The captain gave the carpenter, Nelson, orders to seal the barrels of rotting beef. Chips willingly did this, sealing them well and marking crosses on the heads of the barrels. Why they were saved and carefully stowed away with their maggoty contents was a mystery that no one could explain.

At this point in our passage we had reached the "playground" of a few months back, where we wore ourselves out bucking head winds and seas. Here too, was the same grim stretch where our beloved shipmate, Frank, had been buried in the sea, wrapped in a canvas shroud. We try, but cannot forget him. Niels and I did not need this realization to remind us of poor Frank, and his painful death under such harsh circumstances. It only made the memory of him more vivid, and caused me to wish that I should never see this corner of the world again.

The mate, with his zealous pride in the ship, kept us at work suijing (washing) and painting the white bulwarks and house. It was laughable to see the mate storm and rage at the passing white squalls which wet the fresh paint as fast as we put it on. The *Forest Pride* would be in Newcastle, he said, and he had no intention of letting her show him up.

Although the cook suffered agony with every step, no one was assigned to give him a hand. Niels and I voluntarily helped him with "washing up" on our watches below, while Paul, our extra man, was kept on deck making "baggy wrinkle" and scraping pitch from the deck seams.

With every slacking of the wind, reefs were shaken out, the spanker set, and the topsails and royals made use of; but with sunset and every passing gale they were taken in. This developed into a set routine, so that the men of the dog watch got into the habit of saying, "Well boys, we'll go take in the fair weather rags" each time they turned to in the evening.

The second mate, Mr. Johnson, continued to receive his daily raking over the coals. Nothing he did seemed to be right. Many times at the change of the dog watch, he came on the poop as I was leaving the wheel, to be met with bitter criticism and curses from the mate, French Louie. "Curse of Christ! You ought to be in an old ladies home, look at those braces," and "you've been playing with these by-the-wind bitches again," and so on, without end.

### July 31, 1926
We were nearing the coast day by day, and a close watch was kept at night for lights. Our search was rewarded just after dark on Saturday when the mate pointed out the glow in the sky of Albany, Warnambool, and other small ports along the coast of Victoria. The next day, Sunday, Cape Wicham light was sighted on the dog watch. This light is located at the Northern extremity of King Island, and marks the entrance to Bass Straits. A feeling of good cheer passed through the ship — here we were in the hated Strait; nearing the gate that was to let us out of a land of hail, rain and cold, driving gales of wind.

### August 2, 1926
Today we lifted Wilson's Promontory with a fine breeze carrying us along as we came within sight and passed West Vancouver Islands, Devils Tower, Curtis Island, Crocodile Rock. At sunset, Deal Island, purple and somber to the southward was the solitary light winking from the very middle of the great oval hump. On reaching these latitudes we found the sun shedding a real warmth that soaked into the body with a most grateful luxury. The air, nipping and fresh, offset the drowsy influence of the sea so that every nerve tingled and gave a great feeling that it was good to be alive and in good sea-health.

Sailing east, close-hauled, we passed the steamer *Gabriella* of Sydney. We saluted. In the evening the captain sensed a hurricane and shortened sail; reefed the jigger, and lowered the mainsail, but the bugaboo turned out to be a little squall. It shaded off into a shift of wind, hauling fair.

### August 5, 1926
The captain had been acting in his usual crude and brutal manner since we first reached the cold latitudes, doing a great deal of unnecessary shouting about the deck, and threatening the second mate with all kinds of violence. But up to this time, no one had taken him very seriously, for with every watch on deck when shortening sail was done, the captain pitched in with the watch and lent a hand. The offensive part of this was the close proximity of the captain, reeking of rum and iodoform. The thought had occurred to us, having been intimate with the cook's Creole woman, he most likely had

contracted the same disease. No matter how roundly the second mate was cursed and abused, he kept silent. It remained for Thomsen (Niels), the youngest man to retaliate.

The incident happened at five in the morning. The yards were braced a trifle, Niels was taking in the slack of the fore sheet, belaying it to the bitts on deck. The turns became fouled and the captain shouted at Niels, following up with a volley of oaths. Niels responded, "You drunken bastard!" in an undertone.

The watch crossed to the other side of the ship, and while passing the fore hatch, the captain leaned towards Niels, and said, "What did you say? What did you say?"

Thomsen said he was doing the best he could, considering the darkness and confused deck. With that, the captain struck at Niels's head, missing his aim, and striking him on the shoulder with his fist. Niels fell against One-Eyed Louie, and they both caught themselves on the fore hatch. Niels was up in an instant. Turning to Louie, he asked,"Did you see that?"

"Yes, I did," Louie replied.

Niels asked the same question of the second mate, who also answered, "Yes." This reply surprised us for it was the first time that he had ever responded in a year of abuse.

At this, the captain flew into a rage, shouting, "What's that? What's that!" and threatening Niels with imprisonment in irons on bread and water rations. His voice rose to such a screaming pitch that we were awakened in our watch below and caught the tail end of the storm. Niels had a Bowditch (a navigation book with many blank pages) in which he kept a documentary list of all the captain's sins, so he entered all the facts of the night's events therein.

While One-Eyed Louie was at the wheel from six to eight in the morning, the captain made a pretext of looking in the compass while asking

Louie what business he had sticking up for Thomsen. Louie replied that he could not stand by and see a man abused in such a fashion and keep his mouth shut. Such were his words, in sturdy American expression.

That evening after supper, Thomsen was called aft to the cabin. He found the captain sitting in the saloon with the log-book before him. The mate (French Louie) was standing alongside. "Listen to this!" the captain demanded.

The entry in the logbook was read to the effect that, Niels Thomsen, a Dane, (we thought him to be an American Citizen) employed on board the *Forest Dream* as an able-bodied seaman, was found to be lazy, insubordinate, an agitator stirring up trouble in the forecastle, as well as an out and out Bolsheviki. Except for a scant knowledge of steering, he was incompetent to fill the place of an able-bodied seaman, and was accordingly reduced in rank from able seaman to ordinary seaman, with a corresponding reduction in wages from sixty dollars per month to forty dollars per month.

When asked if he had anything to say to this, Niels replied simply that he protested the captain's action and went forward. The wage reduction was back-dated to the time we arrived in Port Louis, three or four months earlier, clearly after Niels had been on the ship for eight months. In Port Adelaide and Port Louis, he had asked to be paid off and get clear of the ship. In all this time the captain should have been able to discover the alleged incompetence and have discharged him.

The injustice of this incident was so plain that Niels resolved all the more to ask for a hearing before the United States Consul. It was plain that the captain had heard what Niels had called him. I asked him why he had gotten into such trouble. He said it was that he could take the abuse but could not stand the second mate being so abused by the captain.

*August 7, 1926*

This morning we learned that we were just abeam of Sydney. Cheering news with Newcastle only sixty miles to the northward. Since his whooping about the decks during these past weeks, the captain has become strangely quiet and solicitous of the crew's welfare, walking about the decks asking them this and that small detail, like a concerned, doting father.

A strong, cool breeze blew from offshore, straight out of the west. No matter how we clawed into it the ship did little more than hold its own. For three days we tacked to and fro, twenty miles or so offshore with the smoke of Newcastle as a distinguishing mark by day and the glow of its myriad lights by night. Steamers came and went in smoky unconcern while we grew weary of tacking ship, hoping for a tug to come out and tow us into the harbor.

*August 9, 1926*

Dusk was shading the sea when we went about after a long tack. It brought us well inshore where Nora Head flashed its amber light. The breeze dropped to the lightest whisper at sunset; the sky barred with a weird effect of crimson and black stripes.

I had just taken the wheel at eight bells when a small steamer showed its lights from the direction of Newcastle. While we watched its easy, gliding motion over the smooth ground swell, the mate remarked that she was a small collier bound for Sydney. But, since everyone was thinking and talking tugboat, I clutched at the hope of it being the longed-for help; especially as I noticed it carried only one mast light. A moment later, she bore down on us, head on, with both her running lights gleaming red and green. The mate called down the after companionway to the captain that a tug boat was coming alongside. The captain came on deck in his green vest with red berry stitchings and a megaphone in his hand. Square sails were soon clewed up with a great deal of relieved singing, while the powerful tug drew within hailing distance.

The tugboat was the first to hail with, "Good evening Captain."

"How are you?" the captain replied.

"Are you bound for Newcastle?" asked the tug captain.

"Yes," replied the captain of the *Forest Dream*.

"Do you want a tow?" asked the tug captain.

"How much?" queried the captain of the *Forest Dream*.

"Two shillings a ton, in and out," replied the tug captain.

The captain did some mental arithmetic of a sort, the resulting total figure evidently giving him something of a scare, for he shouted, "What is the usual price?"

"That's the fixed price," returned the captain of the tug. Silence for a few moments - more arithmetic. "We are going to have a change of wind," rasped the captain of the *Forest Dream*.

But his hopes of a reduction in charges were rudely dashed when the captain of the tug replied, in a bored voice, "This time of the year we have nothing but westerly wind." A consultation between the captain and the mate followed; the mate taking no interest in the matter, through sheer disgust.

"All right, hook on," our captain answered.

"Do you want to take my towline?" asked the tug captain.

"Yes," replied our captain.

"That will cost you five pounds more," said the tug captain. This last almost staggered our captain; pounds and dollars were reeling about in his head in a kind of devil-dance. With the finances of the ship in such a state as they had been, each additional charge came like a blow to a winded fighter.

However, the long wire towline was made fast and the tug bore off. When we had gone a mile, the towline parted a fathom away from our towing bitt on our forecastle head. It was discovered that the line had been made fast by the manila tailrope which was spliced into the eye of the wire. As soon as the heavy strain came upon the rope, it parted, dropping the long wire into the sea. It took two hours for the tug to reel in the wire towing line. The tug came alongside for a second time; the wire was taken on board and made fast properly to the bitts, and the ship headed for Newcastle.

At one A.M. of the tenth, we picked up the pilot from a small dory, the pilot steamer riding free a hundred yards off our weather bow. Nobby Head loomed up like a blunt-bowed battleship, her lights blinking signals to the pilot boat; plus others, red and green, which indicated the depth of water according to the stage of the tide. A short white lighthouse flashed at regular intervals.

After proceeding up the channel for a short distance, the starboard anchor was dropped with a short lead, the towline let go with a snake-like writhing, and all hands scrambled aloft to make sails fast. With only a few hours left until daylight no anchor watch was set, one man agreeing to keep a lookout until time to call the cook. Safe in Newcastle Harbor after a passage of only forty-two days from Mauritius.

### August 10, 1926

In Newcastle. At eight bells this morning, all hands went aloft to furl sails. From the royal yard I could look all over the harbor, up the winding Hunter River, and across the slender peninsula on which the "Sailor Town" of Stockton is built. A great steel mill sprawled over the countryside to the westward, making the sky grey with its smoke and grime. On our port beam lay Newcastle with its brownstone buildings terraced upon the hills.

At King's Wharf lay a Swedish four-masted bark with heavy square yards and grimy rigging, unloading rock salt. Through our glasses we made out her name, the *C.B. Pedersen* of Goteborg,

Sweden. Across the river on a small slip-ways there was a perfect toy of a small topsail schooner of two hundred tons, white hull with little black ports painted along her sides, oiled spars and hand-kerchief sails, the very antithesis of the big, sullen-looking bark across the way. Her name was the *Louis Theriault*, owned in New Zealand, but still carrying the port of Weymouth, Nova Scotia, carved on her stern, a wanderer far from home.

In the morning two tugs made fast alongside while we got underway for Stockton, the waiting berth for sailing ships since time out of mind. Trim little houses stood row on row, the river bank was green, blooming with yellow daisies, cattle grazed with old pensioned nags in the fresh green grass, children romped with their dogs, all sweet sounds to our sea-tired eyes and ears. We had hardly put our lines ashore, when a swarm of small boys came on board, asking for stamps, coins, and souvenirs. Sailors are alike the world over, and the boys went ashore with their hands full of seashells, stamps, and cigarette cards.

In the evening a group of men came on board for a visit from a Finnish bark, the *Woodburn*, which lay just ahead of us awaiting orders. Between yarns, we learned that she had come from New York, and expected to be sold in Levuka in the Fiji Islands, to be dismantled and made into a coal barge. As the week rolled by we patched sails, overhauled running gear, went swimming in the surf, or strolled down to the Seaman's Mission in the evening. On every hand we found the people friendly and gracious. We were invited into their homes and made to feel that our troubles were theirs.

On Saturday we went aft to ask the captain for some money but were told that no answer to his cablegram had been received. Since there was no money on the ship, all hands would have to wait. We had a good deal of practice doing that, so we settled down for an endurance contest.

Although the captain made countless trips

between ship and town, the best news he could come up with was a half-hearted statement that the problem of money was almost solved. This meant exactly nothing until he showed us a cablegram from Victoria advising that the ship should be libeled, which showed us that the charterers had abandoned the entire enterprise. No mention was made of money, but a line of credit was established at Dalgety's Ship Agents, or so the captain said.

### August 19, 1926

During this period, Niels had been busy filing his charges of assault and mistreatment by the captain, with the American consulate in Newcastle. A clear case of the circumstances of the assault, ("on the high seas") as Niels phrased it, along with names of witnesses was put into the consul's hands. On the morning of the nineteenth justice was to be meted out to a sailor at the consulate, a thing hitherto unheard of in the Merchant Marine. Besides the prime witnesses, One-Eyed Louie, and the second mate, the rest of the crew forward were also summoned to appear as witnesses, in the event they could cast some light on the case.

We were shown into a large room with a heavy table in the middle. Trade journals of every description were neatly arranged in rows, completely covering the table. A dozen chairs were placed around the walls of the room. The captain and the consul retired to another room, the holy of holies, where they held a lengthy pow-wow. When they came out of the room, the consul snapped open his gold watch and remarked that he only had a few minutes before lunch with the mayor of Newcastle, so the case at hand would have to be hurried up.

The charges against the captain were read, and the first witness, Louie, was questioned. He declared the facts stated were true. Second Mate Johnson was called, and he too confirmed the correctness of the charges. The consul stated that he would defer judgment in the assault case until he had heard the case of the disrating of Thomsen, another charge that Niels had filed. It was obvious to all of us that, while the consul may have on occasion held court involving the illegal acts of seaman, he had never heard of an instance involving a complaint against a captain by a seaman. He was somewhat confused as to procedure.

According to the logbook entry which the captain read out to him, Thomsen had been disrated to ordinary seaman, the reduction to date back to the previous May, three months before the entry was made in the log. The consul questioned us as to Thomsen's ability as a seaman. He was told that he had always held up his end of the load during the year he had been on board the ship.

All of our evidence, according to the consul, was from Thomsen's friends who were inspired by emotional impulses. It was for that reason rejected as being irrelevant. He ruled that the captain's word was final. That if he ruled a man to be incompetent and chose to disrate him, no evidence to the contrary could alter the captain's decision. Niels was not even allowed to stand an examination to prove his ability. In addition, the consul ignored the fact that Thomsen had asked to be paid off in both Adelaide and Mauritius, and was refused in both instances. If he was incompetent, why had he not been allowed to quit the ship.

"The disrating of Thomsen stands," said the consul. Louie and Johnson were told to come back the next day, when the assault charges against the captain by Thomsen were to be heard.

In the hallway, we protested against such summary methods of dealing with Thomsen, but the consul was adamant, adding that Thomsen's case was weak because of some doubt as to whether or not he was a United States citizen. The consul went on to question us as to why American sea captains did not care for American crews, a statement that sounded strange, coming from him. We said that the dislikes, if such a dislike existed, might arise because of the peculiar American characteristic of sticking up for one's rights.

As for claiming money, the consul pointed out that since the ship was neither loading or unloading, and had no charter, we could not legally demand any wages. A strange and ridiculous ruling, no doubt invented by the consul on the spur of the moment for want of a better reason. With such a ruling we could wait forever. We appeared to be powerless against bureaucracy. The following morning, Thomsen and his witnesses, Louie and the second mate, having been directed to appear before the consul, were on arrival at his office told that the case had been dismissed by the consul. So much for justice.

A few days later the captain had us all back at the break of the poop, where he dramatically asked, "Who wants to be paid off?" We all raised our hands, after which he dismissed us with a "That's all," and a wave of the hand. Later we learned that he had received a cablegram asking for a statement of wages due the crew, and a total of outstanding bills against the ship. This request came from the owners of the ship, not the charterers. Of course, the fate of the ship and the final outcome of this tangled web of affairs filled our days. Nothing else was talked of, and this was only heightened by the news that the captain had secured a charter for New Guinea where we would pick up a cargo of gold ore.

Prospect of an advance on our wages was later knocked in the head, when we heard that the charter had been made in the owners' names without their knowledge. It had been cancelled since the vessel was still in the hands of the charterers. It appeared that the New Guinea charter had been secured under false pretenses. Other charters for Mexican ports were drifting about, but nothing came of them.

We had become depressed and weary of hearing rumors about money. Up to now not a member of the crew had received a single shilling of their wages since our arrival in Newcastle. The captain made several pilgrimages to Sydney, but returned each time with nothing except negative news. Since we could not predict the outcome of the present situation, none of us proposed working for nothing. We went aft in a body one evening and proposed to the captain that we only do the necessary work about the ship, such as filling tanks, washing down, cutting firewood, and other simple chores. He hemmed and hawed, and beat about the bush so that most of us gave up the talks in disgust and went forward determined to stop work. Archie and I remained behind to wring a final word out of him, but he dodged about so that the incident ended with him telling us to take our troubles to the consulate, and make our statement there.

There was a topsail to be finished, a matter of a few hours work. We were asked by the mate to finish that job, and we did. We mended the topsail and bent it on the yard.

### September 15, 1926

Aware of our circumstances, the ferry captain had long since allowed us to ride free on the ferry. In a body, we went to Newcastle and made our proposal to the consul. He told us that the matter was between the captain and the crew. As for the question of our wages, he advised us to appeal to the Seaman's Union for assistance. It was obvious that he was eagerly looking forward to seeing the last of us. We acted at once, and after a talk with the secretary of the union, we were taken to the office of the president. We met Mr. Tom Walsh. It took a matter of only an hour to put our grievance into the hands of the union's solicitor.

The union solicitor gave us a typewritten form empowering him to represent us and take action on our behalf. The mate was the only man who refused to sign the form, giving as his reason that he intended fighting his battles at home.

We had now met the captain halfway, and our

next problem was to push for libel proceedings. But, after checking with the union solicitor's office, we were told the captain had pointed out that the ship, being a foreign vessel, could not be libeled without the captain's permission. The solicitor was letting things slide pending the arrival of the mailboat *Aorangi* from Sydney, which might bring a new captain, or other good news. The solicitor also advised us that we were not in a position to libel the ship, that only local creditors could take such action. They were not inclined to do so, considering the trifling sums involved. We were now back to square one.

### September 25, 1926

This morning, our sistership, The *Forest Friend*, arrived with a partial cargo from Noumea, New Caledonia. This arrival created a change in our status, for the local agent of the owners of the *Forest Friend* were also the agents of the owners of the *Forest Dream*, on instructions from the owners, our credit for meat, fruit, and vegetables was withdrawn.

According to Niels, our "sea lawyer" who was always perusing the shipping articles, we now had clear grounds for libeling the ship because of a broken clause in the articles. It stated that when in port, the crew must be provided with fresh meat, fruit, and vegetables to offset a diet of non-fresh foods served at sea.

The mate talked to the consul, and he was advised to pursue libel action. The captain, true to form, attempted to forestall this move by asking the U.S. Government to provide aid through the Consul General in Sydney. This was refused because we were not technically destitute in the legal sense of the word; we had a place to sleep, and we had salt horse, salt beef and beans, food of a sort. After calling up Mr. James, the union solicitor, in an effort to speed up the libeling, we were sent to the office of Captain Robson, the agent for the *Forest Friend*.

When we arrived at his office we found our captain there. A few words sufficed to explain why our ship's credit had been stopped. It appeared that the credit obtained by our Captain Myers was in the name of the ship's owners, not the charterers, who were responsible for all of the ship's bills under the terms of what is known as a "bare boat" charter. When faced with this charge, our captain had nothing to say in his defense, except mumbling something about his being made the "goat."

When all the dealings of the captain came out, the atmosphere grew too hot for his comfort and he left abruptly without ceremony. It was revealed to us how the captain had cabled the charterers, stating that he expected to go to the hospital, demanding his wages, and so to speak, desert a sinking ship.

Furthermore, he told them how he had tried to forestall libel action on our part, and how he had tried to have Cook Timerman signed clear of the ship in order to avoid hospital expenses. All this came out, showing us how the land lay. It was due to the efforts of Captain Robson that the spurs were put to the lawyers handling our libel case.

As luck would have it, the solicitor was in Sydney at the time, which simplified the serving of the writs. A long distance message was all that was needed. The facts of the stoppage of food supplies was given, and on the evening of the sixth of October, word came that the ship was now formally libeled.

### October 7, 1926

This morning bright and early, the deputy marshall and his bailiff came on board to affix the writ to the mainmast in traditional style. The marshall spent only a few minutes on the ship, while his bailiff, a sort of glorified watchman, settled down for a comfortable stay. He was a little, broad-shouldered, sunbrowned man with a hook nose and a wide smile. A weathered, double-breasted reefer jacket was as much a part of him as his silvery grey hair. After a cheery "Good morning," he went on to assure us that we should easily recover our wages from the old ballyhoo. "A Master Mariner I am, Sir, but brought up in the foc'sle, and loving the forward end of the ship the more for it too. Skipped out from Jersey Island when just a little nipper, etc. etc."

While the *Forest King* lay at King's Wharf, Newcastle, several of us found a few days work on board the vessel, painting the hull, as several of their crew had paid off following their arrival here. The few men who had left the vessel, told us she was a "proper madhouse." The mate, a Mulatto, had found his hands full handling the men, a difficulty that was brought about on his attempting to be a "hard case," soon after leaving the Pacific Coast.

During the *Forest Friend*'s stay in Stockton, there was further trouble. On one occasion the mate knocked the cabin boy down, kicking him in the head. The boy brought the affair to the attention of the American consul, but the only satisfaction he received was permission to sign off the ship.

A few days later, just after breakfast, we had the pleasure of witnessing a fight between the aforementioned mate, and one of the ordinary seaman. Their differences were settled on the grassy riverbank beside the *Forest Dream*, and ended in victory for the ordinary seaman, who was a big strapping lad. This was followed by a fight between the second mate and another ordinary seaman, following some impertinence on the boy's part. This resulted in the second mate displaying a lovely "shiner" for a week or two. All this in one morning. After all this commotion, the affairs of the ship settled down to an even tenor again.

### October 12, 1926

The days rolled on. The entire town learned of our plight and asked sympathetic questions at every turn. Our ship became known as the "Yankee Poorhouse" and the people showed all kinds of ineffectual indignation at the selfish aloofness shown by the owners and the charterers of the ship. They began having us to dinner occasionally.

Acting under the impulse to save something for himself out of the libel action, our captain decided to file his own claim. On the thirteenth, another writ was attached to the ship, setting forth the captain's claim for one thousand pounds for salary due and other expenses. The addition of this writ, caused us no concern, as our claims had to be met first, and if there was any surplus, his claim might be met.

Up until this time, we had managed to keep body and soul together by scraping up the remnants of the ship's stores. There were days when we had no bread, and as for meat, we had become true vegetarians with no vegetables. We had a small income, as Niels and Paul had found several days work a week in the "open hearth" at the steel mill across the river, and Niels, together with Paul were fishing for shrimp in the river at night. This brought in a few shillings. But we were running low on salt beef, salt pork and beans, only a week's supply left. We again approached the consul, who told us that the captain, as agent for the ship, was liable for a fine of $100.00 a day for failing to supply the crew with provisions. Also, the ship's crew were entitled to fifty cents (.50) per day extra for recreational purposes. But all this conversation was not filling our stomachs.

### October 29, 1926

This morning Captain Robson suggested that matters could be speeded up a bit if the ship's logbook and articles could be brought to the Sydney court by the ship's mate, along with one man as witness. There followed a spirited attempt on the part of the mate to bring the captain around to this point of view, but to no avail. The captain flatly refused to go to Sydney, or to allow any of the ship's papers to be removed from the ship. He declared that only a court summons would budge him. Arrangements for summoning the captain, along with needed articles and logbooks were being made, when news arrived from Sydney that the Admiralty Court would hear the case of the ship *Forest Dream* on November 18th. Twenty days hence! Justice in Australia is not only blind, but woefully slow at best. But at least something was happening.

*October 29, 1926*

The captain brought on board a prospective buyer, looking at the hold, rigging and gear. There was talk of the ship's sale bringing in two thousand and five hundred pounds from this buyer. Everyone's spirits took a rise on hearing this, as it meant that all of our claims would be met.

*October 30, 1926*

This morning we are driven to the necessity of finding some solid means of subsistence. The captain, being in the same boat as ourselves where a shortage of food was concerned, has agreed to accompany three of us to the American consul for some help in obtaining subsistence for the crew. Nothing could be done, insisted the consul. Because of certain technicalities he was unable to provide us with any relief. He suggested that we all go to the local police station. The captain went back to the ship, and the rest of us trotted off to the police station in Newcastle. In twenty minutes our case was laid before the Sergeant of Police, ration bills were issued, and we were on our way to the welfare office, accompanied by a policeman. We were each given a one week ration chit in the amount of five dollars and thirty-five cents.

Under police escort, we were taken to a grocery store, where we bought rice, beans, sugar, flour and bread, all approved by our escort. By pooling all our rations with the remaining ship's stores, we were able to keep the wolf, or dingo, from the door. The captain and mate were told if they wanted to eat, they would have to contribute. They elected to pay the $5.35 rather than accept the humiliation of a welfare chit. Almost every day the children of Stockton were sent to the ship with gifts of home-baked bread and cakes for the crew.

We have lost two of our shipmates to wanderlust. Niels and Paul, bored and frustrated with inaction and problems besetting the ship, decided to explore the "Back Country" by following the dirt road that borders the Hunter River heading inland. Niels requested and received from the Police, a months advance on their chits, bought groceries, took along some canvas for a tent, several pots and pans, waved "Goodbye" and disappeared up the road. They planned to be gone for at least a month.

There has been trouble about cooks. When our jewel of a cook Timmerman left for the hospital, the galley was at a loss for direction. Some of us made attempts at cooking, but the results were terrible, so the captain engaged a cook at union wages.

The new man, a slight dark chap with curly hair, seemed made for the galley. He came on board, straightened up things in fine order, and we looked forward with anticipation to a proper "Timmerman" supper. After getting the galley in shape, he went aft with a list of stores he wanted for the days meals. We all had some misgivings, so we came up on deck, praying for the best. Then came the explosion!

The cook came flying up the captain's companionway, three steps at a time, shouting that he, and only he, was going to boss the galley. He passed through the port galley door and out the starboard door, and with his old felt hat and a Boston bag, was over the gangway and halfway down the river bank towards the ferry, when the captain came out of the companionway, asking, "What was the matter with that fellow, anyway?"

The next candidate was the very opposite, big, stolid and grizzled. Every move was deliberate, but Tom produced some very good dishes during his brief reign. He was with us only three weeks, and finding out that the chances of ever receiving his pay are questionable, he made an effort to pry his wages out of the captain. It was like trying to get blood out of a stone, so Tom gave up in disgust and left threatening to sue the ship. He ended up by joining a coastal steamer, where stores were plentiful, his wages good, with the certainty of being paid.

Our old cook, Timmerman, now recovered from his wasting illness, had a part time job ashore and was living in a pleasant little place on King Street. In spite of all that he had endured at the hands of the captain, Timmerman was ready to come back, so strong was his attachment to the ship and the crew forward. It needed but little pursuasion on our part to bring him on board, bag, baggage, and phonograph.

The stodgy old ship's cat, Victoria, showed signs of new life when Timmerman stuck his head over the bulwarks. Victoria, too, had lost weight. The captain was only too glad to have him back. Our galley problems were now at an end.

### November 3, 1926

Word from our solicitor informs us that our case will be heard on Friday the fifth. The captain will report to Sydney, taking all ship's papers with him. Within sight of the end of our long, weary journey to this hearing, we thought it best to find out what our solicitor's fee would be. Our second mate, who had some experience in libel cases, said it was usually ten percent. Our solicitor told us that he expected the same.

### November 5, 1926

The wage claims of the crew versus the Barkentine *Forest Dream* was heard before the Supreme Court Judge in Admiralty at Sydney, New South Wales. An immediate sale of the ship was ordered. Formal notice and advertisement appeared in the *Morning Herald* of November 10, 1926, to the effect that Frazer, Uther and Co., Auctioneers,

invited tenders for the *Forest Dream*, announcing that the ship's sale is set for November 23rd, at noon. The captain was called to Sydney to place all accounts before the Registrar of the Court.

### November 23, 1926

All of our hopes lay in the owner of the *Forest Dream* making a successful bid, for such action seemed wise. Freights were high at twenty-six shillings a ton to the west coast of South America, and the *Forest Dream* could continue under her old house flag, as well as the United States flag. Indeed, we were all so sure that the sale would wind up in such a manner, that we made no effort to prepare ourselves to leave the ship.

Imagine our complete surprise, when we learned that the ship had been bought by the mate and second mate of the *C.B. Pedersen* for the paltry give-away sum of one thousand pounds ($5,000), a ship worth at least $100,000. We were all outraged. This meant that all hands would be evicted, and the Swedish flag would be flown over the ship. Moreover, after court costs, harbor dues, etcetera were deducted, the remainder would scarcely cover half of the wages due us.

But there was no time for lamentations. As we were now by law distressed American seamen we went in a body to the office of the American consul, where after a few minutes talk, the Consul made arrangements for our board and lodging until such time as we received our wages, whatever that might amount to.

We had come to love the ship, and we were dismayed and felt insulted over what had occured. For the first time we sensed we had the sympathy of the consul. But now we were his problem. Abandoned American seamen are the responsibility of the United States of America.

### November 24, 1926

The official report of the sale of the *Forest*

*Dream* was confirmed today at a session in our solicitor's office. The Registrar sat in the inner room and checked each statement of wages due, taking each man in turn. Three of us had left allotments to our relatives in the United States. Some time before, Thomsen had received notice from his mother that no allotments had been received since last May, over six months ago. In making out the statement of wages due, the captain had deducted these allotments, stating he thought they had been paid.

The Registrar refused to accept the captain's deductions. He would not countenance the disrating of Thomsen and the carpenter, nor the reduction in wages nor the petty fines that the captain had imposed on Thomsen. Also disregarded were the fines meted out to the second mate for taking days off in Mauritius.

*November 25, 1926*

This morning, all hands were busy packing their gear. Suitcases, seabags, trunks, chests, and whatnot, were passed over the rail to the waiting launch below. When loaded to the gunwales with men and baggage, the wheezy old launch bore off downstream, while we all stood up and gave three cheers for the good ship, *Forest Dream*. Niels and Paul had not returned from their trip up-country, so I placed their possessions with a mutual friend in Stockton. We hoped they would return while we were still in Newcastle, but this was not to be. Thus, by force of circumstance, we were obliged to desert our ship in a foreign land, the voyage unfinished, our plans and dreams torn to shreds.

CHAPTER SEVEN

# NIELS
# ABLE SEAMAN

*STARBOARD WATCH*

The voyage from Port Louis to Newcastle was made in forty-five days. Although the wind was abaft of the beam most of the time, it was a rough and stormy voyage, for we had sailed too far to the south after leaving Mauritius seeking the "Roaring Forties", with its gale force winds and gigantic seas. Life was miserable for One-Eyed Louie, Paul and I in the second mate's starboard watch, as the captain had taken complete control of the watch from Mr. Johnson, the second mate. There was scarcely a day that the captain did not have his beak in the barrel of rum brought aboard in Port Louis. Louie and I had become accustomed to his abuse, but it was difficult to absorb the vile treatment he heaped on the timid, compliant, second mate, a kindly person whom we were fond of.

I rebelled on a number of occasions, and in one instance when he struck me, I retaliated verbally with the consequences of bringing on another of the captain's *Mutiny on the Bounty* pet scenarios. I was called to the after cabin, read the ship's log, charged with being a Bolshiviki, and received yet another fine. So I wrote down several more particulars on the spare sheets of my Bowditch, where I chronicled all the captain's sins. I looked forward with inner satisfaction to the day when I would have him brought to justice. I was determined that in some way he would pay for his drunken derelict action at the wheel which had cost my dear friend Frank his life.

Outside of Newcastle we were met by a tug, which towed us up the Hunter River. We moored along the river bank near the small community of Stockton. A small ferry made the five minute trip across the river to the City of Newcastle. Three other large sailing vessels were moored nearby. A branch of the Seaman's Church Institute, a British world-wide Seaman's Welfare Association was located in Stockton. It was managed by a delightful English couple with a family of three daughters. The eldest was Cora, twelve years old, with one eye blue and the other brown. They lived at the Mission House where open house for seamen was held every evening except Mondays. Seamen of all nationalities were warmly welcomed.

Mac, Paul and I spent many of our evenings there, playing cards with the children and the local young women, closely supervised by the manager and his wife. Stockton was a very friendly community, the populace going out of their way to welcome us and take us into their homes.

The three other large American sailing ships moored along the bank of the river opposite the little village of Stockton were the *Forest Friend*, the *Forest King*, both sister ships of the *Forest Dream*. All three vessels had been built in Aberdeen, Washington, for the lumber trade. The *Forest Friend* had arrived with a part cargo from Noumea, New Caledonia, where it had delivered a cargo of lumber from the Northwest.

There was much disharmony between the officers and the crew forward. The first week of their arrival, we had a front seat to four or five fistic exhibitions on the grass banks opposite the *Forest Dream*, with resultant bloody noses and black eyes. At least, we on the *Forest Dream* had managed to avoid such conflict. In addition to the American ships, there were two other sailing ships, the Swedish four-masted bark, *C.B. Pedersen*, loading coal for the west coast of South America, and the *Woodburn*, a Finnish bark, also taking on a cargo of coal.

Joseph W. R. Bone, a New Zealander, was one of the able seamen on the *Woodburn*. We became friends.[1] An able seaman named Harry Lundberg from the *Forest Friend* became a close friend in later years.[2]

Our moorage was near the edge of the village. Further along the road from the village stood a small red school house. The school children had to pass by the ship on the way to school, as did the school teacher, a pretty young woman whom we all followed with our eyes when she passed by the ship. She ignored all our artful attempts to engage her in conversation.

--------

[1] We met again later in Seattle, Washington, were roommates in the Thirties, and partners and companions in the fifties, sixties and seventies.

[2] Harry became a world-renowned legend in his lifetime as organizer and head of the powerful Sailors Union of the Pacific.

I thought up a plan to attract her attention. There were three little boys who on their way to and from school, always paused to watch us as we sat on deck sewing sails. I selected a particularly bright young seven year old and taught him a rhyme to recite to his teacher, which went as follows: "There was a queer bird called the pelican, whose beak could hold more than his belly can. He could hold in his beak, enough food for a week, and I don't see how in the helican." A week later, a ruffled, irate, pretty young school teacher, came to see the captain and wanted to see the man who had taught a little boy a rhyme he had recited in her classroom. She wanted him punished.

And that was how I met Doreen Marlborough, with whom I spent many happy hours at the beach, and enjoyed occasional Sunday dinners at the home of her parents.

One day we were called aft and told by the captain that the orders to load a cargo of coal for South America had been cancelled. The charterers of the *Forest Dream*, as a result of the financially disastrous seven months' voyage of the ship to Mauritius, had gone into bankruptcy. The ship was to be sold at public auction, and there were no funds with which to pay the crew their wages for the thirteen months they had served on the vessel. It appeared that once again we would find ourselves penniless seamen in a foreign country. He said we would be permitted to live on board the *Forest Dream* until it was sold. Pending the sale of the ship, it was likely that some arrangements would be made for subsistence, with help of the American consul or local agencies, all subject to reimbursement from the proceeds of the ship's sale. Later, arrangements were made for the crew in the company of a police constable escort to visit the grocery store nearby, where welfare credit vouchers would be issued for food.

We received no cash which was a sore point with us. When we returned to the ship after our initial food issuing excursion, we had a meeting in the foc'sle on the subject of cash flow. After some discussion, we hit on the plan of surreptitiously peddling any saleable item of ship's gear we could remove from the ship. At night we would clamber aloft to cut down running rigging and remove blocks, all of which had a ready market ashore. The proceeds from the sales would be shared equally amongst the crew forward, including Timmerman, the cook. In a short time, most of the ropes, paints and tools disappeared from the ship, and we all had a bit of pocket money.

The captain and the mate were furious, but they could not keep watch on us twenty-four hours a day. Every morning they would come on deck and make notations of what they thought had been removed during the night.

When the *Forest Dream* first arrived in Newcastle, I had filed assault charges against the captain with the American consul, as well as protesting fines and disratings that the captain had imposed on me during the trip from Mauritius to Newcastle. Much time was spent on this matter which eventually came to naught.

The details concerning the matter have escaped my memory. I do recall that Malcolm was keeping a written account of these happenings in his journal, the contents of which he usually shared with me.

There was not enough money to go around, so with Paul, I paid a visit to the steel mill across the river. The manager listened to our tale of woe and sent us to the foreman of the open hearth, a kindly man. He agreed to employ us on an alternate basis, Paul one night and me the next night. We worked in a section of the mill called the "open hearth" where roaring furnaces and streams of glowing molten metal were evocative of Dante's inferno. We lasted only ten days, unable to stand the heat. Our next venture was fishing for shrimp in the river. Paul and I made some nets and spent hours every night up to our necks in the river seining for shrimp. We cooked and hawked these about Stockton.

Fishing at night in the cold river was gruelling work, so we decided to discontinue fishing and explore the interior of the country by following the dirt road that bordered the bank of the Hunter River. We made a trip to Newcastle and talked to the chief of police. Explaining what we had in mind, he agreed to our request for each of us to receive one month of welfare food chits in cash. This amounted to six pounds, almost thirty dollars. With provisions, a piece of ship's canvas and a couple of pots and pans from the galley, we headed up the river road. The sun was bright, the days long, the road dusty, and the countryside wooded. We encountered very few farms, only three or four each day. I can recall that there were many kookaburas (laughing jackasses) along our route, who made loud cries that sounded like a person's loud laughter.

Paul and I were happy and healthy, not a care in the world, no concern for the future, just looking forward eagerly to the next turn of the road or bend in the river. At the end of each day, we would put up our homemade tent by stretching a rope between two trees, preferably across the road from a farmhouse. Invariably, no sooner was our tent up, than someone from the farmhouse would approach us and invite us to dinner and to stay the night. All the families were eager to visit and talk with us, which was understandable, strangers being a rarity. Paul entertained them with stories of Mauritius and I with tales of ships and the Pacific Northwest. We began to think of ourselves as two medieval story-tellers, wandering about the countryside performing for our food and lodging.

One late afternoon we came to the small village of Raymond Terrace. Just before entering the village we had to cross a small stream about a foot deep which ran across the road. On entering the village, we noticed a group of perhaps thirty men standing around a large corral, where an auctioneer stood on a raised platform. We stood near the edge of the group and listened to the bidding.

The last horse to be brought out was a small, almost miniature, scrawny and dilapidated animal. As he was led about in a circle, there was much laughing, but no one bid on this little creature who trod wearily around in a circle with such a dejected and unwanted demeanor that I felt a flow of sympathy. I shouted, "Sixpence!" at which point the auctioneer quickly slammed down his gavel and said, "Sold!" much to my astonishment and amid much laughter from onlookers.

We learned later that the animal was regarded as a public nuisance, which no one had the heart to destroy. Almost every farmer in the community had owned it at one time or another to transport their children on its back. So it was hopefully included at the end of every horse auction.

The auctioneer was so delighted at the prospect of the horse leaving the community, that he threw in a bridle, a piece of rope, and a gunny sack for saddlebags to contain our stores and culinary equipment. I received a pink bill of sale that read, "Sold to Niels Peter Thomsen of California, U.S.A. one taffy gelding, "X" on the rear left shoulder." Appropriately, we named him Sixpence.

After purchasing a few provisions, we headed out of the village, no longer penniless wanderers, but two men of substance, the proud owners of a horse. At the outskirts of the village we stopped by the small stream, upended Sixpence and scrubbed him down with branches. He accepted our beauty treatment in a docile, friendly manner, making us both feel that he really felt like he was one of us.

We made saddlebags out of the gunny sack by closing both ends and splitting the sack down the middle. The sides were filled with pots, pans, and provisions, and we took off down the road. Paul led Sixpence, and I brought up the rear with a long willow switch urging him along. Sixpence looked happy. We felt great.

There was only several hours of daylight left, so we made our way to the riverbank, rigged up our tent, built a small fire and had our evening meal. Sixpence munched on some oats we had bought in Raymond Terrace. As we traveled further inland the distances between farms became longer, the woods thicker, and the road became more like a trail for a horse and cart.

The people were outgoing and hospitable, and we had no concerns about food. We were offered fresh-baked bread, butter, milk, chicken and meat at almost every place we stopped. We had many offers of employment, which we graciously refused with the explanation that it would soon be time for us to return to our ship. We followed the river road for a week, the farms being in some cases miles apart. We could not always depend on being near a farm when we stopped for the night.

We came to a large estate owned by one of the earliest settlers in the region. It consisted of hundreds of square miles, and the home base, next to the river, was a massive stone house with many outbuildings. The family name was "Robards", and the head of the family was an active, white-bearded man in his eighties. His wife, also in her eighties, with four sons and four daughters, all unmarried, comprised the family. They welcomed us as though we were visiting grandsons. They said that every six months they sent a scow loaded with produce and livestock down the river to Newcastle, an eight day trip, stopping at several river towns enroute to sell and barter. The next trip was to be in ten days, and we were asked if we wanted to make the trip back to Newcastle. It was high time we returned to Stockton and the *Forest Dream*, so we decided to leave on the scow, taking Sixpence with us.

We rode horses, swam in the river, fished, and in the company of the sons, we rode to outlying work stations which were a part of their empire. In the evenings we were pampered and fussed over by the four daughters. The evening meal was served in baronial fashion at a long table, seating at least fifty people. At the head of the table sat Mr. Robards and Mrs. Robards. As guests, Paul and I sat on either side of them. Then in order came the family members, followed by the foremen and lesser employees, some sitting "below the salt."

About two weeks after our arrival, the scow set out for the journey down the Hunter River to Newcastle with a full load, including Sixpence. We made a number of stops at small towns, Paul and I helping the two Robard brothers with the steering and taking care of the livestock. We kept to the middle of the tree-lined river, flowing slowly at a speed of three or four miles an hour. This was a speed that Paul and I were familiar with on the *Forest Dream* in light airs.

On arriving at Newcastle, after thanking them for their many kindnesses, we solemnly said our goodbyes to the Robards. When they had disposed of their goods and the scow they would be heading back home. Paul and I, along with Sixpence took the ferryboat across the river to Stockton, tethered Sixpence in a pasture next to the *Forest Dream*, and reported on board the ship. To our dismay the only persons on board were the captain and the mate, French Louie. The ship had been sold, and the week before, the crew had been required to register with Mr. Rankin, the American consul in Newcastle, whose jurisdiction we were now under.

Malcolm Chisholm, One-Eyed Louie, Archie Horka and Chris Jorgensen had already been sent back to the United States bound for San Pedro, California. Timmerman the cook and Hubert were ensconced in a hotel in Newcastle, waiting for passage to a ship bound for New York. The cabin steward was an Australian who had been sent to Port Adelaide.

Paul and I were devastated over not having been able to say goodbye to our shipmates. I would have insisted on going with Mac, for whom I had a worshipful attachment. I was never to see or hear from him again.

The following day we were instructed to register with Mr. Rankin, the American consul in Newcastle, to be assigned a hotel room, and stand by for an assignment to a vessel.

*As I near the end of this narrative, I ask myself, "What about the mate, French Louie?" One would have expected him to be the key player in this chronicle of the Forest Dream. The answer to this question is that he was the Eminence Grise behind the throne, a very clever scoundrel, who manipulated the captain, essentially a stupid man. I can still see French Louie's speculative, glinting, black eyes studying and planning the captain's next move. He was like a spider in the center of a web, weaving, watching, and encouraging the captain in his follies. He was by far the most dangerous of the two, and it was only because of the hundred cases of whiskey that we were saved from his personal attentions.*

After a week of saying goodbye to our friends in Stockton, and having climbed aloft to the royal yard to look over the steel mill, Newcastle and Stockton for the last time, Paul and I were assigned to the American freighter *Chincha*, loading coal for Montevideo, Uruguay on the east coast of South America. After discharging our cargo of coal, we were to proceed to Buenos Aires, Argentina, to clean holds and load a cargo of bulk wheat for Bassens, France, a small town on the Gironde River which flowed into the Bay of Biscay. I shipped as an able seaman and Paul as an ordinary seaman. Paul had many relatives in France, and we felt the world was waiting for us.

We gave Sixpence to a friend in Stockton. The last time we saw him, the new owner was leading him about in a small pasture near the *Forest Dream* with a young boy on his back. To Paul and me, he would always be a cherished memory.

As the ferry carried us across the channel to take

us to another ship and another age, I looked for the last time at the *Forest Dream* with its towering foremast and four guardians etched against the evening sky. I knew that her image would forever be engraved upon my soul, and a profound wave of sadness swept over me for the boy I had left behind.

CHAPTER EIGHT

# DECK LOG OF ARCHIE HORKA
## ANOTHER CREW MEMBER'S VIEW:

*The author corresponded with Archie Horka, another member of the crew after finding him once more forty years later. Horka joined the crew in Adelaide, Australia and sailed to the end of the voyage at Mauritius. His thoughts give insight to the men and the diarists of this voyage. He describes with greater detail certain events and activities Chisholm and Thomsen overlooked. Horka was probably the last of the crew to see the* Forest Dream. *The vessel was sold to a Swedish company five years after this voyage and eventually destroyed by fire.* Editor

MARCH 4, 1926, Thursday: Today I signed on the barkentine *Forest Dream* bound for Mauritius in the Indian Ocean. It has been three months since I paid off from the Norwegian bark *Skaregrom*. I had been living on the American barkentine *E.R. Sterling*, paying the steward and his wife for my board. One of the seamen on the *Forest Dream* had fallen from aloft and been killed, and I would be taking his place in the crew of six sailors. I arose early this morning and headed for the outer harbour where the ship was moored. On coming on board I was assigned a berth by one of the crew and put on my working clothes, turning to painting the hull of the ship. It felt good to be working again. At noon I met the crew, the five sailors who would be my shipmates for the next few months.

The one who made the greatest impression on me was an Alabama chap named Chisholm whom we called "Mac". We found that we had interests in common, he being an excellent water colorist and fine sketcher, fond of poetry and literature. Then there was the youngest man on the ship, Niels Thomsen of Danish descent, and the handsomest young man I have ever set eyes on. His hair was a flax like shock of wildness, and out of his lean, bronzed face shone a pair of bright blue eyes. He,

unlike Mac, was an irresponsible young fellow, caring little for the future and seeking only freedom and adventure.

There was Louie, aka "One-Eyed Louie", an old time sailing ship sailor with a great wealth of experience. Another sailor was a black-haired Dane who rarely spoke a word and was poor company. The remaining sailor was a cheerful, gregarious German. It appeared that it might be several weeks before the ship put to sea again.

MARCH 17, 1926 — Wednesday: Early this morning we were towed out about two miles and anchored abreast of Semaphore Beach, not too far distant from a Norwegian bark named *Pamilia*. She is bound for Callao, Peru, to load a cargo of guano (bird dung) for the United States.

While laying at anchorage there came to our ears some disquieting rumors that the owners were bankrupt. That unsettled our peace of mind and made us doubtful if we would ever get to Mauritius. Rumors are usually rampant when a vessel is beset with such mischances as had been the lot of the *Forest Dream*.

MARCH 24 — Wednesday: The carpenter has orders to fire up the donkey boiler, and it looks like business tomorrow.

MARCH 25 — Thursday: The mate rouses us out at 6:00 A.M. to get underway, the wind being southeast and promising us a good start. A nippy bite in the air sent us about our work with alacrity. Besides, there was the desire in everyone to get out of this bight and be on our way. With the fore-topsails, headsails and three lowers she was brought around to head southwest by south. Sail after sail was crowded on, and at 8:20 A.M., we cleared decks and went to breakfast. Everything was on her except the gaff topsails. Close by the wind she threaded her way down St. Vincent Gulf under a freshening southeaster. Gradually the buildings of Adelaide were lost in the morning haze. Before sundown we had passed the blink of St. Althorpe Island Light and were now practically clear of narrow waters. Everyone was jubilant at such a feat, so neatly and quickly executed. The men's spirits revived and some even ventured to say that it looked like the vessel had a change of heart. For myself, she exceeded expectations.

MAY 1 — Saturday: The days are cloudy though the nights are brightened by a full moon, and we peer our eyes out looking for Rodriguez Rock. Our search is unsuccessful, and everyone is cast down in despair. The low morale and low spirits are not sweetened by the pessimism of the first mate, French Louie, who is constantly slurring the captain and his sloppy navigation. He hints that we will be picking up coconuts in Madagascar, yet. Such talk in the hearing of a restless crew by the chief mate certainly does not make for harmony. How ignorant these men are — not to understand the simple rules of ship psychology. What possible wasp's nests may they be poking at by these stupid tactics?

But the wind holds true, and surely we reckon that they need only to ascertain the latitude of the island of Mauritius and run it out. This hope sustains us in spite of pessimistic moanings that we may miss Mauritius. All these problems have been caused by the captain's mishandling of the ship's chronometer during his days of drinking. Many birds about. Tropic birds and terns which signify that land is not far distant.

MAY 3 — Monday: We all have had a very nervous night peering expectantly into the darkness for a light that should be flashing or some other sign of land. But we have a premonition that land is just over the hump.

With daylight we experienced the thrill that comes only to those who voyage under sail. Days of weary plodding, then a period of uncertainty, speculation and wonder if we will make it. Then, suddenly it presents itself on the horizon and all doubts and fears about the faulty chronometers vanish. We have arrived, and once more in touch with civilization, an exhilaration that one never feels on a precise, mechanical operated steamer.

Shortly after six in the morning we sighted a smear across the horizon ahead. We had often been deceived by clouds that looked similar. But there was a dimness and a shade to this smear that differed from the clouds about it. The captain rushed up from the cabin at the shouts of land, and with a smile verified our discovery. Soon after, a range of peaks reared themselves from the water to the southward of the first clump, and he recognized Mauritius. The smaller clump had been Round Island. We jibed ship, stood north parallel with the land now about 25 miles off, and though we moved aggravatingly slow in the light breeze, the land grew more and more distinct and large. We had cheery news for the watch below when they rolled out of their bunks for breakfast. They scarce believed us.

There was little or no wind and we drifted about until dark with the island tantalizingly near. The word was passed that we would lay off the island until daylight before heading into the harbour of Port Louis.

What an impressionable night that was! An

oppressive silence, the ship quiet and unreal as a shadow, silhouetted boldly against a bejewelled background of myriads of stars, rising and falling to a gentle ground swell. The island, lying to the eastward loomed darkly and dangerously near in the deep tropic night, its jagged pinnacles enshrouded in a night mist lending it a distorted, mysterious appearance. And in one's nostrils came the fresh, invigorating breath of vegetation, of river beds and jungle growth and an aroma of wood smoke intermingled into a delightful smell which one never encounters except when approaching land after months at sea.

Under the blinking stars the ship lay like a seabird at rest with head beneath its wing and awaiting dawn before it takes wing again. Now and then the stillness is interrupted in its work of hypnotic obsession by a creak of spars and the clank of metal aloft in the rigging or a disturbing splash of "dugong" (sea cow) gamboling about the ship. Then, being at the wheel, one was brought to the realization that he was a part of all this, by the "clomp, clomp, clomp" of the second mate's heavy shoes as he paced the poop deck.

MAY 7, 1926 — Friday: We have been having head wind for the past three days unable to get close enough to Port Louis to pick up a tugboat to tow us into the harbour. Most discouraging. At daylight a slight breeze came up in puffs, and we managed to get closer to the harbour. The forenoon wore well on, the watches laboring to take advantage of each gust or breath of wind. Then about ten o'clock what looked like a small boat coming out to us, then another smaller boat, and the ship was agog! At last we were to be spared further agony of baffling currents and frivolous light airs. The outer world was reaching out a helping hand.

Though small, the boats slowly moved us towards the harbour entrance. Mr. McNeil, the owner's agent, was on board one of the boats. We

were three months overdue, and he had been waiting for us that length of time. The boats were manned by diminutive Hindus with delicate handsome features and slight frames. We were towed to a small corner of the harbour where we dropped our anchors and ran stem lines out to two buoys astern. Meanwhile the crew rolled up the sails on the yards and thus ended a voyage of "tradewind days" with a run that was one day over the record in mileage from Australia, the trip taking forty-three days from Adelaide. Had we not spent four days trying to enter Port Louis, we would have made the trip in thirty-nine days.

Foremost in the minds of the crew was the hundreds of dollars of wages that they expected to receive. The ship's articles stated that the crew would be entitled to one half of the wages due them when the cargo commenced to be discharged. However, it appeared that the owner's credit at the Bank of Canada was in trouble. The captain was much wrought up at our request for money and had to admit that he also did not like the look of things where money was concerned.

The captain told us that he had cabled the charterers bank for funds and had been told that the Bank of Vancouver had promised him a reply. When he gets funds, he will do what he can. Now we have been told that no money will be forthcoming from the bank. Saturday he gave us each some rupees, which amounted to $28.00 with the promise that we will get more when he receives some. Previously we had discussed among ourselves in the foc'sle head and decided that if money was not forthcoming we would stop working. However, we would be patient for another week. We shall see.

All this week Hubert and I painted the yardarms aloft. Chris and Louie mended sails. Mac was assigned as night watchman and Niels was over the side chipping anchor plates. With all this air of uncertainty and inaction hanging over the ship, everyone felt sullen and disinterested. Even the first mate, usually full of ambition and alacrity went about sullen and indifferent. Work proceeded steadily but leisurely for it looks like we will have a long stay here in Port Louis.

MAY 16, 1926 — Sunday: Mac Chisholm and I, finding each other's companionship harmonious and congenial, chose this day to take a walking trip through the limits of the town and into the countryside on roads that were bordered with palms and eucalyptus trees. We are both distressed and ill at ease over the disturbing rumors that there is no market for our cargo, insolvent owners, etcetera. All these problems are uppermost in our minds. Also, Niels is sick with a fever and is reduced to staying in his bunk. He is a very ill man. The mosquitoes which attack a person sleeping on deck are a real white man's pitfall in the tropics.

MAY 19, 1926 — Wednesday: A veritable army of small black fellows came on board to work cargo. They shift the deckload by sliding plank after plank over into the lighters and no machinery is needed. This is all right for the 2"x 6" boards, but wait until they have to unload the 12" x 12" timbers. An air of activity pervades the ship once more with white clad, helmeted tallymen and agents about and bustling little black fellows sending timber over the side.

MAY 21 — Friday: Niels is so ill with fever that we advise him to ask to be sent to the hospital. He broached the subject to the "Old Man" (captain) who callously tells him that he has no time for him. But when the young fellow went down the gangway with the intent of going ashore to tell this to his doctor, our good captain found time to write him a hospital slip. Armed with this, Niels visited the port doctor. After some deliberation on the agent's part, he was admitted to the paupers' ward at the Civil Hospital. That evening Hubert and I visited him and found him feverish, but at least under skilled care and attention. His only complaint was that there were no dainty female nurses to attend to him.

MAY 25 — Tuesday: Last night about eleven o'clock I was awakened by a lot of loud talking and yelling on deck. I rushed out and saw the captain lying bleeding on the deck and the first mate standing over him. Mac was nearby and told me the two had been fighting. The captain was unconscious so I fetched a bucket of water and began bathing the captain's head when the mate, who was pounding his chest and shrilly shouting that the French lion was superior to the British: "The French lion never dies!"

Seeing us administering to the captain, he seized the bucket of water and dashed the contents in the captain's face shouting, "This is the bucko' way of applying smelling salts." The Old Man, drenched and artistically bespattered with blood was helped to his cabin. But the mate would not help — not he. All he wanted was a bucket of water to clean himself up. The smoke began to clear by now and later the captain called for the mate and an understanding was arrived at. The mate, still stirred up, came forward to the foc'sle to have more vino with the crew and assured us that save for a black eye he was still the "top dog".

The next morning the Old Man faced the world with a smooth, serene though bloody face, but the mate, poor man, had a big black shiny starboard eye.

JUNE 7 — Monday: The first letter arrived from Grimstad, Norway, where I had spent two months on board the *Skaregrom*, my last ship. From Gudvig, of course, and after reading its contents, I was greatly depressed. She persists in sorrowfully maintaining that she cannot allow me to address her in affectionate phrases as before. I am vexed at trying to find out the problem. Is it all maidenly pretense, a pretended indifference, or is it a change of heart that is passing from one fancy to another?

JUNE 10, 1926 — Thursday: Today the captain brought news that we have received orders to go to Newcastle, Australia, to take a load of coal to South America. The news is received in various ways, some happy at the thoughts of Chile and the Spanish girls, while others are cast into the depths of the prospects of another protracted voyage. Some letters were received after much waiting and watching, but none from Gudvig.

JUNE 13 — Sunday: Mac, Niels and myself have decided that we will scale the local peak, the highest on the island called Le Pouce, "the thumb". A local person will be our guide. We have with us our lunch and an American flag to plant on the top. I will also bring my camera.

Thus fortified we prepared for the ascent; the real climb was up the steep rock the final 500 feet. We left our bags behind, taking only our camera, binoculars and an American flag. The pinnacle was approached from the south side through a steep, dense jungle. Then suddenly the peak thrust itself before us, the vapor drifting past and sometimes hiding it completely. We were now anxious for the final scaling. We had romped with the abandon of goats, for with the wine and the mountain air, we were fairly intoxicated. Our guide told us we must be careful during the scaling, leaving all monkeyshines behind. This sobered us up, and we set to the task of climbing.

We crept up the steep path on hands and knees, clutching at tufts of grass often at the very edge of an abyss that yawned before our eyes. For ten minutes we crawled and finally emerged with a cheer of exultation at the summit. Atop was planked a square cement pedestal about three feet in diameter and four feet high, which had been formed

here by the crew of a French ship in 1881. We planted the Stars and Stripes in the hole in the pedestal and sat down on the few feet of safety. In truth we were perched upon a very limited square of safe footing.

The information on the concrete informed us that the height was 3,500 feet. All about us was grey fog. The mountain mist hid the world below, but we sat about until well after noon when the sun thinned the vapors away. We then beheld a grand spectacle. To all sides rolled the green isle; close at our feet the rugged sister hills of Le Pouce, farther west the city of Port Louis running out to meet the broad sheet of blue Indian Ocean that rose to meet the sky. To the south was stretched miles of geometrically arranged sugar fields watered by streams whose courses could be traced by dense growths of trees. No matter where one pursued the landscape, it always terminated in the sheet of blue. We had before us the entire island of the Isle de France.

We carefully retraced our steps down the side of the pinnacle, sliding on our spinal ends and muddying ourselves. It was all sport and fun, and we had a jolly laugh even when we sat for photos in a rain squall. It was a rich and satisfying experience.

JUNE 14 — Monday: An exceptionally hard day. We lowered the cargo booms, dismantled all the gear and strapped it up neatly, falls, guys and topping lifts; then bundled the whole lot into the bos'un's locker. Also hoisted two tons of coal on board for the ship's galley. All preparations being made for going to sea. Royal, upper topgallant sails and spanker bent in the afternoon.

JUNE 15, 1926 — Tuesday: All clear for sailing but still no action. Mac and I visited the sailing ship *Favell* tonight, the Finnish school ship with the forty man crew whose company we have enjoyed for the past month. We borrowed the cook's wind up gramophone and had a jolly good time.

Youth! We showed them our photographs and Mac's sketches. We had made some good friends on the ship and we promised to keep in touch. The *Favell* will always have a warm place in our memory.

JUNE 20, 1926 — Sunday: Together with the strapping fellows from the *Favell*, Mac, Hubert and I tramped to the Pamplemousse Botanical Gardens where we had visited in the early part of our stay in Mauritius. The sun tried to discourage us with its broiling rays but there were many water spots along the way, so we did not mind. The road led through many villages where our mass formation, our outlandish clothes and manners caused the villagers to gape in wonder. We had a plentiful supply of food and drink in our packs which we spread on one of the park's tables. After viewing the gardens we started on our return to Port Louis. On the way back we sang marching tunes and sea chanties. We all enjoyed the outing.

JUNE 23, Wednesday — *Prince of Wales Birthday*: Holiday on board. Mac, Niels and I are invited to the cadet quarters at the Lime Police Barracks to spend the day with our cadet friends. The cook again graciously loaned us his wind up gramophone which proved the hub of activity. Without it we would have had to fall back on our powers of entertaining, so this is a rest for everyone. The room was about sixty feet long and there were billiard tables, chess and card tables. It was just a crowd of young men. We had a good time dancing the quadrille. They saw us off to the ship at the dock and bade us farewell. The wine and vermouth had given me a splitting headache.

JUNE 27 — Saturday: The Old Man was hardly ashore an hour before he hurried back all in a sweat, bursting with news. We saw the mate hoist the Stars and Stripes and come running forward to tell us that the ship had been released and was free to sail. A

feeling of joy and relief swept through the ship. Even Second Mate Johnson said, "Dot's a blessing."

AUGUST 6 — Saturday: We have been making great progress towards the Antipodes this past few weeks with mostly strong westerly winds and the ship averaging over ten knots. Today we have light northerly and northwesterly winds, and we have sighted Jervis Bay. During the morning watch while handling the braces to square the yards, the captain, in a fit of temper made a faux pas. Young Thomsen was not belaying the sheet fast enough to suit him, so snatching the rope out of Niels's hands, he struck him violently in the chest with his fist sending him hard against One-Eyed Louie, upsetting them both.

Thomsen immediately asked old Louie, "Did you see that, Louie?"

Louie confirmed, "Yes, I did."

Niels turned to the second mate Mr. Johnson and asked the same question. He received the same reply.

The captain, who had been drinking, seemed to take notice that his act would have to be answered for. After this incident he treated the watch with more civility.

Another such incident sobered him still more. The following night he was abusing the docile old second mate, who finally to our great surprise retorted that when we got to Newcastle he would see to it that this business of knocking people about and calling them names was made known. More words followed, but the direct result was noticeable as the captain spread sugar profusely, even beginning to behave like a doting father.

AUGUST 9, 1926 — Monday: The succeeding 48 hours were an ordeal. We cruised about the bight, tacking every four hours, sometimes twice in a watch, trying to get closer inshore against a strong westerly offshore wind. The wind and the current would not let us get within ten miles of Newcastle, but the wind is clear and dry.

AUGUST 10 — Tuesday: Spent the day tacking back and forth, and by dark we were about eight miles outside the harbour. The day closed with a glorious red sunset, and we made preparations for another night of pulling braces and handling sails.

We had finished supper, and the sun had just dropped below the horizon when someone on deck shouted that a small steamer was making for us out of the dark background of Norah Point. As it came closer we made the vessel out to be a tugboat, and there was joy throughout the ship. He passed us a towline in the dark, and no one noticed that it was the tailrope of a wire hawser that we made fast to the ship's towing bit. We had been expected to make fast the wire, but in the darkness had mistaken the rope splice for the wire. It was another hour before we again received the towline and began heading under tow to Newcastle Harbour. At three A.M. we dropped anchor in Newcastle Harbour, furling our sails enroute, having made a record passage from Port Louis to Newcastle in forty-two days.

AUGUST 11 — Wednesday: We hove anchor this morning and were towed a short distance up the Hunter River to the small village of Stockton where we moored to some pilings next to a green meadow. Out went the gangplank.

NOVEMBER 4 — Thursday: Three weeks ago Niels and Paul, bored with lying about in Stockton, decided to go on an extended exploring trip by following a trail up the Hunter River. They departed with a canvas tent, pots and pans and headed up the river. Today they showed up, having floated down the river on a produce barge. They had a wo-begone little old horse with them named Sixpence. It seems they had bought him at an auction in a small town about fifty miles up the river. By dint of much exertion they managed to make the horse carry all their baggage heaped upon the feeble old horse. Niels gave it to a local person who rode his children about in a nearby field.

NOVEMBER 23, 1926 — Tuesday: This evening Niels (who had signed on the American steamer *Chincha*) came on board in a great hurry to tell Paul that he had made arrangements with the captain to ship him as an ordinary seaman on the *Chincha.* The captain will sign him on at sea as there is no time to check with the consul. Therefore, Paul packed hurriedly with my help and left with Niels. The family is breaking up.

DECEMBER 15 — Wednesday: Today Malcolm Chisholm shipped out in a coastal ship *S.S. Monarch* on voyage to Port Pirie. I wonder if I will ever see him again.

DECEMBER 21 — Tuesday: This afternoon the barkentine *Forest Dream* which had lain framed in our window for over a fortnight, let go from her moorings and was towed out of the harbour. We watched her make sail, first the main, then the mizzen, jigger and spanker. When well clear of the land and making the fresh northeaster fair, she shook out her square sails that we had overhauled so neatly. Old Johnson, the second mate, came up for a look through the glasses and bitterly remarked, "A fine ship gone to hell."

We followed her until the housetops hid her from view. And didn't she look pretty? Though far off, we could see square upon square of canvas forming in silhouette against the eastern sky as the toy like fabric pitched and reared to the swell.

Thus ended the episode of the *Forest Dream* so far as we were concerned. Never had we dreamed it would end thus, but good luck to her. She is in her

element at least, and though it is under a foreign
flag, *she is a windjammer at sea.*

PART III

*CHAPTER ONE*
# U.S. MERCHANT MARINE
# S/S CHINCHA

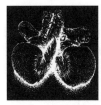 Two individuals in the crew of the *Chincha* stand out for me, for antithetical reasons. The Irish bo'sun, Nolan, a 230-pound, thirty-five year old bully who took particular delight in assigning me to the most miserable tasks, and the other person was an ex-prizefighter from Boston, about fifty years old, named Callaghan. Callaghan had taken a lot of punishment during his years in the ring, boasting two cauliflower ears, a broken nose, plus scars and broken teeth. He loved to show his scrap book and talk about his boxing career. He neither smoked nor drank, was a fine shipmate, and well liked by all. Callaghan thought I moved quickly and might have some potential as a boxer. We soon became good friends, and we shadow-boxed, punched the bag, and skipped rope all the way from Australia to South America.

On arrival at Montevideo, Uruguay, the crew received an advance of fifty dollars, and all hands went ashore the first evening to look the city over. Most of the sailors headed for the red-light district. It was dark when Paul and I came ashore. As we walked along the darkened waterfront street, a man came running out of an alley flashing a gold watch that he said had been stolen. He offered it to us for twenty dollars. I was able to get him down to twelve

dollars. Further along the street, a man ran out of an alley exhibiting a diamond ring, also said to have been stolen, and offering it for twenty-five dollars. After some discussion, Paul bought the ring for eight dollars.

What simpletons we were. We had a drink in a restaurant bar and returned to the ship by way of the red light district, alive with wide-eyed adventurers of all nations. We passed hundreds of open windows displaying enchanting, partially clad women extending invitations to one and all. It reminded me of the windows in the home for delinquent girls in Fresno, California, where as a ten year old boy, I had to pass on the way home from school.

When we arrived back on board ship, we examined our purchases, congratulating one another on our maturity and shrewdness, having spent our money wisely, instead of foolishly on wine, women and song. There were twelve berths in the sailors' foc'sle, mine being a top berth in a far corner. Parallel to my berth ran a series of steam pipes, a good feature in cold weather. The disadvantage lay in that the insulation surrounding the pipes was the home of thousands of cockroaches. When I slept, they would crawl all over me in their nightly search for food.

About four in the morning we were awakened

by noisy exclamations from five or six sailors grouped around the table in the center of the room. Listening to their conversation, we learned that each of them had purchased either a ring or watch the previous evening, paying as much as twenty dollars for a ring, and thirty dollars for a watch. Subjected to the bright light on board ship, the watches were found to be of brass, and except for the hands on the face of the clock, had no works. The diamond rings were also of brass, set with cut glass. Paul and I said nothing about our shoreside business acumen. In the morning we quietly gave our jewelry the deep six.

We spent a month in Montevideo, arranging to take night watches, so we could spend the days strolling about the colorful city, mingling with the friendly people. Paul and I usually had lunch in a cheap restaurant, drinking local wine, and sitting on a park bench admiring the beautiful, black-stockinged Uruguayan women walking by as on parade. After unloading our cargo of coal, we proceeded up the River Plate to Buenos Aires, Argentina, where we would remain for almost three months, cleaning the holds and loading bulk wheat for France. Paul and I spent the first week sightseeing. The piers berthed scores of ships from as many different countries, and the Seaman's Welfare Center held amateur boxing matches every Friday night.

Callaghan thought his protege needed testing, so he arranged a match for me with a sailor from a German ship, who was my weight of 125 pounds, with a body like Hercules. Callaghan was ecstatic in his role as my handler in the ring. The match was to be four three-minute rounds with each of the participants to receive ten dollars. The German sailor was a rough customer, and I was fortunate to survive the four rounds on my feet. By the time the last bell sounded, Callaghan had come to the conclusion that my hands were too light-boned, and that perhaps we should abandon his dream of my

having a pugilistic career. With swollen lips, ringing ears and sore ribs, I whole-heartedly agreed. Poor Callaghan, the gentleman he was, refused the five dollars, not abiding by our arrangement that we would share my ring earnings equally. This was our first and probably his last fight promotion venture.

Buenos Aires was clean and beautiful. The center of the city was full of spacious parks, holding many statues of the country's heroes. It was a seaport with many attractions for seafarers. A typical dance hall, of which there were many, consisted of a gigantic dance floor with a large second floor balcony at one end, where sat fifty or sixty attractive young women, each equipped with a violin or cello. The strings of the instruments were soaped so no sound could be produced, the music being generated by five or six legitimate musicians in the group. The girls would alternately saw away for an hour, and for the next hour, scantily dressed, would mingle with the patrons on the dance floor - a veritable sailor's paradise.

One evening on our way to the Seaman's Church Institute, Paul and I had dinner at a small restaurant which boasted a four piece stringed orchestra. One of the violinists was a dark haired, petite, very pretty girl of about eighteen. I fell instantly in love. The following evening I came alone to have dinner and sent her a red rose in exchange for a smile. This went on for four nights when the restaurant owner took pity on me and invited me to have dinner with the orchestra during their intermission.

Her name was Marita, and there was a slight problem that would require delicate handling. Her brother arrived at midnight every night to escort her to the bus station. Marita arranged to come to the city every afternoon at three o'clock. We would meet at the bus station, and after coffee in a small restaurant, we would spend three hours in the park before she reported for work. We wandered about the park, holding hands, thrilled at being close to each other, saying and doing all the things that innocent young lovers say and do. In the evening I would show up at the restaurant to have dinner with the orchestra in the back room, and later in company with her brother, escort her to the bus station. The custom of the country did not permit her to be alone with a man after dark, so our romance was a harmless, happy interlude. After seventy years I can still see her face and hear her happy laughter. We always found something to talk about, although she spoke no English, and my Spanish was even more limited. When we sailed from Buenos Aires, we exchanged photos, and I promised to return.

The voyage from Buenos Aires to France took three weeks. On arrival at the mouth of the Gironde River in the Bay of Biscay, a French pilot took us up the river to the small town of Trompelou, not far from Bassens, where we moored at some pilings along the river bank. Several days later we commenced discharging our cargo of bulk wheat that would take many weeks. The unloading was performed entirely by women carrying the wheat ashore in baskets perched on top of their heads.

A short distance from the ship was a local restaurant and bar in which most of the crew gathered every evening, drinking beer and socializing with the local farmers. True to my usual custom, I spent my time in a far corner with the innkeeper's youngest daughter. With a dictionary between us we did our best to communicate. I can recall the only complete sentence I memorized, "Donnez moi un mille baisers," (give me a thousand kisses).

The chief mate announced that the ship's next port of call would be New York, and that we should anticipate leaving France in about two months. Paul's mother was from a socially prominent family in Paris, and he had promised to visit them while in France. He had never met his cousins, and asked me to accompany him, but the bo'sun refused

to give me the time off. So Paul made arrangements to visit Paris before the ship was to leave.

One Saturday afternoon, Paul, two sailors from the ship and I took the bus to the nearby town of Bassens, stopping at the first bar we passed. To our surprise, who should be sitting in the bar but the bo'sun, Nolan, with an attractive young woman of about twenty at his table. It was an informal establishment, so in a conversation with the proprietor I learned that the young woman was his eldest daughter. She was a bareback rider with a circus during the summer months, who had come home for the winter to help him in the bar. I could not resist openly admiring her, which she could not help but notice. At our table, we sat around for an hour socializing and drinking wine, when I saw the lady at the bo'sun's table leave and go upstairs. A few minutes later, with no thought of the girl who had preceded me, I had need to visit the bathroom, and started up the stairs.

We met half way up on the narrow stairs, stopped, and then without a word, she took me by the hand and led me into a bedroom, locking the door behind us. She sat me on the bed and began undressing me. It was my twentieth birthday, I had been going to sea for five years, and I had never known a woman. My initiation lasted almost an hour, and to this day I remember it as one of my life's memorable experiences. We came separately down the stairs to find the bo'sun purple with rage, and I was to feel the brunt of his wrath all the way to New York. At every opportunity, I rubbed salt in his wound with a knowing smile as I hugged to my breast this precious gift from the lovely, circus bareback rider from Bassens.

On arrival in New York the ship's crew was paid off. Paul had become ill while in Paris with his cousins and was forced to check in at the Marine Hospital. I stayed at the Seamen's Church Institute rooming house on Front Street near the Battery. The rooms were a dollar a night for a single room, and fifty cents for the dormitories where, at five-thirty in the morning the room clerk would pound on the door with a large rubber hammer, announcing that the rooms must be vacated by six o'clock. I was in the chips, so I opted for a single room and slept until eight.

The following day I registered at the Sailors' Union Hall, and then went out to the Marine Hospital to see Paul. We agreed that I was to try for a ship to the West Coast, and he would contact me through the Sailors' Union Hall in Seattle when able.

I went to look up Frank Garlock's father, a janitor in a large apartment building in New York City. I recognized him immediately when I saw his round Polish face, the image of Frank. He was delighted to see me, we had a cup of coffee and I told him about Frank, leaving out the gruesome last hours of his life. I gave him Frank's watch and personal papers, along with the six thousand dollar insurance policy I had been carrying around for fourteen months.

Three days later, after paying Paul a goodbye visit at the hospital, I shipped out as a quartermaster on the intercoastal passenger liner *Finland* bound for San Francisco via the Panama Canal. The *Finland* carried six quartermasters who shared the same room at the end of a passageway. The quartermasters, whose duty was to steer the ship, were divided into three duty watches of two men in each four hour watch; midnight to four A.M., four to eight A.M., eight to twelve A.M. I was assigned to the four to eight watch.

At five A.M. nearing the anchorage off the eastward entrance to the Panama Canal, the engineers opened the steam valves to the anchor windless forward. The steam pipe leading through the quartermaster passageway burst. The door to the quartermasters' room was open and all four quartermasters were cooked to death instantly. I never even knew their last names. Their bodies were shipped back to New York.

The *Finland* arrived in San Francisco on April 24, 1927, eighteen months having elapsed since I sailed from Victoria on the *Forest Dream*. I paid off the *Finland* and took a Greyhound bus to Seattle.

A week later I shipped out on the passenger vessel *Emma Alexander* as quartermaster. The *Emma* was a coastwise ship of the Admiral Line which plied between Seattle and California ports via Vancouver, British Columbia. I sailed on the *Emma* until I came ashore in Seattle on the twenty-fourth of November.

At the union hall I ran into Joe Bone[1], an acquaintance from my days on the *Forest Dream* in Newcastle, Australia, and we became roommates. It was a cold winter in Seattle. Joe and I lived at the Columbia Hotel at First Avenue and Seneca Street, just around the corner from the hall of the Sailors' Union of the Pacific at 83 Seneca Street. The union agent was Pete Gill. We hung around the hall, but shipping was practically non-existent. After getting up in the morning we would walk down to King Street for breakfast at a Japanese restaurant, stop by a friendly, sociable owner of a second hand clothing store, where we would spend an hour chatting, and then move on to the union hall to sit until noon. Joe would smoke his pipe in some corner, and I played chess or cards.

One evening while strolling along King Street (skid row) I saw the back of a man's head that I recognized instantly. He was standing up against a counter that opened on to the street, where he was having a bowl of soup. It was old One-Eyed Louie from the *Forest Dream*, whom I had not seen since Paul and I had left the ship to go exploring up the Hunter River in Newcastle, New South Wales, Australia. It was a joyful reunion. When he learned that I had little or no money, he took from his

---

[1] For more information on Joe Bone see the long footnote at the end of this chapter.

pocket eight twenty dollar gold pieces and gave me three of them; all the while apologizing that this was all he had left after being paid off his ship the previous week. He knew that I would have done the same for him.

This was the breed of sailors that no longer exists. We were always paid off in gold coins before the shipping commissioner at Colman Dock. The ship's captain and the commissioner sat at the end of a long table with stacks of gold coins of five, ten, and twenty dollar denominations.

We who sailed in sailing ships thought of ourselves as a cut above the men who sailed in steamships. Instead of sensible canvas seabags, we carried heavy, wooden sea chests from ship to ship, and we shunned rubber boots (preferring high leather boots that had to be kept soft by rubbing with saddle soap or grease from the ship's galley.) For a week, the three of us, Louie, Joe and I, met every day in the Sailors' Union Hall to reminisce and exchange information on old shipmates. A carefree wonderful existence.

Joe kept me afloat by footing the costs for food and room rent, marking down my share in his book of accounts that he always carried with him. He even noted the five cents for a newspaper I might ask him to buy. It never occurred to him to buy one for himself. We ate all of our meals in the Japanese restaurant, Joe paying and entering my share in his little black book of accounts.

Paul and I had exchanged a number of letters. He had shipped out on a British freighter for Europe. On his return to the United States he planned to come across the country by bus, meeting me in Seattle. On January 10, 1928, I shipped out as a quartermaster on the U.S. Army Corps of Engineers hopper dredge *Culebra*, based in Aberdeen, Washington, where it was dredging Grays Harbor.

One historic event took place in the three months I spent on the dredge. Reason long forgotten, I had a circumcision. The ship tied up at the dock in Aberdeen every Saturday morning for the weekend in port, so I made an appointment to have the operation performed in the doctor's office on a Saturday morning at ten o'clock. I left the doctor's office, boarded a street car to the end of the line, and from there I had to walk over a mile to the *Culebra*. Halfway back the Novocaine started to wear off, and I hobbled the rest of the distance to the ship. I spent a miserable week. At night my penis would swell up and tear at the stitches. To get some relief, I would sit on the edge of the bed with my feet on the cold steel deck to reduce the swelling. Steering the ship two four hour watches each day, I stood with my legs wide apart, jumping with pain every time the wheel made contact with that bruised, pitiful, little object hanging between my legs.

The crew found the spectacle amusing. I have always felt a special attachment to Aberdeen, where a small but relatively once important piece of my anatomy is hopefully, enshrined. I left the *Culebra* in February and returned to Seattle, checking in at the Columbia Hotel. I paid off my debts. I had to practice frugality, as Joe Bone, my banker, had shipped out on a vessel bound for the east coast.

Shipping was slow at the Sailors' Union Hall, so I began walking on board laid up ships in Lake Union and found a part time maintenance job scraping rust and painting on a small freighter, the *W.A. Perkins*, anchored in Lake Union. The wages were only three dollars a day, and the work only from Monday through Friday, taking home fifteen dollars a week. It would take care of my room and board, but I would have to forego even an occasional movie. It was a hard winter for seafarers and other waterfront workers.

JOSEPH W.R. BONE. During the period the *Forest Dream* was moored in Stockton, New South Wales, Australia, I became acquainted with a New Zealander, Joseph Bone, a seaman on another sailing ship, the *Woodburn*, Joe and I were the same age, and on meeting again in the Sailors' Union Hall in Seattle we decided to team up together. This arrangement was somewhat like the "buddy system". We sailed on the same ship whenever possible, and when ashore, roomed and had our meals together. It may have been for a feeling of security, and to help overcome the loneliness of not having any family.

We were complete opposites in temperament. Joe had been reared in an austere, religious orphanage, devoid of warmth or love, and he had run away to sea at the age of thirteen, sailing on small sailing vessels on the coast of New Zealand. He was mild-mannered, righteous to an extreme degree, illiberal, filled with prejudices, and deeply scarred by his early life experiences. Why we were attracted to one another I really never understood. He was introverted, rarely spoke, and had difficulty communicating. I felt very protective towards him as I imagine one would feel for a brother or a sister. I am certain that had any occasion ever put his life in danger, I would have risked my own life for him. He was penurious, hoarding every penny, while I was a spendthrift, spending every dollar as it was earned; a trait I have never been able to overcome. I have never placed any value on money. Whether or not I had any, never seemed to seriously concern me, even to this day.

Irrespective of all our shortcomings, we were bonded in some inexplicable fashion. Joe always opposed anything I said or did. I made all the decisions and he always followed along in a grumbling way with dire predictions of disaster. He never took a chance on anything in his life, except once, when I induced him to buy stock in my small steamship company. I was just the opposite, always ready to gamble my last dollar. I would give anything to hear Joe's analysis of me, which I am sure would be more hypercritical than my description of him.

I lost track of Joe for about sixteen years from 1938 to 1954, when I formed Aleutian Marine Transport Company and bid for the mail contract to service forty isolated native villages in the Aleutian Islands and the Alaska Peninsula. While creating the shipping company I thought of Joe. Through a mutual friend I located him on the east coast, having been an employee of the Gulf Oil Company for ten years as a ship's bosun. I induced him to become one of my partners in the mailboat venture where he served with me as a seaman on the mailboat *Expansion* for the ten years of the mail contract. When I decided to go into the fishing business and founded Aleutian King Crab in Dutch Harbor, Alaska, Joe came with me as night-watchman at my processing plant. When the company was sold five years later, his investment of five thousand dollars had increased to three hundred thousand.

After the sale of the company in 1969, I moved to the West Indies and Joe moved to San Francisco. He made his home in a third rate transient hotel on Mission Street, a place like the old Columbia Hotel on First Avenue in Seattle where we had roomed together forty years earlier. He still lives there after twenty years of retirement in a small room overlooking an alley, no private bath or telephone, still wearing a hickory work shirt. He eats in cheap restaurants and has a net worth of over two million dollars. On rare occasions when I can reach him on the hotel desk telephone, three flights of stairs from his room, the first thing he says is,"This is the hotel phone and we can only talk for three minutes." He takes pride in telling me that he can live on his Social Security check. For several winter months he goes to Los Angeles and lives as a paying guest of some friends I introduced him to fifty years ago. Poor Joe, never to have loved a woman of his own, have children to love and cherish, or anyone to care for and protect. Joe is my oldest friend and companion of my youth, and at his instigation we are irrevocably estranged. I miss him now in the winter of my life.

CHAPTER TWO

# THE CAPTAIN'S TABLE

 It was March 1928, and shipping at the Sailors' Union Hall at 83 Seneca Street was non-existent. I had been on the beach a month, and a week earlier had found a job scraping rust and painting bulkheads on the *W.A. Perkins*. Returning to my suite at the Columbia Hotel with my week's wages of fifteen dollars, I stopped at the desk to pay my weekly room rent of four dollars. I rarely received any mail, so I was surprised to be handed a letter postmarked Newcastle, New South Wales, Australia. The letter stirred up memories, it being over twenty months since I had left the five-masted barkentine *Forest Dream* in Newcastle, where it had been seized in a bankruptcy action. None of the crew had received pay for their fourteen months on the vessel.

The letter was from the United States Consul General in Newcastle. He informed me that the proceeds from the sale of the *Forest Dream* had been allocated, and that a portion of my back wages, amounting to four hundred and fifty dollars (a small fortune) was being held for me by the State Department in San Francisco. I was almost penniless, having just paid my hotel bill, and owing six dollars to my Japanese restauranteur on Jackson Street, my weekly food bill. I would be left with only four dollars. Four dollars would not get me to San Francisco on the bus or by train, and none of my close shipmates who might give me a loan were in Seattle. I had no hitch-hiking experience.

The thought occurred to me that perhaps I could stow away on one of the passenger ships of the Admiral Line. It made weekly sailings to San Francisco via Victoria, B.C. Telephoning from the hotel desk phone, I learned that the *S/S H.F. Alexander*, the largest passenger ship of the company was due to sail for California at midnight on the following Wednesday. I had never served on the vessel, but I had been on board on several occasions to visit shipmates so I had a picture in my mind of her deck layout.

To carry out my plan I needed an expensive looking wardrobe and a presentable leather bag. I took a walk down First Avenue to talk to Sam Cohen, the pawnbroker who was the temporary custodian of my only suit and my father's gold watch and chain. I showed him the letter, and with the promise of a twenty dollar bonus, he agreed to return my suit and allow me to buy a Harris tweed overcoat, a Borsalino hat, and a fine-looking leather bag — all to be paid for when I returned to Seattle. I had hoped to retrieve my watch. Sam thought I did not need a watch and insisted on keeping it, probably as additional security.

All that now remained was to get on board the ship on Sunday night, and to conceal myself until the ship had left Victoria B.C. the next forenoon. I had work clothes in my bag, expecting to be assigned to scrubbing decks, scraping rust, or washing bulkheads at such time as I was discovered to be a stowaway. I felt certain that would be shortly after departing from Victoria. Even if I were not found to be a stowaway, I still had to eat. If unable to find a way to provide myself with meals for the next four days, I would have to turn myself into the chief purser or chief mate. At any rate, the situation would cease to be critical once we had left Victoria astern enroute to San Francisco, but I would cross that bridge when I came to it.

Late Wednesday evening, carrying my bag and bedecked in my fashionable Harris tweed overcoat and Borsalino hat, I walked to the pier where the *H.F. Alexander* was moored. The ship was aglow with lights, a band was playing and scores of passengers were streaming on board. The ship lay alongside a large building. Inside a sloping ramp about 300 feet long led up to the gangway of the ship. At a table halfway up the ramp stood two assistant pursers who examined passenger tickets. I waited at the bottom of the ramp for a time, and when a group of six or eight college students started up the ramp, I followed thirty feet behind. I lingered until they had been waived on by the ship's pursers. As I approached the table I motioned in the direction of the group ahead, pointed to my bag, saying, "Carrying this for my friend," and kept on going.

After walking on board I began looking for the men's lavatory. I quickly found just the type I desired. It had five or six booths where the doors extended to within two feet of the floor. I entered one of the booths, placed my bag on the seat, locked the door from the inside, and crawled out under the door. I then went into the lounge, hung my overcoat on a rack, and mingled with the crowd of passengers and visitors.

Shortly thereafter a deck steward moved about the deck sounding a melodious tune on a xylophone-like instrument while announcing "All visitors please go ashore." I remained in the lounge until the ship cleared the dock, enroute to Victoria. The weather was misty, and a light rain was falling. Most of the passengers had retired to their staterooms. Seeing no crew members about, I put on my Harris tweed overcoat and went out on deck to explore the after cargo deck. Under a canvas cover I found an unlocked Cadillac sedan with several blankets on the back seat. I brought my bag from the lavatory, placed it in the car, rolled up in the blankets and slept soundly until seven in the morning. I was awakened by the sounding of the ship's whistle entering Victoria Harbor.

An hour later, the ship sounded its departure whistle from Victoria. After surveying the immediate deck area, I crawled out of the car with my shaving gear and refreshed myself in the men's room. Now that the ship was underway to San Francisco, it was no longer of any great concern were I to be exposed as a non-paying passenger. There were no laws which carried a penalty for being a stowaway on board ship, and our next port was my destination. Should I be discovered, I would be put to work for my passage, in which case I would be provided with meals taken with the ship's crew, thus solving a problem which eventually would have to be faced. My plan was to render myself as inconspicuous as possible while I figured out how I would eat, having only four dollars.

After making certain the coast was clear, I donned my Harris tweed overcoat and my Borsalino hat. I took a stroll about the decks, including going up to the navigating bridge, giving the officer on watch a morning salutation and commenting on the fine weather, as any first class passenger might have done. On the way back from the bridge, I passed three common stowaways being kept busy scrubbing the decks under the watchful eye of the ship's bo'sun.

While in the act of hanging up my overcoat in the lounge, an announcement came over the loudspeaker that breakfast was being served in the dining room. Passengers should seat themselves at any available table. I was ready for breakfast, so I followed a group of passengers to the dining room. On entering, I saw an attractive brunette seated alone at a table. I asked for and received permission to sit at her table, and in the course of having breakfast we discovered that we were both traveling alone, and that we possibly had some interests in common. Her name was Anita Williams, a traveling sales representative for a cosmetic firm in Toronto, Canada, on her way to a convention in Los Angeles.

After breakfast while walking about the deck, an announcement came over the speaker requesting all passengers to form a line at the purser's office to make permanent dining room seating arrangements. We walked to the purser's office where I noted that no one was presenting tickets or identification. Anita and I took our places in line with the other passengers and were issued a table for four.

In the short period we had known one another, our friendship was blossoming rapidly. Thinking it might be a good investment, I asked the deck steward to have two deck chairs with blankets placed side by side in a sheltered deck area. This expensive gesture cost two dollars leaving me with only two dollars of working capital to invest in project Anita.

Having thrown caution to the winds, I decided that there being nothing to lose and just perhaps something to gain, I might as well assume the full-fledged role of a first class passenger. By this impulsive decision, instead of becoming the least, I unwittingly became one of the two most conspicuous persons on board the luxury liner *S/S H.F. Alexander*. This was hardly in keeping with my

original plan. Anita and I parted, agreeing to meet in an hour by our deck chairs.

On arriving there an hour later, we found a third chair next to ours, occupied by a distinguished middle-aged gentleman. He introduced himself as Henri de Ligne, a French architect, who had just completed a major hotel building in Vancouver. We told him we had only just met, and like many men of his age he seemed interested in promoting romance between two young people.

In the ensuing conversation among the three of us, I implied that I was the scion of wealthy parents and had done a great amount of international traveling. He would mention a certain restaurant in Bordeaux or Buenos Aires and I, having visited these cities as a seaman, would counter with the name of another restaurant or bar on the same street.

Feeling a warm friendship developing among the three of us, Anita invited Henri to join us at lunch. She appeared to be most favorably impressed by two sophisticated world travelers. In the mid-afternoon while seated in our deck chairs, we were approached by an assistant purser who, after excusing himself, addressed Anita, saying, "The captain presents his compliments and requests the pleasure of your company at his table during the voyage."

Anita was a trifle flustered and replied, "I am together with this gentleman," indicating me.

The assistant purser immediately replied, "He is included in the invitation."

It is traditional and customary for the captain of a passenger ship to select and invite one or two of the most attractive women passengers to dine at his table during the voyage, as well as persons from a V.I.P. list of passengers presented to him by the chief purser on the ship's first morning at sea.

At this point I must confess that I was beginning to ponder about my true status as a stowaway. I wondered if I might not be getting into water far over my head. Strangely enough, I was beginning to feel more and more like a first class passenger. I liked the feeling. Contemplating the enchanting possibilities that might develop in my growing relationship with Anita, I could not muster any resistance.

That evening I sat opposite from the captain at the captain's table, with Anita sitting on his right. A bejeweled dowager V.I.P. was on his left. I had the chief engineer on one side of me, and the chief mate on the other, both in full dress uniform.

I thought I looked quite presentable, having shaved in the men's room, and sporting a clean white shirt, albeit a bit wrinkled. I conversed with the captain, the ship's officers and the dowager, trying my best to appear totally ignorant about ships, just in case one of the officers might recognize me as having been a crew member on another ship of the same company. The evening went beautifully. Anita and I danced until midnight, and strolled about the deck until two, said goodnight, and I retired to my comfortable bed in the Cadillac. The following day Anita invited me to her stateroom for afternoon tea. Several glorious days rolled by. As we strolled about the deck, we were openly referred to as the honeymoon couple. I had completely forgotten that I was a stowaway. Best of all, my two dollar investment was paying dividends.

The day before the arrival of the ship in San Francisco, Anita and I were dancing at the afternoon tea dance in the lounge, when I noticed that the piano player was constantly eyeing me. Suddenly it dawned on me that he and I had served on the *S/S Emma Alexander* at the same time for one or two trips over a year ago. I had scarcely met him or socialized with him, so I felt he probably would not recognize me. During an intermission, he came over to me and asked if I had ever sailed on the *Emma Alexander*, as he thought he recognized me as someone he knew. I made a colossal mistake of denying I had served on the *Emma*, when I should have acknowledged him. But the damage had been done.

The next morning as we were passing through the Golden Gate entrance to San Francisco Bay, with the three of us in our deck chairs, one of the assistant pursers approached me and asked if I would come with him to the purser's office. Excusing myself, I accompanied him, knowing what to expect. I was not particularly disturbed, as the worst that could happen was I would be questioned and released.

The purser's office reached all the way across the ship with a door to the main deck on either end of the room. Standing in the office was the chief purser, Mr. Gillespie, the chief steward, Mr. Presser, and the chief officer, Mr. Stevens, all my erstwhile dinner companions. I leaned against the desk, one leg partly on the edge, smoking my remaining cigarette. In retrospect, thinking about my behavior in this confrontation, I feel ashamed at my callow effrontery, which for me was out of character. Mr. Gillespie was a fine person with whom I had shared a number of pleasant dinner conversations. He would be the most vulnerable to official criticism as a result of my exploits as a stowaway.

I could sense that all three department heads were embarrassed, and concerned over what the consequences might be to each of them personally, should the captain discover that he had been sitting opposite and entertaining a stowaway at his table for the past four days.

They wanted to know how I came on board, where I had slept, and how I had arranged for my breakfast and lunch. They knew where I had dined the past four evenings. I gave them an honest and detailed account, minus any reference to Anita. All this time, I was sitting with my back to the door, which was of the Dutch door type, consisting of upper and lower half-doors. The purser asked me where my luggage was located, and when I did not readily reply, he said, "Mr. Thomsen, we are not planning to keep your luggage, just tell us where it is. We are only interested in seeing that you are the first person over the gangway. Bring your luggage to this office, and as soon as the gangway is out, the assistant purser, carrying your bag, will accompany you to a taxi at the pier entrance. He will pay the fare to wherever you are going." There were no recriminations from any of the three officers, and I could almost hear sighs of relief.

I slipped off the desk, turned about, and to my horror, Henri and Anita, with whom I had been living a double life for the past five days, had been standing behind me at the open half of the Dutch door, hearing my entire confession. Seeing my expression of dismay, they assured me they thought the entire affair amazing, and me quite an admirable fellow. Henri asked me if I had any plans about where I would be staying in San Francisco. On learning I had no plans other than to collect my money from the consulate and return to Seattle, he said, "I have a double room at the Union League Club. Why not stay with me until you return to Seattle." I happily accepted his offer.

Henri left Anita and me to say our goodbyes. I never saw Anita again. When the gangway was secured, I reported to the purser's office. The assistant purser, with my bag in hand, was waiting for me. We were the first persons off the ship. The assistant purser was quite companionable. As we walked through the building to the Embarcadero Street entrance, I said to him, "The chief purser sat next to me for four days. Why did he not look me up on the passenger list?"

He replied, "He told me to look you up on the list, and I reported to him that there were four passengers named Thompsen on board. We did not know that you spelled your name Thomsen."

Outside the pier entrance, the purser hailed a taxi, and asked for my destination, whereupon I replied, "The Union League Club." He looked startled, and respectfully paid the taxi fare. We shook hands, and up Market Street I headed for my suite at San Francisco's oldest and most exclusive

men's club, still traveling first class.

I stayed at the club with Henri for four days, collected my four hundred and fifty dollars from the consulate. I checked with the Admiral Line and learned the *Dorothy Alexander,* a smaller passenger liner of the same company was due to sail from San Francisco to Seattle in four days. On sailing day I bade goodbye to Henri de Ligne, shipped my suitcase to Seattle by parcel post, and walked on board the *S/S Dorothy Alexander.*

There was a large, raised observation room on the fore part of the main deck containing leather chairs and couches. After leaving the dock, I made myself comfortable in the observation room where, except for trips to the restroom, I remained until ten in the evening. The weather was very rough as we headed for Seattle, bucking into heavy northwest seas with heavy sprays on deck.

I was feeling hungry so I headed for the lounge where I was the only occupant. I removed my overcoat, made myself comfortable in an easy chair and rang for the steward. I explained that I had been seasick and missed my dinner. Could he bring me up a platter of chicken sandwiches and coffee? He happily did this for a one dollar tip.

After my meal, pocketing the extra sandwiches, I retired to the observation room. I was the only passenger on the ship not in his room. I slept comfortably on one of the couches. In the morning it was still very rough. I saw only two passengers up and around, so I walked into the dining room and was served a hearty breakfast. I returned to the observation room, still the only occupant. This routine was followed for the entire five days of the voyage with my meal of sandwiches in the evenings, breakfast in the dining room, chicken sandwiches for lunch, and an occasional chocolate bar for dessert.

The trip to Seattle was very rough, bucking head winds and seas. Most of the passengers spent the entire voyage in their berths. When the vessel docked in Seattle, I was the first person over the gangway. Except for the night steward, I had not spoken to anyone during the voyage. No one ever knew that a non-paying passenger had made the trip to Seattle.

I checked in at the Columbia Hotel at First and Seneca, then set out to re-establish my credit at my favorite Japanese restaurant. I went to Sam the pawnbroker to settle my account and retrieve my father's gold watch and chain in the process. Two weeks later I shipped out as an able seaman on the oil tanker *Los Alamos*, making several relief trips to Alaska. On my third trip back to Seattle I paid off the *Los Alamos*.

# CHAPTER THREE

# ARCTIC FUR TRADING SCHOONER C.S.HOLMES

While taking a walk along Seattle's waterfront on a lovely spring day a week after I paid off the oil tanker *Los Alamos*, I spotted a four-masted schooner alongside the wharf at Colman dock, loading cargo. My heart missed a beat as a longing for the *Forest Dream* days engulfed me. Inquiring of a man standing on the dock, I learned that it was the fur trading schooner *C.S. Holmes* being readied for her annual six month cruise to the Arctic as far north as Point Barrow, the northernmost tip of the United States.

As I stood there, a racey Stutz Bearcat roadster pulled up near the ship. A man in his twenties walked on board. The man I had been talking to said it was the captain. I walked over to the ship's side and asked the man who appeared to be in charge and whom I took to be the mate for permission to come on board. I received a nod of assent. I asked if the ship had a full crew. He replied that they needed two sailors, and if I was interested he would take me to the captain in the after cabin. After answering a number of questions as to my experience, Captain John Backland, Jr. took me on as able seaman. I turned to the following morning, May 16, 1928.

The first mate (to whom I reported in the morning) was a tall, heavily-built Swede with a hangover from what must have been a week or two of drinking and carousing. He had a mouthful of Copenhagen snuff, some dribbling from the corners of his mouth, and he reeked of alcohol. The rest of the crew looked to be in the same condition.

Mr. Gus Carlson was a man of limited education, a quiet man of great competency in his profession. He had served as first mate on the *Holmes* for many years under the command of Captain John Backland, Senior. His seamanship skills and local knowledge of the Arctic Ocean and Bering Sea made him indispenable for this Arctic voyage.

Captain John Backland, Jr. was 26 years of age. This was his first voyage as Master of the *Holmes*. His father, John Backland, Sr, in his early sixties was a legend in the Arctic fur trading industry. He was terminally ill with cancer. He had turned his Arctic interests over to his only son who had made several trips with his father to Point Barrow.

John Backland, Junior, had led a privileged lifestyle, a product of the University of Washington where he had held the heavyweight boxing championship. One could sense that he was apprehensive in his approach to his responsibilities as master of the vessel. I found him to be a capable shipmaster, introverted, pragmatic and reserved.

This was his first command, and if he was aloof to all of his crew, except to Gus Carlson, his mentor, this was understandable.

The second mate, Mr. Clark, was the opposite of the first mate in temperament, professionalism, and Arctic experience. A rosy-cheeked, talkative man in his fifties, he was much too timid and ineffectual to be a competent officer of a sailing schooner setting out on a six month Arctic trading voyage. He reminded me of the second mate, Mr. Johnson on the *Forest Dream.*

On completion of loading our cargo at Colman Dock, we were towed to an anchorage in Elliott Bay to take on explosives. These consisted of dynamite and black powder to be used should we become trapped in ice floes enroute to Point Barrow. The captain's family was on the pier, his father in a wheelchair, for a last look at his ship and only son.

We spent the night at anchor in Elliott Bay. The following morning at daylight we were taken in tow to the open sea off Cape Flattery where we hoisted our sails enroute to Unimak Pass and the Bering Sea.

The crew member that stands out in my memory was an able seaman in his early thirties. Billy Buckmaster had been born and brought up in Nome, Alaska, during the rugged environment of the "Gold Rush" days and gave the impression of being a "tough customer". He had spent some years as a third rate prize fighter, and displayed a formidable scrap book of newspaper clippings attesting to his prowess in the ring.

It was soon obvious to all of us forward, the donkey man, the cook, two younger sailors and myself, that it was Buckmaster's intention to be the "cock of the foc"sle." I had a strong premonition that he and I would have a confrontation before we reached Unimak Pass, a month's sail from Seattle. Despite strong headwinds and resultant constant tacking into the wind, the passage was without incident, making the voyage to Unimak Pass in four weeks. We saw very little of the captain who rarely

came on deck other than to take navigational observations when weather permitted. Before entering the Bering Sea, we lay to in the lee of Unimak Island for two days, fishing for codfish, filling some thirty barrels of salt cod for our own use and for trading purposes. We also took on an extra dozen barrels of codfish from the cod-fishing schooner *Wawona* fishing nearby.

True to his bullying nature, Buckmaster had lost no time in demonstrating by his actions that he intended to take command of the foc'sle. He left the two older men more or less alone, but lorded it over the two younger seamen who deferred to his whims without challenging him. It was another situation where I was concerned. His fighting capabilities impressed me, and I hoped we could live in peace, but I had no intention of going along with his arrogant dominance of our everyday lives. I pointedly ignored him.

One day, while sitting on the bench in front of my bunk, Billy Buckmaster, perhaps out of frustration at my attitude, struck me in the face as he passed by. I leaped to my feet and we exchanged blows. The donkey man reported the incident to the captain who ordered us to the quarterdeck. I was never to fully understand what impelled Captain Backland to arrive at the decision that we should settle our differences by staging a boxing match on the main hatch the following Sunday. He may have been bored and longed for some entertainment, plus the fact that he had been boxing champion at the University of Washington.

He decreed that the bout was to be fought under the Marquis of Queensberry Rules (whom I had never heard of), and that we would wear canvas work gloves. These gloves were so abrasive, that it would have been kinder to have used bare fists. Sunday morning before the bout, he called me aft to his cabin, and asked me to sign a document that I willingly assented to the match. He seemed somewhat distant about the whole matter and expressed no concern about my improbable survival. It was an attitude I thought strange and did not fully appreciate.

The four days prior to the bout were full of unusual and extra-curricular activities, supervised by the captain. The second mate was in charge of preparing the boxing ring, putting posts on each corner of the hatch and encircling it with rope. There were mixed feelings in the foc'sle. The two younger seamen, while I had their sympathy, were not about to openly express their feelings with regard to the outcome of what they thought was a "David and Goliath" contest — they were stuck with Buckmaster for four more months.

George, the cook, and Hans Anderson, the donkey man openly supported me, but solemnly predicted that I would be chopped to pieces in the first round. All week Buckmaster spent his spare time skipping rope and shadow-boxing about the deck, apparently looking forward with great anticipation to the following Sunday.

There was nothing mixed in my state of mind. I viewed the construction of the ring with the same feelings as a convicted criminal on death row might view the erection of a gallows-tree. I went back in my mind over all that Callaghan (of the *Chincha*) had taught me. I thought of my fight in Buenos Aires where, after three rounds my arms had felt like leaden weights. I believed that if I could make it through the first three rounds, because of Buckmaster's physical condition caused by his smoking and drinking lifestyle, I might have an advantage. So I planned a totally defensive fight until the last round, and I prepared myself for a beating. But I had survived beatings before this.

At ten o'clock on Sunday morning, all the ship's crew, with the exception of the mate on watch and the helmsman, gathered about the main hatch forward of the quarterdeck. The captain appointed the donkey man to be time-keeper with instructions that there would be four rounds of three

minutes each. He was provided with a watch and a cooking pot from the galley to use as a bell. The captain would be the referee and count for the knockdowns.

Promptly on schedule, Buckmaster bounced into the ring, dancing about and punching the atmosphere with great gusto. I was a little slower entering the ring. We put on our canvas work gloves and the bell sounded. To make a long story short - I was battered about for the first two rounds without striking a return blow, while Buckmaster danced about the ring, belaboring me with punches. In the last half of the third round, Buckmaster hit me on the Adam's apple and I still recall the pain. I went down, but at the count of seven was on my feet and managed to hang on until the bell.

Then came the last round. Buckmaster was breathing heavily and it was plain to see that he could scarcely lift his arms. I closed in and battered him with ferocity. He could not retaliate and went to his knees. I was so exercised that I kept on punching him while he was down, until the captain intervened.

Buckmaster and I never became friends, but he never bothered me or any of the crew for the rest of the voyage. Several years later we met on the Seattle waterfront where he was a longshoreman working on a ship on which I was an officer. I felt no animosity as we talked of old times, and I am sure he felt likewise.

Since entering the Bering Sea, we had experienced light airs and calm seas. We were in no haste as we had to wait for easterly wind to open a passage between the ice pack and the shoreline. As the ice moved out, we would move North close to the shore between the grounded icebergs and the beach to keep from being crushed should the wind shift to the west. The *Holmes* had two small motor launches hung in davits alongside. These were used to move the ship in close quarters and calm weather, as well as towing barges and skin boats between ship and shore.

We met our first ice floes off Nunivak Island and drifted about for a week waiting for the seasonal (offshore) easterly winds to push the ice floes from the shoreline. Finally the channel between the ice and shore widened to allow us, with the help of the launches, to thread our way north. Having spent two weeks of idly laying-to waiting for an opening, it now became urgent that we make all possible speed to Point Barrow and get out of the Arctic Ocean, without being trapped in the ice by unseasonal westerly winds and resultant closing in of heavy ice flows.

Our first two stops were the villages of Savoonga and Gamble on the island of St.Laurence. We delivered our freight and began our first fur trading. The pelts were mostly white and red fox with an occasional cross and silver. The average red and white fox pelt brought at least seventy-five dollars on the Seattle Fur Exchange. Silver and cross fox brought over one hundred dollars each. The natives were paid fifty dollars in trade goods which, in the main, consisted of supplies of food, clothing and gasoline for their outboard motors. The ship also carried many kinds of notions, including silk stockings and many items of hardware. The fifty dollars in trade represented twenty dollars in cash, resulting in a handsome gross profit of over five hundred percent to the trading vessel. The normal winter catch for a trapper was approximately fifty pelts, which meant an income of one thousand dollars annually. Our next stop was Cape Prince of Wales, where a tin mine was in operation at Tin City.

From Cape Prince of Wales we moved hastily to the village of Shishmaref, and on to the village of Kotzebue, the largest settlement in the Arctic. Captain Backland's main trading post, the Midnight Sun Trading Company, was located there. Two brothers of Scottish extraction, Archie and Warren Ferguson, formerly of Oregon, operated the general trading store. Archie was unmarried, and Warren was married to the daughter of the local chief of the main tribe in the area. Hadley was a tall, intelligent, native woman held in great respect by natives and whites alike. There were three children of the marriage. This union enhanced Warren Ferguson's position as the largest and most affluent trader in the area.

Because of the shallow water in the bight, it was necessary to anchor the *Holmes* about ten miles from the village. Two major rivers flowed into Kotzebue bight, the Kobuk and the Kougarock. During the three summer months, hundreds of natives from the interior, some from as far distant as four hundred miles, would converge on the village of Kotzebue to fish for salmon, barter their winter catch of furs, and participate in group activities that took place in what was a traditional annual pilgrimage to the sea.

After anchoring the *Holmes*, we lowered one of the launches and the captain set out for the village, the donkey man operating the launch. I was selected to go along in the launch to assist in the operation of towing a scow back to the ship. The village was not visible, so we steered in the direction of smoke on the horizon, caused by the scores of cooking camp fires located on the beach.

When within sight of the village, we were met by the Ferguson brothers in their powerboat, along with thirty local walrus-skin boats (umiaks) full of people, all laughing and cheering. Captain Backland spent several hours with the Fergusons at the Midnight Sun Trading store. In the evening we returned to the ship towing two small cargo scows. It should be borne in mind that these summer months were a period of continuous daylight, the sun below the horizon for only an hour or two each day.

Discharging cargo at Kotzebue took six days. Captain Backland assigned me to supervise the unloading of the scows on the beach in Kotzebue, and as we were using two scows, I spent the six days ashore. This gave me time to walk about the village to observe and converse with the local people. Wherever I went I was followed by twenty or thirty children, all wide-eyed and curious. Living in Kotzebue at that time were six whalers who had come to the Arctic in the eighteen hundreds on New England whaling ships. They had left their vessels and married local native women. These men were all in their eighties and nineties, full-bearded and mostly bedridden, living quietly with their wives who took care of them. I spent most of my spare time listening to their stories.

I slept and had my meals at the trading store and inn kept by Tom and Molly Berryman. Tom was an Englishman, and his wife, Molly, was a local native who weighed over two hundred pounds. They had several trading posts, one on the Kobuk River and another at Selawik Lake. Their two daughters were Mabel and Esther, both attractive.

Another individual I recall was the federal commissioner, Judge Southworth, a dignified, older man with a neatly trimmed spade beard. He introduced himself to me on my first day in the village, principally to inform me that he was the law in Kotzebue. If any man from the *Holmes* was found to have had intimate relations with any of the local women, he would be removed from the ship and a marriage would take place, which he would perform. The culprit would not be permitted to leave the Kotzebue area. This announcement tended to cool the enthusiasm of all potentially shore-bound romantic adventurers, including yours truly.

The two Berryman daughters had entirely different personalities. Mabel was eighteen, had bobbed hair, was very friendly and was looking for an state-side husband. Esther was seventeen and beautiful, tall and slender with black shining hair that fell below her waist. She never spoke to anyone other than a local person. She was unapproachable, and I am certain that had she smiled on me, I would gladly have become a permanent resident of Kotzebue.

On departing Kotzebue, we headed for Point Barrow, stopping at Kivalina, Point Hope, Cape Lisburne, Icy Cape and Wainwright enroute. While anchored off Blossom Shoals at Wainwright, a strong westerly gale sprang up, and the *Holmes* began dragging her anchor towards the shoals. We paid out more chain to no avail. We put out two kedge anchors, but she still dragged. To save the ship, we slipped the hawse-pipe anchor and chain, cut the two kedge anchors loose, and headed for Point Barrow, where we anchored.

After the gale blew itself out, a steady, un-seasonable wind sprang up from the west, causing the major ice flow to surround us completely. As far as the eye could see, there was nothing but solid ice, spotted with large humps of bergs. The mate told us that there was a better than even chance that we might stay frozen in for the winter. If the ship was pushed towards the north, or east of Point Barrow, we would have to abandon the ship and be stuck in Point Barrow until spring. Captain Backland looked very concerned. We discharged the ship's cargo on dog sleds to be delivered to the village.

Tom Brower was the owner of the only store and trading post in Point Barrow. The Presbyterian Mission and a weather station operated by the U.S. Army were the only non-native facilities. The *Holmes* brought ten tons of coal for the store, which we regarded as a joke, as there were large coal outcroppings a mile from the village, available with a pick and shovel.

Except for a few inches of thawing during the summer months, the ground was frozen hard for ten months of the year. If a person died during the winter, his body would be placed in a flimsy wooden box and set on the ground just outside the village. It was normal to see the dogs running about the main street playing with the skull a week later, the flesh being stripped off. The natives regarded death as an utterly natural process of life, not having the morbid outlook of our advanced society. I made several daylong walrus-hunting forays out on the ice with some natives, all very exciting. I was given a pair of tusks as a trophy, which I still have. After about a week, the wind shifted to the east, and the greater part of the ice flow moved westward, leaving us locked in ice a mile from open water.

Freeing the ship from the ice pack became our one and only project, and we lost no time in breaking out explosives from the lazaret. We commenced at the edge of the pack and worked towards the ship, using quart bottles of black powder, fused and attached to twenty-foot long poles that we had on board for that purpose. The poles were shoved under the ice and detonated. The dynamite was placed on top of the ice. Twenty or more native boats (walrus skin umiaks) powered by outboards, were kept busy towing chunks of ice to open water.

The wind held easterly, and two weeks later we entered open water. It had been a narrow escape, as three days after we left Point Barrow, we had word that the pack has closed in on the shore permanently.

It was high time to leave the Arctic Ocean, and the *Holmes* headed South, stopping briefly at each port of call. At Kotzebue, we took on board a tall, raw-boned Swede, Fred Forslund, a giant of a man, who had just married a pregnant Kotzebue native woman named Clara. He was to be dropped off at Point Lay where he would open a trading post for the Midnight Sun Trading Company.

We unloaded Fred's winter supplies, dog team and building materials, staying three days. All of the sailors went ashore to help Fred construct his home. Except for four native families living within a one hundred mile radius, Fred would see no other human beings until we returned the following summer. That winter Clara would give birth to a daughter, and Fred would be faced with unforseen challenges that would require great courage and momentous decisions.

The homeward voyage from St. Laurence Island via Unimak Pass was fast and uneventful. We had been absent from Seattle for six long months, and all hands looked forward eagerly to arriving in Seattle. The voyage had been a great success with no major or lasting setbacks. Captain Backland came out of his shell, showing another and more cheerful side of his nature, and I had to revise my initial analysis of him. I came to the conclusion that his former withdrawn and austere behavior was due to grief over his father's terminal illness, and the burden of responsibility that went with command of the *Holmes*.

Knowing that I planned to sit for a mate's license, the captain gave me instructions in navigation, permitting me to use his sextant in taking celestial observations, a very generous act. He did not mention that he might have plans for me on any future voyages of the *Holmes*.

Inasmuch as we had no radio, the normal procedure on entering the Strait of Juan de Fuca was to signal the Cape Flattery Light Station to arrange for a tugboat from Port Townsend to meet the ship and tow us to Seattle. However, on the morning of our arrival at the entrance to the Strait, the weather was clear and a fair wind was pushing us into the Strait at a speed of eight to ten knots. The captain decided to proceed under sail to Port Townsend. This was not to be, as after several hours, the wind hauled ahead and a dense fog set in, forcing us to tack into the wind, zigzagging back and forth from one side of the Strait to the other. We tacked ship each time we picked up the sound of the surf on the beach. It was a very tricky business.

Considering the dense fog and unknown tidal currents, we could never be certain of our position, so this was at best a hazardous operation. Late in the afternoon, while on the starboard tack heading towards the Canadian shore, we struck and slid over a reef in the vicinity of Race Rock. The ship lay tilted against a large sloping rock which we later learned was called Church Rock. The ship was not taking water so it was in no danger of sinking for the time being. The fog was dense, and at intervals we kept sounding our fog horn. From the ship we could barely make out the shore line.

After about a half hour, an Indian in a canoe came paddling out to the ship. The captain asked him to send word to the naval station at Esquimalt, near Victoria, that we were in need of a tug to pull us off the reef.

When the tide changed and a swell came up, the ship began pounding its side against the smooth slope of Church Rock. This caused most of the crew members to think that staying on the ship was not safe. Together with their belongings, they left the ship and scrambled upon the rock, leaving the captain, Mr. Carlson, and me as the only crew members on board. It was a miserable night with none of us on the ship or on the rock getting any sleep.

At daylight the wind died down, shifted to the west and the fog lifted. The swells had abated, and all the crew returned to the ship. Although we had a ten or twelve degree list, the cook arranged for coffee and sandwiches.

About ten o'clock in the morning, a large Canadian naval tug from Esquimalt arrived on the scene, her decks lined with eight or ten gold-braided dignitaries. Following a conference between Captain Backland and the master of the tug, a decision was made that being high tide and the *Holmes* practically afloat, an immediate attempt to pull her back over the reef should be made.

The *Holmes* was pulled free on the first try, and although Captain Backland requested to be towed to Port Townsend on the American side of the strait, the Canadians commenced towing us to the Esquimalt Naval Base at Victoria.

I was at the wheel, steering behind the tugboat. The captain and Gus Carlson, the first mate, were pacing to and fro on the quarterdeck. The captain was very disturbed over being towed to a Canadian port, certain that a salvage claim would be made, not only on the vessel, but on the one hundred thousand dollars in furs, ivory and whalebone in the hold. I was drawn into the conversation, and seeing we were heading into a strong breeze that could take us to Port Townsend, I said to them, "Why don't we cut the towline and sail to Port Townsend on the American side?"

They both looked a bit shocked, but after they conversed for ten minutes, the sails were hoisted and boomed amidships, stand by the jibs was ordered, and the towline was cut. The wheel was put hard over, and under full sail, including topsails, we turned about and headed for Port Townsend. The tugboat assumed that the towline had parted, but by the time they had reeled it in, we were five miles away making ten knots for Port Townsend. The next morning a small tug towed us to Seattle.

I was told later that Captain Backland had settled a salvage claim with the Canadian Navy, the ship's cargo not being a factor in the settlement.

After the crew was paid off, Captain Backland took me aside and said that if I obtained my mate's license he would like to have me on the *Holmes* as a mate the next season, if I would agree to certain provisions. He explained that the Maritime Laws required a sailing ship the size of the *Holmes* have on board a licensed master and a licensed first mate. Mr. Carlson had served on the ship as first mate for many years, but he did not have a license. To evade this requirement, it was necessary, as a subterfuge, to hire a person with a mate's license to sign on as first mate, when in actuality he would act as second mate on the voyage. He explained that his father had carried on this arrangement for many years in the case of Mr. Carlson, and that Mr. Carlson was indispensable. The young captain wished to continue the arrangement, and asked if I would agree to such a condition. I told him that I had great respect for Mr. Carlson as a man and as a mate, that we got along together very well, and I would be happy to serve under him, though I officially signed on a first mate.

It was arranged that I was to keep him informed of my progress with respect to acquiring a license, and contact him in Seattle in the early spring.

I was low on funds, the wages on the *C.S. Holmes* having been only sixty dollars a month. After several weeks, Joe and I had resumed our "banker/client" relationship with Joe having the last word on whether I would be having one egg or two eggs for breakfast. Joe was content with a dish of oatmeal and prunes, his favorite breakfast.

In those days an examination for a mate or master's license included an oral examination by a board of three shipmasters. In addition to tests in seamanship and navigation, they explored your character and evaluated your moral fitness to become a Merchant Marine officer - a far cry from the marine license examinations of the 1990s.

I passed my examination with high marks,on January 24, 1929, after graduating from Captain Taylor's Nautical Academy. His advertisement in the San Francisco Examiner read, "CAPTAIN TAYLOR WILL LIFT YOU FROM THE DEPTHS OF IGNORANCE TO THE HEIGHTS OF KNOWLEDGE IN SIX WEEKS." I received my second mate's license, and on the following day, Joe and I took the bus to Seattle and checked in at the Columbia Hotel on First and Seneca. We were happy to be back to our favorite restaurant where a dinner which had cost twenty-five cents two years earlier, now cost fifty cents, including soup, and for dessert, apple pie a la mode.

I called at the offices of the Pacific Coast Steamship Company. Three days later I was assigned as third officer on the cargo steamer *Curacao*, for a round trip to Southeastern Alaska. It was my first trip as an officer, and I was fortunate in that the captain was a true gentleman named Tibbetts. He was very considerate and understand-

ing. We returned to Seattle on February 8, 1929, and several days later I called on Captain Backland at his home on Magnolia Bluff, advising him that I now had my mate's license and was ready to ship on the *Holmes* as a mate.

Captain Backland instructed me that on March first I should report to the *Holmes*, moored in Lake Union, to assist Mr. Carlson in preparing the ship for her May departure on the annual fur-trading voyage to the Arctic.

With the cooperation of Mr. Carlson, I was able to acquire an able seaman's berth for my shipmate, Joe Bone. Having served on the ship the previous year, I knew what my duties as a mate would be.

Joe and I had a month of leisure ahead of us. We would be leaving for the Arctic in May on a sailing ship on which I would be an officer. It was a great feeling, almost as thrilling as reporting to the Barkentine *Forest Dream* in Victoria four years earlier.

Two weeks later I met my old shipmate from the *Forest Dream*, One-Eyed Louie, in the Union Hall. I arranged with Captain Backland and Mr. Gus Carlson to take him with us as able seaman. This meant that two of the four sailors forward would be old and trusted friends.

This trading voyage was to be a repeat of the previous year. As a mate I now berthed aft in a tiny room next to the after cabin companionway. For the entire voyage my relations with the captain and Mr. Carlson were excellent. Time passed quickly, and under the tutorship of the captain, I took navigational sights whenever weather permitted. Thus began my interest and love for the art of celestial navigation. It was to stand me in good stead in later years, particularly during World War II in the South Pacific.

The voyage was routine and uneventful except for our stop at Point Lay where Captain Backland had established a new trading post on our homeward-bound trip the previous year. We had stopped there for several days to build a house for Fred Forslund, who was to spend the winter with his pregnant bride whom he had married in Kotzebue. Fred was a former seaman on the *Holmes* who had been left in Kotzebue several years earlier. He was a giant of a man, well over six feet four and weighed perhaps two hundred and twenty pounds. After we anchored, Fred, along with several natives, came out to the *Holmes* in his outboard boat. He told us that he had a most successful trading season with a total of over four hundred white fox skins together with a number of silver and cross fox.

He had a story to tell that I can still recall word for word and I quote him: "During the coldest winter month with only the two of us at the trading post, Clara began to have labor pains. This was her first child, and I did not know what to do to help her. None of the things I had been told to do by Clara's mother and her sisters in Kotzebue seemed to work. For three days she screamed in pain, but the baby would not come. Finally, in desperation, I tied her hands to the ceiling rafters above the bed, with her knees resting on the bed. I got behind her, and with my wide belt across her stomach, and my knee in her back, I squeezed the baby out. It was a healthy baby girl."

The whole of our trip was otherwise routine, and financially very successful. The winds were astern all the way from St. Laurence Island to Cape Flattery, where a tug took us in tow.

The *Holmes* arrived back in Seattle from her Arctic trading voyage on October 8, 1929. Joe and I stayed at our usual Seattle lodging, the Columbia Hotel. After spending two weeks applying for an officer's berth with a number of Steamship companies with negative results, I arrived at the conclusion that San Francisco, the headquarters of some large oil companies, might offer more opportunities. Joe was waiting for a possible berth as an able seaman on either the *Commodore* or the *Vigilant*, both five-masted sailing schooners sailing out of Bellingham in the lumber trade to the Hawaiian Islands.

I was anxious to sail on my license, so I boarded a bus to San Francisco. This was a time of depression, and shipping was scarce. Unexpectedly on December 17, 1929, I was hired as third mate on the Standard Oil tanker, *W.S. Rheem* for a round trip to Bayonne, New Jersey. I joined the ship in Richmond an hour before sailing time and reported to the captain. He gave me a large brass key, along with instructions to unlock the pilot house door. The key broke in the lock, and the sailing was delayed for the forty minutes required to repair the door — my first official act as third officer. On our return to San Francisco, my status was made permanent, with the vessel regularly on the intercoastal run. The round trip generally took sixty days via the Panama Canal, with a two day stay on the east coast and a five day layover in the San Francisco Bay area, loading. The captain was named Blumchen, a kindly man, who reminded me of Captain Dawson of the Sloan's liniment incident on the *S/S Dilworth*, five years earlier.

# ADDENDUM

*The following biographies of some of the crew members of the Forest Dream were written by Captains Thomsen and Horka, many years after their voyage together. They are not intended to be inclusive, but lend insight to this crew and their eventual futures. Information was collected from the four corners of the world and family members. Most are self explanatory.*

# Excerpted from the Seattle Times - August 25, 1925

Barkentine leaves to encircle the globe.

FOREST DREAM will carry lumber to Mauritius and bring back hardwoods and sugar.

Beginning a voyage during which she will circle the globe, the five-masted Barkentine FOREST DREAM left Seattle at noon yesterday for British Columbia, where she will load for Port Louis, Mauritius Island in the Indian Ocean east of Madagascar. The vessel has been chartered by Imported Hardwoods, Ltd. of Vancouver, B.C. from the owners, the Grays Harbor Motorship corporation. She will load one million feet of ties and shipments of canned salmon and flour in Vancouver and on the Frazer River for Port Louis.

## TO LOAD SUGAR AND COPRA.

After discharging the ties, which are to be used by the government railroad on Mauritius Island, and the flour and canned salmon, the FOREST DREAM will load sugar and copra in Port Louis and then voyage across the Indian Ocean to Singapore, where she will complete her homeward cargo with hardwood. From Singapore the vessel will head for Vancouver and Seattle via the transpacific sea lanes, the longest voyage from the North Pacific in many years.

The FOREST DREAM is commanded by Walter H. Myers, a veteran sailing ship Master of Seattle, who was formerly in the services of the Northwestern Fisheries Company, and at different times the sailing ship ST. PAUL and the bark GUY GOSS. He was master of the North Sea trawler IMBRICARIA which recently went from Seattle to Japan to act as convoy ship for Major Pedro L. Zanni, Argentine Army aviator, who was attempting to circle the globe in an airplane.

## MATE IS OLDTIME SEADOG.

Issac Hanson, Mate of the FOREST DREAM, is a picturesque "Iron Man of the Sea," who has spent many years aboard ships. He visited Mauritius Island twenty years ago as a quartermaster of the three-masted British MOUNTAINEER, which voyaged from Great Britain to East London, South Africa and Mauritius island, and carried sugar from Mauritius to Dunedin, New Zealand, where she loaded wheat for Liverpool. "We may make the voyage in three months, but most likely it will be six months," said Captain Myers. "It depends on what luck we have with the weather. In all probability it will be a year, before we sight Cape Flattery Light on our homeward voyage."

"When I was in Mauritius twenty years ago, there was nobody there but Coolies and Indians," said Mate Hanson. The Island produces sugar, and is in a high state of cultivation.

## MATE RECALLS LONG VOYAGE

"How long will it take us to make Port Louis? That's hard to say. If we're lucky we will be there in three months. The longest voyage I ever made was in the old full-rigged ship OCCIDENTAL. We were one-hundred and fifty-three days from Liverpool to San Francisco with a cargo of coal. By the way, she was a sistership of the ORIENTAL of the Seattle fleet of Libby, McNeil & Libby."

It is 12,500 miles from Seattle to the Island of Mauritius, just halfway around the earth by the Cape of Good Hope route, and about 11,500 miles by the Northern Australia route. Mauritius has a population of 425,000 including about 10,000 whites. The British Government maintains a large naval coaling station at Port Louis, and controls the Island, although it formerly was known as Isle de France.

## PICTURES

1. Issac Hanson, the original First Mate of the FOREST DREAM. He quit the ship in Victoria, and Captain Myers hired Louis Huet (French Louie), an old shipmate.
2. The FOREST DREAM moored in Lake Union preparing for her long voyage.
3. Captain Walter H. Myers of the FOREST DREAM.

### SHIP FOREST DREAM HELD ON DEBT LIBEL

Victoria, B.C. October 12, 1925

Special Sheriff H.W. Goggin barred the departure for sea today of the American Barkentine FOREST DREAM, laden with 2,000,000 feet of lumber for Port Louis, Mauritius. The FOREST DREAM detained over a claim by the International Towing Co. Ltd. Of $1,255.00 for towing services by the tugs Caesar, and Masset between Seattle and Vancouver. The owners of the Barkentine dispute the claim, but must pay the amount into court, pending the settlement of the issue at law, or the vessel which now lies in the harbor here with a full crew on board and provisioned for four months, will be indefinitely delayed.

VICTORIA, B.C. October 17, 1925

The Barkentine FOREST DREAM, sailed today, bound for Mauritius, with 2,000,000 feet of lumber.

# MALCOLM MCDOWELL CHISHOLM

*The astonishing account of how a portion of Chisholm's journal
became a part of this narrative of the voyage of the* Forest Dream.
*Written by Captain Niels Thomsen.*

In 1925 while the *Forest Dream* was moored in Stockton, Newcastle, New South Wales, Australia, and Paul Gueho and I were on an exploring expedition up the Hunter River, the U.S. Consul shipped as destitute seamen the American crew members Archie Horka, Louis Gimel and Malcolm Chisholm back to the United States on an U.S. ship bound for San Pedro, California. Several weeks later when Paul and I returned to Stockton via a river barge, we were saddened to learn that our shipmates for the past fourteen months had left the country without us. I was especially grieved that I had been separated from Malcolm, my best friend and mentor whom I idolized. I was never to see or hear from him again.

Fifteen years elapsed. In 1942, as a lieutenant in the U.S. Coast Guard stationed in Ketchikan, Alaska, on communications duty one Sunday I noted an item in the "Walter Winchell gossip column" of the *New York Times.* It referred to a certain Congressman by the name of Gautier from Pascagoula, Mississippi, who was involved in a minor Washington scandal.

The name Gautier struck a chord in my memory, and I recalled that while the *Forest Dream* was tied up in Australia, Malcolm often gave me letters to mail to a woman in Pascagoula addressed to Fairfax Gautier. I wrote that Sunday to the Congressman asking if he had any knowledge of Fairfax Gautier or Malcolm McDowell Chisholm.

The Congressman replied to my letter with the information that Miss Fairfax Gautier was his cousin, that she had never married, but had been engaged to Malcolm Chisholm. Chisholm had lost his life in the Spanish Civil War of the late 1930s while a member of the Abraham Lincoln Brigade fighting against Dictator Franco.

I eventually contacted the archivist for the Abraham Lincoln Brigade who transmitted the following information from their files:

"On March 2, 1937, Chisholm was issued passport #370880 and sailed with about 100 other volunteers on the *S.S. Washington* on March 10, 1937. His age was given as 36 years and the address listed on his passport was 17 Spooner Street, Huguenot, Long Island, New York. The next entry we have for him is that he was killed in action shortly thereafter at the Battle of Brunete, Spain, in July of 1937.

"A propaganda pamphlet dealing with American units in Spain were strictly volunteer units and were not as structured as you might envision a regular US military unit."

The archivist wrote in 1995, "I suggest that you check back with me in about six months time, hopefully, our organization will have received the complete records on microfilm of the entire international brigades. The records were shipped off to Moscow as the war in Spain was winding down and have not been viewed by western scholars for almost 60 years."

The further details have, not yet, been received.

I began my first effort of recording *Voyage of the Forest Dream* in 1990 solely as a chronicle of my life for the edification of my grandchildren. It was entirely from a memory going back almost seventy years.

In July 1992, a neighbor gave me a copy of an East Coast maritime historical pamphlet wherein I noted a letter to the editor from Captain Harold Huycke, a well-known collector of sailing ship memorabilia, which made reference to the sailing ship named *Moshula*. One-Eyed Louie, a sailor on the *Forest Dream* had once sailed on the *Moshula*.

By coincidence, Captain Huycke lived in the same Washington State city as me. I telephoned him, asking if he had ever heard of One-Eyed Louie. In the course of our conversation, I mentioned having sailed on the *Forest Dream* in 1925.

Captain Huycke informed me that some thirty years ago he had come into possession of a portion of the journal of Malcolm Chisholm, written while on the *Forest Dream* on a voyage to Mauritius in 1925.

I recalled that while the *Forest Dream* berthed overnight in San Pedro, a newspaper reporter had suggested to Malcolm that he keep a diary. Malcolm complied, and on many occasions during the voyage would read me passages from it. Captain Huycke recognized my deep emotional involvement and graciously made the diary available to me. I found references to myself on most of the pages, describing long forgotten events of seventy years ago. It was like a letter from the grave.

The reader will not fail to discover some variances of our versions of the events that transpired on this fourteen month long voyage. In particular, Mac makes no mention except by vague references to the primary reason for the unusual conduct of the captain and the first mate. I attribute Mac's not mentioning the hundred cases of whiskey to the fact that the twenties and thirties were years when prohibition was the law of the land, and that of the entire ship's crew was a participant in a serious criminal violation. We could have all faced prosecution.

If Mac intended his diary for possible publication, being a prudent person and in order to protect his shipmates, he might well have refrained from mentioning the attempted smuggling of 100 cases of scotch whiskey into the United States.

Any differing views, especially in our descriptions of the captain and the mate (French Louie), can be accounted for by the traditional sailing ship watch and watch system. It was like working for two different employers. On the *Forest Dream* the strong and capable first mate ruled the port watch, while the weak and ineffectual second mate supervised the starboard watch under the tyrannical, absolute control of the captain. It was my misfortune to be in the starboard watch.

The first mate would never have permitted the captain to interfere with any of the men in his watch, especially not Malcolm whom he regarded and respected as an outstanding individual and who was his obvious favorite. Malcolm was thus never exposed to ill treatment by the captain.

On the other hand, the sailors in the starboard watch, due partially to the timidity of the second mate, had no protection from the captain's brutal, drunken behavior. To survive and retain our sanity we had to fight our own battle against abuse and degradation.

The reader will see the captain and the first mate through two different pairs of eyes; one from a mature, gifted, well-educated man of twenty-five, and another through the soul of a vulnerable eighteen year old romantic, determined to challenge his tormentor again and again.

Were you to read Malcolm's diary only, you would find the behavior of the captain and the first mate of the *Forest Dream* almost unbelievable and bordering on a ghoulish nightmare. The revelation of the one hundred cases of whiskey adequately provides the answer to this enigma.

Except for some minor editing, sentence reconstruction and a few well-remembered descriptive explanations, Mac's story has not been altered. After seventy years, it is with a feeling of wonder and reverence that I undertake the telling of this story of two men who in their youth spent fourteen months together. Here is our story, told by the last survivor of this voyage of the *Forest Dream*.

# MYSTERY OF MALCOLM CHISHOLM'S LOST DIARY

While the ship lay alongside the dock in San Pedro, a Los Angeles newspaper reporter named Waldo Drake came on board the Forest Dream and asked Malcolm to keep a diary of the voyage and later send it to him for newspaper publication. The following is a copy of a letter written by Malcolm to Waldo Drake.

Port Louis, Mauritius
15 May 1926

My Dear Drake:

Here is the opus — with all the attendant crudities, but facts, Facts, Facts.

The photographs, unfortunately, were all foggy, due to aged films the local photographer tells me; however, I shall stock up on fresh ones on the return, and the gods willing, get some good sea snapshots. I am sending a handful of sketches to make up the loss.

Of course the thing has been a labor equal to the well-known task of Ulysses. At times I was tempted to heave the whole thing over the side - then again — well, you know how it is.

The two drawings of the ship — I made it with lines in mind. "It was sometimes only six hours between all sails set; and hove to under single lower topsail".

Perhaps the sketches of the men will be of some interest. Do you think an article on Mauritius; it's people, customs, etc., would be worth while? At any rate, I shall work up something, and send it along.

We expect to be here at least two months, with Newcastle as the next probable port, probable, mark.

On my return to the much desired United States I will come down to San Pedro and see you — there are some frank opinions I should like to get.

But my address is below, and I would be much obliged to you for a reply to this narrative that I am sending under the same cover — with most of the editor's "strongest ones" deleted. Until that time I am sincerely yours.

                                                                                       Malcolm M. Chisholm


Barkentine Forest Dream
Care of Imported Hardwoods Ltd.
Vancouver, BC Canada

NOTE: Mr. Waldo Drake did receive the above letter, but was never again contacted by Malcolm. A Mr. Robert Weinstein, a maritime historian and collector in the Los Angeles area, somehow acquired Mac's diary, and in the late Eighties sent it to Captain Huycke in Edmonds, Washington. It appears that for half a century Malcolm's diary lay in unknown hands.

## PAUL GUEHO

*The author corresponded with the U.S. Embassy in Port Louis, Mauritius, May 1988, seeking the whereabouts and disposition of his friend and crewmate Paul Gueho with whom he had lost contact in New York in 1925. Gueho had been travelling by bus across Canada to join Thomsen in Seattle when his wallet was stolen and he was promptly deported to the British Isles for lack of proper identification.*

The embassy located Gueho's son, Joseph Gueho residing in Mauritius. He responded with the two letters following these two documents concerning my search.

May 1, 1988

U.S. Embassy
Port Louis, Mauritius

Dear Sir:

In 1926 I was a seaman on the five Masted Barkentine, FOREST DREAM, an American Sailing ship from Puget Sound, Washington.

During my three month stay on the Island, I was the guest of a family named GUEHO, and when the ship left Port Louis I stowed the son of the family, Paul Gueho, in the chain locker, and Paul and I experienced many adventures in Australia, South America and France. We lost contact in new York, and the last I heard of him was that on his way by bus to Seattle to meet me a month later, his wallet was stolen and he was deported to the British Isles.

I would be very appreciative if you could locate any of his relatives who may have knowledge of his whereabouts.

Thanking you,

Niels P. Thomsen, Captain
U.S. Coast Guard, (ret)

**United States**
**Information**
**Service**

*Embassy of the United States of America*
*Fifth Floor, Rogers House*
*Port Louis*

*Telephone: 082347*

June 6, 1988

Captain Niels P. Thomsen
U.S. Coast Guard (ret)
5604, 16th Avenue N.E
Seattle, Washington 98105

Dear Captain Thomsen:

We have been in contact with Mr. Joseph Gueho, son of your
friend Paul Gueho, who died some years ago.  Mr. Joseph Gueho,
who is a researcher at the Mauritius Sugar Industry Research
Institute (M.S.I.R.I.), clearly remembers his father telling his
children about the "Forest Dream".  After leaving the "Forest
Dream", Paul travelled to Canada where, in a train, he was
robbed of all his papers.  He nevertheless crossed the seas to
France where he studied accountancy.  At about the age of 30, he
travelled back to Mauritius where he worked as an accountant,
married and raised a family.  Paul Gueho never left Mauritius
after that.  His son Joseph has found an old passport of his
father and has promised us a copy of the photo that's attached
to the passport and that portrays Gueho as a young man.  We will
send this to you as soon as we can, together with some relevant
dates and further details.

Sincerely,

John A. Quintus
Public Affairs Officer

I

Mrs Liliane Berthelot,
American Embassy,
Port Louis.

Joseph Guého
27 Darwin avenue,
Quatre Bornes

2nd June 1988.

Dear Mrs Berthelot,
Thank you for your phone
call following the querry of the
Captain of the "Forest Dream" about
my father Paul Guého who sailed
with him to America.
Actually father died on the
17th February 1964 at the age
of 57 leaving his wife (born Lise
Bestel) a daughter (Monique,
now Mrs Maurice Randabel) and
three sons (Joseph, Jean and
Jacques). I am enclosing

———————

II

photographs of my father's
sailor passport to the Americas
in case you would like to
send a copy to the Captain.

My father left in with a
wooden box he used to carry
along with him on his voyage.
It contains postal cards from
America and incidentally he
had written the name "Forest
Dream" on the inside of the cover
of the box with a mention
that he left home on the 18th
June 1926, reached Australia
in August. He left in November
and reached Montevideo in
December. In Jan-Feb. 1927 he

III

was at Bueno Aires ... etc

That is about all he left us
with as concerns this voyage
except that as typical of
sailors he liked to play the
flute at home and had
amongst his possessions a
strong needle and good thread
reminiscent of his job of
sewing sail on board!

The captain would perhaps
like to hear that father
married on the 21st September
1936 returning from France
where he had practised
accountancy during a few
years. He later enrolled in
the 8th Army Pioneer Corps

IV

and had the grade of Sargent.
(Please find also annexed a
photograph of him at this
time).

Please send my best regards
to the Captain of the Forest
Dream and tell him that it
was nice of him to think
about his old mate Paul Guého
and that I would be pleased
if he could give me more
details about his own career
at sea.

Thanking you for your
kind consideration

Yours sincerely

Joseph Guého

Joseph Gueho
27 Darwin Avenue
Mauritius
Indian Ocean

12 May, 1991

Captain Niels P. Thomsen
U.S. Coast Guard (retired)
3798 N.E. 97th street
Seattle, Washington  98115
United States of America

Dear Captain Thomsen:

It is with much pleasure and emotion that I am writing today in response to your letter dated the 15th of march last, the long delay in answering being due to my spending a few weeks in MALAWI on a Botanical Congress held there lately.

I quite understand that it was a very hazardous undertaking to try finding trace of a friend somewhere over the planet, and it is sad that my father, Paul, could not tell you of his joy at knowing that you are now safe and sound and living in Seattle at the antipodal from us here.

My most sincere thanks to you for having so kindly presented me with excerpts from your autographical account entitled "Journey of an Impatient Heart." On reading this most wonderful tale, impregnated with such a high degree of humanity and moral strength, drawn at times from the inevitable sorrows of life, I could not refrain from telling you how much I admire your inborn gifts of outstanding character and continual youth of heart. My father would have been extremely happy and proud at the news that you had made a meritable and accomplished career at sea and on land as well, and so much so that you had been a dearest friend of his in his youth.

As for myself, it is most gratifying to be able to send to you our most sincere congratulations and how much comforting to know that from the sailing crew of the FOREST DREAM I could still write to someone who has loved my father's companionship and shared his aspirations at a most enjoyable and critical period of his life.

He has kept an unforgettable souvenir and impression from his voyages on sail, and he mentioned to us at home that he had a friend, Niels, who had stayed at his home in VACOAS before his departure for Australia. It is only after sending your autobiography that I can at last fit together the bits and pieces I gleaned form him and realize what a hard, but at times so marvelous adventure it must have been to travel such a long way to the Americas on or under the tall masts and sails.

Your horse "SIXPENCE" is as famous to me as ROSSINANTE was to DON QUIXOTE, and how much fun it must have been to your colleagues on the wharf to see you both coming back to port from your rambles inside Australia. Anyway, out of it all, father had acquired the custom of ever being amiable, helpful and kind to all, and every person he met was always greeted with a smile first.

Unfortunately for us, our dear father left us too early. In his very last years he was really tired, but heroically kept us going through his toil til 1964, when he died at the age of fifty-seven. He had served with the 8th Army in Africa during World War Two, and the drinking water available was not of the best quality and he had suffered from amoebic dysentery there. In consequence, his liver had apparently been affected, and since then, a very slow but inexorable process of weakening health took place over the years.

On his return from France he worked for a company owned by the Closel family in operating the sailboat WANETA traveling to the oil Islands and Madagascar, and bringing hardwoods back to Mauritius. He was then the manager of a sawmill located in Port Louis near the harbour. Thereafter, and for a good many years, he was a cashier and the accountant for the "Magasine Closel," a well furnished establishment in Port Louis. However, on his return home from the war, being of a clever and inventive mind, he worked with the fabrication of wooden structures and furniture needed for new houses, schools, public buildings, and what not, for a company owned by Georges Randabel, his brother in law, at a time when the country was going through a very important process of development and increase in population. In such a small country we are now numbering around a million five hundred thousand souls.

I hope one day the family here will have the immense pleasure of welcoming yourself and your wife on a visit. This can easily be planned and arranged to the best anytime you may decide to come and spend some time in the Island on holiday. I am very glad to hear that you have much appreciated staying in the Yorkshire dales in England, and should you settle there, I am sending very good wish to you for a happy life there. The brief confines of this letter does not allow to send at one time, the so many aspects I would have liked to share with you abut ourselves and Mauritius. I am ending my letter by giving you some news about myself and my day to day activities.

I have always had an interest in nature, and with heaven's help, I have made a career in the botanical field, exploring mountains and island of this region to this day.

I am presently the curator of the Mauritius Herbarium, housing some thirty thousand plant specimens from the Mascarene Islands, Agalgo, St. Brandos, Chagos, etc.

I shall be fifty-four next august. Am married to Chantal Martial, a cousin of mine, and have one son age fifteen, whom we christened Jean Paul after his grandfather. He looks a little bit like him, and next time I shall be sending a photograph of the family.

Has your project of publication of your book come to completion yet. Should you need any further information or documents from here please let me know, and I shall do my utmost to obtain them for you.

I leave you now, Dear Captain Thomsen, sending you my best regards and hoping to hear from you.

Yours Sincerely,


Joseph Gueho

P.S. It was the time that my father was planning to settle in Canada that he was robbed of his wallet on the bus and could not meet you in Seattle, and finally came to Mauritius, where he spent the rest of his life.

## "FRENCH LOUIE" HUET
*Written by Archie Horka*
*July 4, 1976.*


Louis Huet, or "French Louie" as he was known among seamen along the Pacific Coast, was a Channel Islander-born from the island of Jersey or "Zrerrzy" as he pronounced it. At Newcastle, NSW, where we were libelled with the barkentine *Forest Dream*, the authorities' bailiff was a man named Hocquard, likewise a "Zrerrzyman". The competition was amusing.

Mr. Huet (we always addressed him as Mr. Huet) was a man of medium build, wiry and well muscled with chiseled features and black, tousled hair. He had incurred a leg deformity from an accident in the four-masted bark *May Flint* years back and it left him with a limp. Oddly enough, many of the "old shells" showed some sign of the wear and tear of life in the deepwater ships. Despite what one hears about the medical skills of the sailing ship skippers, a casualty usually resulted in some crippling or the poor man came out "feet first".

Huet was aloft in the foretop of the *May Flint* when that ungainly ship lost her rigging in one of her several dismastings. It was likely the September 8, 1897, casualty as recorded by Lubbock, page 86, in *The Downeasters*. As Louie described it for us, "men were lying in the waterways like flies." Lubbock is silent on this.

The "mate" usually wore a black and white checked lumber jacket, white trousers and the crown of a white uniform cap, a rig so characteristic of the man that, at this long-removed day, I cannot see him dressed otherwise. He was rated by his peers of the Coast as a sterling seaman, a reputation of which he was very proud. Ofttimes, when feeling "matey" he would ask old Louie Gimel, our "patriarch": "Louie, ain' I a good seaman, eh? Sometime ees no work but we always mak' him go, eh Louie?"

Usually in control of himself, he finally burst his bounds when he and the Old Man, Captain Walter Meyers, celebrated Queen Victoria's Birthday, May 24, 1926, while the ship lay in Port Louis, Mauritius. Too much stimulant was the main cause and old scores were being settled as is often the case after long days at sea. The Old Man had his mate flat on the deck-load, sitting astride and waving us off with, "This is my affair."

We had gathered around, blindly assuming that the presence of the hands forward would bring the two "officers" to their senses. The mate was screaming, "The French lie-on can beat the Dutchman anytime!" The skipper was a Boer, incidentally.

With a tremendous effort Louie threw off his assailant and in the ensuing grapple, the Old Man fell to the deck load, striking his head with a sickening crack, extinguishing all his lights! We fellows became alarmed and Mac Chisholm rushed for a bucket of water, shouting, "Gentlemen, gentlemen!"

The mate seized the filled bucket and dashed it's contents into the face of the fallen skipper, shouting for our benefit, "The Dutchman can nevair beet the French Lie-on."

The dash of cold water revived the skipper in a moment, and we were relieved to see him open and blink his baby blue eyes. Refusing our efforts of assistance, he tottered aft to his cabin, only to emerge shortly after, flexing his muscles and calling for the watchman. He would show the people that he was still "in charge" but he wore a sore head for some days after that.

That was really a birthday celebration aboard the *Forest Dream!*

At Newcastle, NSW, the affairs of the ship took on a grim aspect. The Old Man could arouse no interest from the owners at Seattle and the ship's people were denied an advance. Food was low, the cook quit and we men took temporary work ashore, maintaining our domicile aboard, however. We had libelled the ship in Admiralty and were enjoined by those acting on our behalf to "stay by" or we could be classed as "deserters". No fear, we stayed.

Huet was understanding and when we declined to perform any duties save sanitary work, he did not press the matter. Later, when we decided to seek legal redress, he joined with us and the action was registered in Sydney as "Huet and others vs. *Forest Dream.*"

Following the ship's sale just before Christmas, 1926, the people scattered to the winds as is the way of sailors but I heard later that Huet and the Old Man took passage home to Seattle in the *Sonoma* or *Sierra*. In a roundabout manner I learned later that Huet never went to sea after that, but took up stevedoring in Grays Harbor in 1926.

I should add the name of *Henry B. Hyde* to the list of ships in which he served and of this ship, the *"Onnery B. Ide"* he spoke with great pride: "Dat was the finest ship wot dem had," he often said.

The mate had his favorites among the people and 'though I was not one of them, he was eminently fair in his treatment of the men and allotted the work according to their abilities. In other Pacific Coasters in which I served, I could not say the same, but then as Fred Klebingat once reminded me, "clannishness prevailed no matter where you went."

**ARCHIE HORKA**

*Letters written by Archie Horka to the author.*

37-02 Ferry Heights,
Fair Lawn, New Jersey-07410
4th.October,1971.

Captain Niels P. Thomsen,
Aleutian King Crab Co., Inc.,
Dutch Harbor, ALASKA.

Dear Captain Niels:

I feel free to address you informally, confident that I have the right man "Nailed down."

Reading an article about Alaska by Alan Villiers in a recent NATIONAL GEOGRAPHIC Magazine, I sat bolt upright at the mention of a familiar name — Niels Thomsen! The author mentioned the schooner C.S. Holmes, 1928, etc., and I rubbed my hands in glee. After a silence of forty years-how in hell are you,fella?

Last time I exchanged letters with you, was when you were in that schooner with Louie Gimel. You were going into buying a schooner and after that I lost all trace of you. From your postal address I assume that you succumbed to "the allure of the frozen North", I believe that is the accepted phraseology. Apparently you did well, very well,indeed and I am glad for you. Good on ye, as we used to say in Australia, 'way back forty years ago. Put down your big crab-trap for a moment and tell me something of yourself. And what of Mac Chisholm and old Louie? Hubert came to this country in 1930, sailed on the coast awhile and became a Union official. Poor fellow passed away sometime in the 1950's. I had a correspondence with Charley Carter (Captain Carter latterly) with whom Mac was pally on the Aussie coast, you'll recall. Charlie too, has passed on but in the interval, he gave it as his opinion that the War likely swallowed up poor Mac.

In the intervening years I remained a sea,with the very same company I joined in 1928, United States Lines. In 1967, after thirty-nine years and at age 65 I retired, full of years, no honors but not without the proverbial "pot to piss in." I delight in my well-planned leisure, do the things I like and have very intention of living to one hundred! If things then look good, I'll consider going on further from there.

Famous "last words" those, just after the doctor declares your cadaver as "excellent autopsy material."

If I have the wrong Niels Thomsen, forgive me but I am betting "hats tore up" that you are that handsome, young fluffy-headed Dane we had with us in FOREST DREAM. Besides, there could not be two Niels Thomsens in Alaska! Or could there?

It is somewhat like asking over the P.A. system at a Welsh football match —"Is Dai Jones here?"

My Good Wishes —

Archie Horka

37-02 Ferry Heights,
Fair Lawn, New Jersey-07410,
18th. January,1974.

Captain Niels P.Thomsen,
Friendship Bay Hotel, box 9,
Bequia, St. Vincent,
West Indies.

Dear Friend Niels, Den Dansk Djaevel:

This note is owing you for a long time, nigh eighteen months but I held off for a reason. From the enclosed clipping you would know that I was aware of your intentions but how could one know where you would light next?

First off — let me congratulate you on having done something with your life, on having made something of yourself. None of us could know, back in those interesting days of 1926, how we would end up. Nor did we much care, wouldn't you agree? On the bone of our arse, we were, selling our ship from under "Unca' Walt's feet but were we worried? Hell, we had youth and exhuberant health and if any man in that strangely assorted focsle held any ambitions, they were not world shaking.

You always had a bent for doing the thing that promised to net you some fun, some adventure and the consequences were "no never mind." Like that time you and Paul Gueho decided to "go bush" while the ship lay idle in Stockton. It seems that you got as far as a place called Tea Gardens, a place where the sun was warm, the women kind to you and somebody was always giving you tea and something to eat. Then one day, we fellows in the ship were astounded to see you two "Sundowners" come a' cantering down Fullerton Road on a swaybacked hoss, waving your sun toupees like a couple of Marco Polos home from an adventurous exploration! The hoss, you"ll remember,was tied up at the foot of the gangway for a long time and even French Louie, crusty, old sailor that he was — took a hand a feeding and watering it.

Then, a long time afterwards, when Paul and you had returned from that steamer trip to France, you were drawn North to Alaska, Louie Gimel and you and Joe Bone in the schooner C.S.HOLMES. In those hairy, scary days, had you any notion of going into the King crab business?

Or into the Coast Guard or perhaps buying a schooner and finally becoming a rich hotelier in the salubrious British West Indies?

No, indeed. You took it one day at a time and,assuming that you hadn't changed much from the time you were a light -headed kid that Mac Chisholm was trying to protect from the world — who could have known what to-morrow would bring?

Your story read like the Great American novel yet you shrug it off and even find it in you to laugh at yourself. Despite your own belittlement of self, I am proud of you, kid! It occurs to me that had you but applied yourself, I mean really buckled down seriously — you could have won the world or anything you desired. However, that was not your way and yet, despite your seemingly heedless manner, all things came your way-and stuck there! You were like the fellow lying in the grass taking the sun and when a stranger came along toting a bag of gold and said, "Hey, mate-you named Thomsen? I got something for ye." Opening one eye, you motioned with your thumb and groaned, "Just leave it there."

Every man has his own conception of "success"and in this Yankee-doodle land we measure it by " How did you do for yourself, mate?" When you tired of chasing the dimes you chucked it, even as now, the hotel business is not for you. Where, I wonder would this note find you? Pain-ridden with your blasted arthritis perhaps, your only concern is to sail away into the  sunset in your schooner,as you had been doing in the Mediterranean these past four years. Good on ye, as we used to say in Australia, remember?

Good Luck to you Niels and again, congratulations on having achieved the means and the time to indulge your every whim. I showed copies of your remarkable letter to everyone I know and all agreed that "one sailor  had, indeed, made it." One of my skipper friends had made a yachting passage out of Barbadoes to the Grenadines and I asked him to stop in at Bequia. Upon his return he told me that, although they did not call in at Friendship Bay, they made inquiries nearby and learned that, "Captain Thomsen was well known and well like by everyone in the area" so you see, your deep concern for the well-being of your hotel employees was appreciated. I hope this mutual regard continued until the time you disposed of the property?

Maybe I am assuming too much? Perhaps things have not moved so fast and you still could be the owner-manager of the Friendship Bay Hotel?

I shall await your reply and if you are still located at Bequia,I shall initiate some action to come down to see you. Wait for me?

Let's see, you should be around sixty-seven years old, right? I am seventy-two and I reckoned you to be four or five years younger. Old Mac was somewhere in between. Good old Mac — I wonder whether he is still in the land of the living. I had a long correspondence with Charlie Carter (remember him?) and it was his belief that "Mac was dead" but I am unable to say what he bases his conjecture on.

Whatever became of old Louie Gimel, would you know? For a time,  he and I exchanged an occasional letter and from last intelligence, Louie had hibernated into the Umatilla Reef Lightship. That's a hell of a time ago and I assume our old friend has now joined "Unca' Walt Leyers out on the burying ground. You and Louie were going out to the graveyard one day and piss on Meyers' grave, remember? Like the old English story has it, Old Man Meyers would likely rear his bald had and utter, "F'r Krissakes, youse fellers, Wobble it around a little. I'm getting all of it!" Aw, well — speak well of the dead.

The last word in your letter,it is likely you had gone back to the Eastern Mediterranean for a look at Greece,  Jugoslavia, Turkey, Sardinia and Sicily and for that reason I am doubtful that this note would readily find you? However, you seem to be a man who always established a "base" so I shall not despair of eventually finding you. I was on the verge of flying down to Bequia when I received your letter and even had Eastern airlines plan an itinerary for me. I had just returned from the Cape Horners' Congress at Copenhagen, Norway and the Western Isles of Scotland so thought it best to rest my weary, wandering legs-and mainly, to allow the yeast to rise in my bankroll !

I am still shaking my head in wonder at this guy, Niels Thomsen. Tell me more.————

Archie Horka.

Would you be interested in a photo of the FOREST DREAM and one of the gallant crew,taken by the newspaper photographers who came up from Sydney whale we were libelling the ship?

Captain Archie Horka                         Gustav Alexandersson
3702 Ferry Heights                           Nordvagen 23
Fairlawn                                     S-132 00 Saltsjo-Boo
New Jersey                                   SWEDEN
U.S.A.                                       5 September 1971

Dear Captain Horka:

Yours of 1 September was duly received, and I thank you very much for the information, and for your kind offer to send me a copy of "Yankees under Sail" by Heckman. I have never seen this article so I would be glad to have it. If any costs are involved, please let me know, I would be happy to send a check.

About Dr. Lyman, our mutual friend, I too am impressed by his knowledge about sailing ships, and find it remarkable how he can be acquainted with not only U.S.A. and English books and sources on the subject, also Sweden, Finnish, and publication in other European countries. I am happy to have a good many of his "Log Chips".

Perhaps you would like to know what happened to the FOREST DREAM. I have seen some papers about her in the Swedish National command 28 August, 1925. When the ship was sold at auction by the Supreme Court of Sidney, N.S.W. of 23rd November, 1926, the crew was as follows — you may remember some of your shipmates: Capt. W.H. Myers, Louis Huet, John Johnson, Emil Nelson, Malcolm Chisholm, Archibald Horka, Hubert Schlee, Christian Jorgensen, Niels Thomsen, Louie Gimel, Paul Gueho and Benedict Thatcher. Your forename was so in the crew list, I understand you always have been called Archie. However the ship was sold for 1,000 pounds to three Swedes — Captain Karl Backstrom 9/20 at 450 pounds, who became her new skipper, Lieutenant sun Tamm 9/20 at 450 pounds. Tamm now lives in Gothenburg, 76 years old. In 1929 Captain Tamm was in San Francisco and bought the ABRAHAM RYDBERG for the Rydberg Foundation, and became her skipper; and the third share-holder was Captain Hjalmar Dahlstrom 2/20 at 100 pounds, famous master of the C.B. PEDERSEN for many years.

FOREST DREAM was at Antwerp from December, 1927 to April, 1928. In January 1929 we find her at port Ste. Louis du Rhone where she laid to October, 1931. FOREST DREAM to her Swedish home port, Stromstad on 6 January, 1932 and was laid up. She burned there in Stromstad harbor 5 January, 1933, nearly a year after her arrival. It was never known how the fire had started, but as there were no guards on board, one theory was that some vagabonds had been sleeping in the ship and that they had caused the fire which was observed in the early morning.

This was just a follow up letter and you must not reply. I thought that you were interested in the fate of the "five sticker", as you once was a sailor and know this ship.

Regards,

Yours Sincerely

Gustav Alexandersson

13-13

(Form No. 18—Consular)
(January, 1917)

# CERTIFICATE OF DISCHARGE OF SEAMAN

## AMERICAN CONSULAR SERVICE.

Newcastle, N.S.W., Australia, November 19, 1926
(Place and date)

Name of ship, _____ Bktne. FOREST DREAM _____

Official number, _____ 219,276 _____

Port of registry, _____ Seattle, Wash. _____

Tonnage, _____ 1604 _____

Description of voyage or employment, from Victoria B.C. Canada to Mauritius
British Possession, Indian Ocean and other ports in South Indian Ocean, and
return to port of discharge on Pacific Coast of America in U.S. or Canada,
via such ports as Master directs, for a term not exceeding 18 months.

Name of seaman, _____ NIELS THOMSEN _____

Place of birth, _____ Denamrk _____

Nationality, _____ American _____              Age, _____ 21 _____ years.

Character, _____ Good _____

Ability, _____ Good _____

Capacity, _____ **AB** _____

Date of entry, _____ October 6, 1925 _____   Date of discharge, November 19, 1926.

Place of shipment, _____ Victoria, B.C., Canada. _____

Place of discharge, _____ Newcastle, Australia _____

Cause of discharge, _____ Mutual consent. _____

I CERTIFY that the above particulars are correct, and that the above-
named seaman was discharged accordingly.

*Niels Thomsen*                                      *W. H. Myers*
_____                            _____
Seaman.                                                      Master.

Given to the above-named seaman in my presence the day and year
above written.

*R. L. Rankin*
_____
Consul _____ of the United States of America.

227-A

Niels Thomsen's discharge from the barkentine *Forest Dream*.

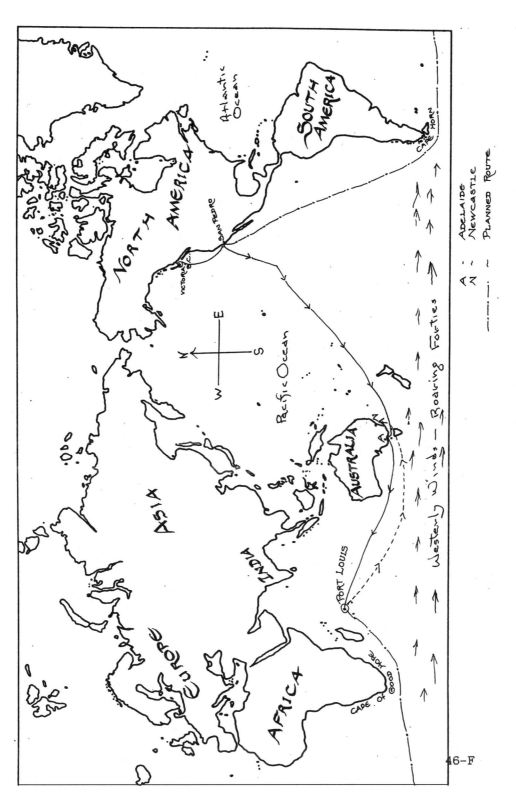

VOYAGE OF THE BARKENTINE FOREST DREAM

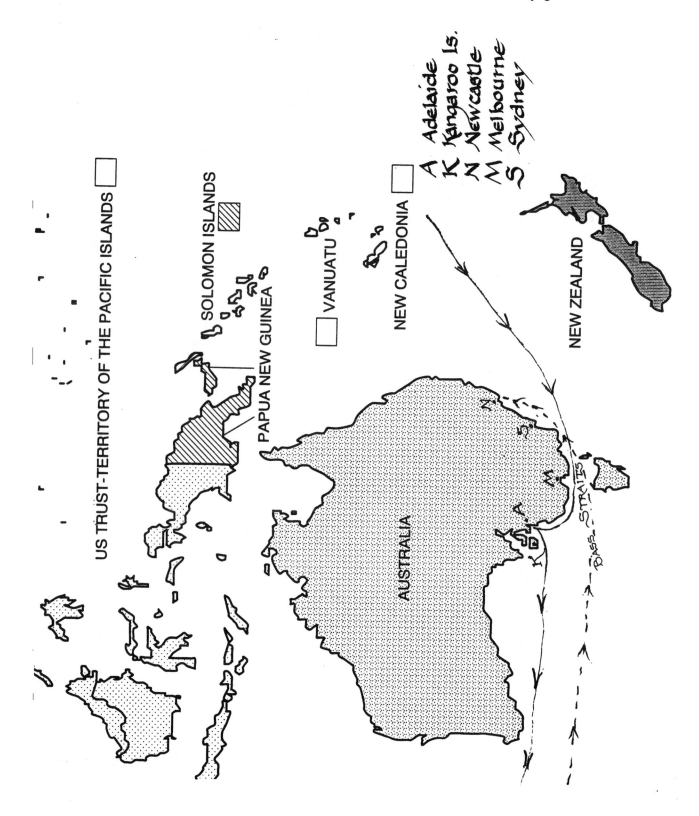

US TRUST-TERRITORY OF THE PACIFIC ISLANDS

SOLOMON ISLANDS

PAPUA NEW GUINEA

VANUATU

NEW CALEDONIA

NEW ZEALAND

AUSTRALIA

BASS STRAITS

A   Adelaide
K   Kangaroo Is.
N   Newcastle
M   Melbourne
S   Sydney

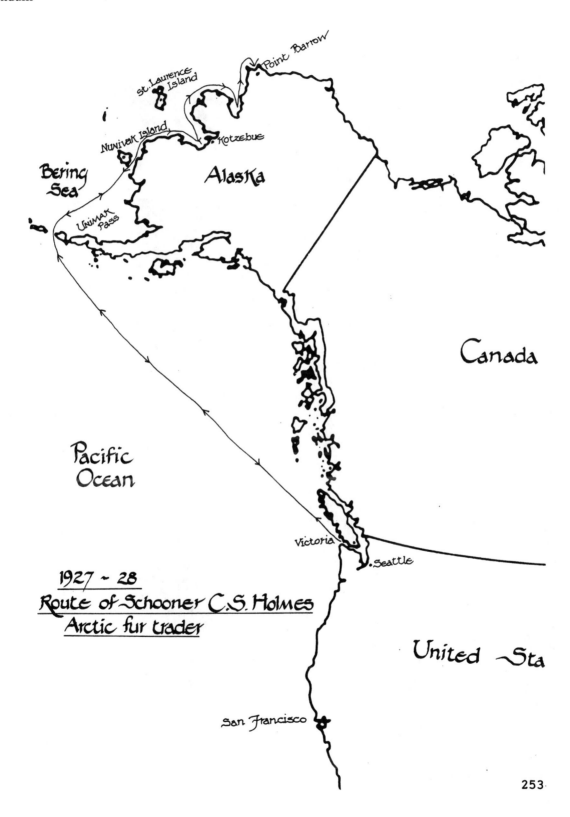

Point Barrow

St. Laurence Island

Nuvivak Island

Kotzebue

Bering Sea

Alaska

Unimak Pass

Canada

Pacific Ocean

Victoria

Seattle

1927 ~ 28
Route of Schooner C.S. Holmes
Arctic fur trader

United Sta

San Francisco

253

Above: Jenny's steamship and railroad ticket to Nebraska. Below: Hendrick Lund, personal valet to four Danish Kings.

A clipping from the Danish Illustrated Journal.

## THE AUTHOR
### CAPTAIN NIELS PETER THOMSEN

Born in Ribe, Denmark 1907
Emigrated to the United States 1912
Attended Jackson Grade School in Fresno, CA until 1922

### BOOK ONE
#### VOYAGE OF THE FOREST DREAM and Other Sea Adventures

**1923-25**    Seaman on coastwise vessels and steamers.

**1925**    One of the survivors of a crew of twelve on the voyage of the five-masted barkentine *Forest Dream* on a 200 day voyage at sea enroute from Victoria, B.C., Canada to Port Louis, Mauritius in the Indian Ocean.

**1927-1928**    Seaman and first mate on the fur trading, four-masted sailing schooner *C.S. Holmes* out of Seattle as far north as east of Point Barrow, Arctic Ocean.

**1928**    Unlimited license as second mate of ocean vessels. Unlimited master and pilot licenses.

**1929-30**    Deck officer, American Merchant Marine

### BOOK TWO
#### MERCHANT MARINE

**1930**    Six months in Hollywood, CA pursuing motion picture career. Protégér of Amy Semple McPherson, noted evangelist, while studying voice, dancing, singing and acting. Extra and stand-in at Warner Brothers Studio

**1931-38**    Deck officer and master in American Merchant Marine

**1934**    Commissioned as ensign in U.S. Naval Reserve.

**1939**    U.S. Lightship Service as master of *U.L.H.S. Columbine*, San Francisco Bay. Naval reserve training on *U.S.S. Nevada*.

### UNITED STATES COAST GUARD

The U.S. Lighthouse Service was absorbed by the U.S. Coast Guard in 1939. Appointed Warrant Deck Officer, and on request assigned to USCG Cutter *Ariadne* at San Francisco.

### WAR YEARS

**1941**    US Coast Guard taken over by the US Navy. Commissioned as Lieutenant (JG) and assigned as Executive Officer USCG *Cyane*. Later appointed director USCG Reserve and Navigational Instructor to Alaska Air Force Surface Rescue Division.

**1942**        As commanding officer USN vessel *Y.P. 251* (85-foot patrol vessel) as senior officer present, and in conjunction with cutter *McLane,* rammed and sank the Japanese submarine *RO-32* off Alaska Coast on July 12, 1942, sinking later confirmed. Subsequently decorated with Legion of Merit with Combat Insignia.

**1942**        Assigned to combat transport *Hunter Liggett* at Guadalcanal in Solomon Islands as Ship's navigator. Appointed staff navigator and chief pilot to Admiral Laurence F. Reifsnider, USN, commander Third Amphibious Group consisting of twelve troop transports throughout the Solomon and Bougainville Island invasions. Letter of Commendation from the commander, Third Amphibious Group.

**1944**        Assigned to Morro Bay, California as commander Local Naval Defense and commander of Coast Guard Patrol Stations at Monterey and Santa Barbara.

## BOOK THREE

**1944**        On request for assignment to Forward Combat Area was given command of *USS Menkar* (AK-123) and on this top secret independent assignment carried out installation of Loran stations in forward areas from Halmahera, New Guinea to Iwo Jima, which permitted high altitude precision bombing of the Japanese home islands. While at anchor in Buckner Bay, Okinawa, the *Menkar* shot down one Japanese suicide aircraft as it dived on the vessel.

**1945**        In July assigned to Alaska as district personnel officer. In August was appointed additional duties of chief demobilization officer of reserve officers and enlisted personnel of Alaska.

**1947**        Commanding officer Coast Guard cutter *Tupelo*, and commander Coast Guard Base, Toledo, Ohio. Invented, developed and patented the mechanical chain stopper and safety lead, now in use by all buoy handling vessels world-wide. Commendation from US Coast Guard commandant.

**1950**        Commander, US Coast Guard base, Ketchikan, AK

**1952**        Combat service connected disability retirement from the US Coast Guard with the rank of commander, promoted to captain on the retired list due to wartime decoration of the Legion of Merit with Combat Insignia.

**1952**        Founded Ketchikan Merchants Charter Association, a small refrigerated shipping service between Seattle and Southeastern Alaskan ports. President and general manager

**1954**        Awarded US mail contract for Aleutian Islands, AK. This contract held until 1964 when boat service was discontinued by the postal department. President and general manager

**1954-64**     Founded and operated the following business enterprises in Seattle and Alaska:
Ketchikan Charter Merchants Association
Southeast Alaska Marine Transport Company
Rainbird Equipment Company
Tiare-Tahiti Sailing Cruises
Thomsen Art Gallery and Appraisers
Salmon Royal Restaurant and Delicatessen

Aleutian Seafoods, Ltd, Salmon curers
Coral Sea Boat Company
Pelican Boat Company
Fairbanks Boat Company
Aleutian newspaper *Mailboat Monitor*, Editor
Aleutian representative of the Bank of Kodiak

**1964**     Successful primary Democratic candidate as State Representative for the Aleutian Islands with a view to unseating the ineffectual Democratic incumbent. Stepped aside to insure election of qualified Independent Alaskan Native. Involved in advancing Alaska land claims movement which ultimately resulted in compensation to the native peoples. Politically active on furthering stricter conservation measures of Alaska king crab resources.

**1964**     Formed Aleutian King Crab, Inc., at Unalaska, Dutch Harbor, Alaska. Major stockholder, president and manager. Mayor of Unalaska.

**1969**     Sold Aleutian King Crab, Inc to Brown and Williamson Tobacco Company in Louisville, KY, for several million dollars. Established tax exempt charitable foundation "Community Cooperative of Seattle" in the form of Halfway House to enable distribution of monies to needed projects, principally in the educational field in the West Indies. This project brought me to the island of Bequia in the St. Vincent Grenadines, West Indies.

**1970**     Purchased and developed Friendship Bay Hotel, a luxury resort hotel on the island of Bequia, representing a private investment of in excess of one million dollars.

**1970-81**  Operated Friendship Bay Hotel and spent time sailing in the waters off the West Indies in my 56 foot sailing yawl *Zorba* and my 100 foot schooner yacht *Lilli* in the Spanish Mediterranean.

**1980**     Married Airdrie Anne Amtmann, artist and illustrator, age 30.

**1984**     Moved to Seattle, WA

**1985**     Civil Service appointment as pilot on US Army Corps of Engineers dredge *Yaquina*, sea going hopper dredge operating on the Oregon and Washington coasts.

**1987**     Resigned from Army Corps of Engineers.

**1990-96**  Author of *Journey of an Impatient Heart, Voyage of the Forest Dream and Other Sea Adventures, The Men of the Menkar*.

**1993-96**  Counsel to Kuye'di Tlingit Tribe of Kuiu Island, AK Financial and economic advisor.

# Index

# Sailor's Lament

The sea no longer does enthrall,
Give me a place where shadows fall,
And even though it be on land,
Give me a steady place to stand.

Like jewels in an inverted dish,
Are starts to grant my every wish,
But I need more to get me by,
Than diamond clusters in the sky.

The sea is countless shades of blue,
But I want birds and flowers too,
I need tall trees and gnarled oaks,
And sometimes all I need is folks.

I need to lie in cool green grass,
And watch the pretty girls that pass,
And sit in the shade of a cherry tree,
And listen to the song of the honey bee.

Niels Thomsen